Plato

and the *Republic*

This Routledge Philosophy Guidebook introduces one of the greatest works of Western thought – Plato's *Republic*. The *Republic* is the most widely studied text in philosophy, and the arguments that Plato put forward in the *Republic* more than 2000 years ago continue to influence debates in nearly all the human and social sciences; familiarity with the text is essential for all students.

Nickolas Pappas's approach allows students both to follow the overarching argument of the *Republic* and to grasp in detail the individual propositions Plato uses to sustain that argument. The opening chapters place Plato and the *Republic* in their historical and philosophical context. By combining careful elucidation of Plato's positions with a critical commentary on his thought, Pappas provides a superb introduction to Plato's lasting philosophical contributions concerning the nature of justice, the difference between knowledge and opinion, and the dangers of poetry.

Plato and the Republic is ideal for students coming to philosophy or political theory for the first time; students already familiar with the *Republic* will find their interpretations challenged and enriched. The profound influence of the *Republic* throughout the history of ideas cannot be overstated; with the guidance of this book, students will have a distinct advantage in their subsequent studies.

Nickolas Pappas is Associate Professor of Philosophy at the City College of New York.

Routledge
Philosophy
GuideBooks

Edited by Tim Crane and Jonathan Wolff
University College London

Locke on Government
D. A. Lloyd Thomas

Locke on Human Understanding
E. J. Lowe

Plato and the *Republic*
Nickolas Pappas

Forthcoming:
Heidegger and *Being and Time*
Stephen Mulhall

Spinoza and the *Ethics*
Genevieve Lloyd

Wittgenstein and the *Philosophical Investigations*
Marie McGinn

LONDON AND NEW YORK

Routledge Philosophy GuideBook to

Plato

and the *Republic*

■ Nickolas Pappas

First published 1995
by Routledge
11 New Fetter Lane, London EC4P 4EE

Simultaneously published in the USA and Canada
by Routledge
29 West 35th Street, New York, NY 10001

Reprinted 1996, 1998

Text design: Barker/Hilsdon

Typeset in Times and Frutiger by
Florencetype Ltd, Stoodleigh, Devon
Printed and bound in Great Britain by
T.J. International Ltd, Padstow, Cornwall

British Library Cataloguing in Publication Data
A catalogue record for this book is available from the British Library

Library of Congress Cataloging in Publication Data
A catalog record for this book is available from the Library of Congress

ISBN 0–415–09531–X (hbk)
ISBN 0–415–09532–8 (pbk)

To the memory of my father,
Steve Pappas (1915–1994)

Contents

12 Plato's abuses and uses of poetry

Preface

Why another introduction to the *Republic*, or rather why any? Plato can engage unprepared readers without help. His lively dramatic conversations, his constant nimble references back and forth between mundane phenomena and their metaphysical significance, his high seriousness before the questions of knowledge, morality, community, and death – all in supple prose that never forgets its audience – have made him one of the most widely read philosophers of Europe's history.

But Plato's dialogical style, however enticing, yields poor results when a reader wants either to get an overview of the territory covered, or to worry a single point in greater detail than a conversation allows, to isolate the premises of an argument and discover which ones are doing the work, to find different ways of putting a single Platonic point and see what consequences follow from each restatement. The important issues in Plato's long dialogues appear and vanish: Plato raises one point only to digress to another, or to attend to a detail of his argument. Eventually the originating issue comes up again, but transformed or disguised. The reader who feels lost among the turns of conversation may wish that Plato had also written a few pedestrian treatises covering the same ground as the dialogues, but more explicitly and, when it is necessary, more tediously.

It is my hope that this book might work as such a guide. For the most part I have stayed close to Plato's own arrangement of his arguments. At each point I spell out his position, then stop to analyze, criticize, or expand on it. (I depart from Plato's expository order only in discussing Books 5–7, which I go through once with an eye to the political theory, then again looking only at the metaphysics.) Thus most of this book – Part Two – is an exposition of the text, with pauses for further discussion. Later chapters regularly refer back to relevant earlier sections, to facilitate the task of putting together different treatments of a subject into a unified whole. Toward that same end, I have identified and numbered ①, ②, etc. what I consider fundamental premises or assumptions in the *Republic*'s argument, and collected them in the book's appendix, both so that I can allude compactly to important Platonic claims, and so that the reader can see steps in the first books of the *Republic* as they function in the later books. Finally, the last three chapters return glancingly to certain general issues that profit from being discussed with reference to the entire *Republic*. They had to be scarcely more than notes, to keep this from becoming some other book, but as first approaches to the issues they show how one may review the whole dialogue.

In addition to bringing forward the *Republic*'s overarching structure, I have emphasized the complexity of its relationship to ordinary thought. It is easy to fall into thinking of Plato as the archetypal (or stereotypical) philosopher of otherworldly ideals, in politics therefore a utopian, in ethics a propagandist for a species of "justice" that has nothing to do with its pedestrian version. But the *Republic* works to keep its arguments intelligible to readers who are not trained philosophers, at the same time that it advocates a perspective of theoretical reason that would leave ordinary thinking behind. This duality of purpose makes for a productive tension in the dialogue, clearly spotted when Book 1 moves from a behavioral definition of justice to an internal one, or when Book 4 tries to accommodate its psychological interpretation of virtue to the ordinary variety, or when Book 5 distinguishes the philosopher from other putative lovers of knowledge. The tension is most dramatic in the *Republic*'s ambivalence about the nature of reason (especially in Book 9); but it is also at play in Socrates' repeated strategy of double arguments, in which he follows a theoretical justification for a view with one that the non-philosopher can follow. While Plato certainly does reach conclusions that at points deny the worth of daily experience, those conclusions would not have retained their power if he had not worked so effectively to motivate them from within daily experience.

In writing this book, I have been guided above all by Julia Annas's *An Introduction to Plato's Republic* and Nicholas White's *A Companion to Plato's Republic*. The reader who knows these excellent works will spot my extensive borrowings from them. In addition to these, the books on the *Republic* by Cross and Woozley, by Murphy, and by Nettleship have greatly molded my views.

In the interests of sustaining a direct and unforced mode of presentation, I have omitted the traditional references with which I would have acknowledged the enormous intellectual debts I have incurred in writing. By way of informal substitute for those references, I close each chapter with a brief list of the books and articles that most informed its interpretations; I consider these the best places for the reader to go first in moving beyond what I have said. The book's bibliography likewise serves the two purposes of identifying the sources I have most relied on, and directing the reader's own further investigations. I trust that the authors listed there will recognize the points at which my treatment has been schooled by theirs.

All quotations from the *Republic* come from Allan Bloom's translation (New York: Basic Books, 1968). I depart from his usage in my discussion only in referring to "reason," as he often does not, and to Plato's "Forms," as he never does.

I owe thanks to two institutions. I planned the book while teaching at Hollins College, which also generously supported me as I wrote the first draft. I then moved to the City College of New York, where I put the manuscript through its stages of revision; I am grateful for its material support for my preparation of the volume.

My other debts can hardly be tallied. I cannot do justice to the influence of Cyrus Banning, under whose tutelage I first read the *Republic*, nor to the lasting instruction I received from Eugen Kullmann, William McCulloh, Martha Nussbaum, Steven Strange, and Donald Morrison. I hope that this book is a credit to my teacher Stanley Cavell, to whom I owe my deepest understanding of what a philosophical theory is, wants to be, and perhaps ought not to be. My colleagues at Hollins College, by advising me through the execution of this project, helped more than they realize to make it a reality. I thank John Cunningham, Peter Fosl, Allie Frazier, and Brian Seitz; although I have left Hollins, their fingerprints remain in countless ways on the pages of this book. I am deeply grateful, too, to Michael Pakaluk, who read a long section of an earlier draft, and not only saved me from errors, but also showed me how to make my argument better. Then there are my students at Hollins and City College. I single out Jennifer Norton and Caroline Smith for their contributions to this book, but I could easily name a dozen others.

I owe immeasurable thanks to my parents, for their contributions to my education, and in particular for their encouragement as I wrote. This book is dedicated to the memory of my father, who died while it was in production. He loved Plato and pressed me to take my first course in philosophy. Finally, I thank my wife, Barbara Friedman, who helped me in every conceivable way over the past two years, reading drafts, engaging me in arguments, and drawing Plato's soul for my book's frontispiece.

Part one

General
introduction

Chapter 1

Plato and
the *Republic*

The life of Plato

The end of Athens' Golden Age

When describing his ideal city in the *Republic*, Plato permits himself a wistful tone, almost a nostalgia for the future he envisions. Without reducing that nostalgia to a purely biographical fact about Plato, we may still recognize in his hope for a perfect city something of his sense of loss for the Athens that had flourished until his early childhood. Born in 427 BC to an aristocratic family, Plato must have grown conscious of his political surroundings during the last moments of the Golden Age of Athenian culture, which had begun with the Greek cities' victory over Persia early in the fifth century. Even as he became aware of Athens' splendor, it was about to disappear. A few years before Plato's birth, Athens and its allies entered into the mutually destructive Peloponnesian War against Sparta and its own alliance, and set about squandering the prestige,

3

the military strength, and the considerable wealth that had accrued to it since the end of the Persian Wars fifty years before.

In the beginning Athens felt so confident of victory that even the war's opponents saw it at worst as an injustice against a former ally, rather than, as it proved to be, the end of Athenian glory. It seemed at first that the war would remain a scrape. When Plato was about five years old Athens entered into a truce with Sparta called the Peace of Nicias, and well-intentioned Athenians let themselves believe that the worst was over. But another six or seven years of scheming led to renewed warfare in 415, when Athens embarked on the disastrous Sicilian Expedition. Two years later – Plato was fourteen – the news returned that Athens' powerful armada had been destroyed in battle, and with it naval superiority over Sparta. The Peloponnesian War would limp along for nearly ten more years before the Athenian surrender, but after the debacle at Sicily most Athenians knew they had no chance of winning.

The dramatic works most sensitive to current events, the comedies of Aristophanes, took on a fresh bitterness after the battle at Sicily, to indicate the change in Athenians' view of the war. Whereas the playwright's first protests against the war satirize Athenian life, they still celebrate the city's fundamental vigor; after the Sicilian Expedition Aristophanes wrote *Birds*, a wish to escape from human existence to some better life, but also a critique of the bullying arrogance of which Athens had grown all too capable. After *Birds* came the anti-war comedy *Lysistrata*, which hints that Aristophanes had given up his hopes for even a respectable defeat.

Plato and Socrates

Plato would have reached adulthood with the wish to find some better political arrangement for his city than it had known and, if necessary, to impose that arrangement on Athens. In this spirit he began to join the company of other young aristocrats who associated with Socrates in the marketplace. Plato was twenty then. His uncle Charmides and his mother's cousin Critias were already among Socrates' friends. It is impossible to say how closely Plato found himself drawn into their circle. Even by the informal standards of that day Socrates was no obvious sort of teacher. Although in Athenian gossip he would have been called a "Sophist" and lumped with Gorgias, Protagoras, and the *Republic*'s Thrasymachus, the sobriquet in that casual sense meant little more than "egghead" does now. The Sophists were itinerant teachers who provided the only sort of higher education available in Greek cities.

We have little information about Socrates' place in this milieu. Plato, by dint of his focus on Socrates and his philosophical authority, has given us the most lasting portrait of the man: Socrates interrogates his fellow Athenians about their moral practices and theories, slyly inserting his own presuppositions into the conversation. In other dialogues he leads his defenseless co-conversationalists through step after step of elaborate ethical and metaphysical theories. In the works of Xenophon, though, Socrates confines himself to mouthing pieties; he is as upright a character as the Platonic Socrates, but for the most part this Socrates adheres to the morality of a traditional Athenian gentleman.

The third portrait of Socrates by someone who could have known him is the *Clouds* of Aristophanes. This Socrates runs a Thinkery devoted to abstruse metaphysical inquiries, where any paying student can learn rhetorical tricks for eluding creditors and moral sanctions. He is as enigmatic as the Socrates of Plato's dialogues, but in every other respect the Aristophanic portrait of Socrates challenges the Platonic portrait. We can only conclude on the basis of this jumble of evidence (1) that Socrates had few doctrines of his own, but (2) queried his fellow Athenians about their moral assumptions, (3) that he probably did not charge a fee for his company, and unquestionably (4) that something about his behavior earned him a number of influential enemies.

If Socrates was no obvious teacher, Plato was equally no obvious sort of student. He had absorbed the ideas of other philosophers before he met Socrates, who seems to have captured Plato's imagination first as the originator of a kind of philosophical question, and secondly as a symbol of the questing philosopher, who follows an investigation wherever it may lead. For Plato, Socrates' courage, honesty, and integrity always overlap with his intellectual virtues, especially his devotion to the truth for its own sake, together with an uncanny cheerfulness in the face of everyone's failure at reaching that truth. This deep unity of philosophy and morality may have been Socrates' most persistent influence on Plato.

Many Athenians, though, grew suspicious of Socrates' open-ended questioning, which looked to them like moral skepticism. And if fear of moral skepticism comes out of a hunch that someone who questions traditional values might be capable of anything, Socrates' associates would have confirmed that hunch, and therefore the suspicions. Alcibiades, for one, seemed for years the political promise for Athens' future, until he talked the city into the Sicilian Expedition; in subsequent years he betrayed Athens more than once, even engineering a coup against its democracy. Plato's relatives, Critias and Charmides, were at the center of a group of conservatives who overthrew their city's democracy at the end of the Peloponnesian War (404 BC) and ruled, as the Thirty Tyrants, for nine corrupt months.

In time every Athenian came to oppose the Tyrants, and after their nine months of misrule they stepped down, in exchange for an amnesty for all crimes committed during those nine months. Democracy returned to Athens. But preferable as this democracy was to rule by a committee of oligarchs, its conception of justice inclined toward vengeance, and after a few years (in 399 BC) the democracy tried and executed Socrates. No doubt mistrustful of the man's association with a crew of reactionaries and traitors, and sick of his questions, the people of Athens agreed with his enemies' accusations that Socrates disbelieved in the gods of the city, that he introduced his own, and that he had corrupted the city's youth.

Plato was twenty-eight when Socrates drank the hemlock; we may well imagine that this event, on top of all the rest, left him more eager than ever to look for a political system founded on, and faithful to, moral principle.

The Academy

There is less to say about the rest of Plato's life, although he lived to be eighty or eighty-one. After the death of Socrates he lived for a while in the Greek city of Megara, and then might have traveled around the Mediterranean. He returned to Athens and bought an estate where he founded the Academy. More an institute of advanced study for those already educated than the site of acculturation that modern colleges are, Plato's Academy was the European world's first such intellectual organization. Plato's most famous pupil, Aristotle, later founded his own Lyceum in Athens; still later, Epicurus and the early Stoics established their schools, and Athens remained a center of philosophical activity until the sixth century AD, when the Byzantine emperor Justinian closed all pagan schools of philosophy.

More politics

Until his death in 348 or 347 BC, Plato lived in Athens and ran his Academy. During this time Greece experienced no upheaval of the magnitude of the Peloponnesian War. After Plato's death King Philip of Macedon, a marginally Greek power to the north, would conquer most of Greece and end the era of the autonomous city-states; his son Alexander would spread Greek civilization to the east, effecting a triumph of classical thought; but no contemporary of Plato's could have foreseen those possibilities. For thoughtful Athenians of this time, the task was to make sense of the changes they had seen in Athens and in Greece at large. The *polis* (literally "city," but for the Greeks a self-sufficient political unit) did not seem to work any more. Athens had wasted its power in the war with Sparta. In 371 Sparta's own loss to Thebes in battle showed that no *polis* was invincible. Should the new alliances among cities grow into pan-Hellenic governments? How much autonomy could each city be expected to give up? What would their internal governance have to be like if they submerged their identities in a larger group?

We have reason to believe that Plato and his fellow Academicians participated in this discussion. According to several ancient accounts, the Academy functioned in part as a political consultants' group, with its members traveling to other Greek cities to reform their constitutions. Two of Plato's associates, Erastus and Coriscus, returned to their native city of Scepsis after studying at the Academy, and persuaded their ruler to adopt a more liberal form of government. City planners, were, as a rule, popular heroes in ancient Greece. Sparta attributed its idiosyncratic constitution to the legendary

Lycurgus. Athens had Draco and Solon. Legend aside, Aristotle (*Politics* 1267b22–29) tells us of Hippodamus of Miletus, who invented the practice of city planning, and who in particular planned the Athenian port of Piraeus. Hippodamus was, according to Aristotle's testimony, a kind of philosopher, the first non-politician to inquire into forms of government. If a political theorist before Plato had applied himself to the details of city planning, then the Academy's constitutional consultants must have belonged to a recognized tradition. We ought to read the *Republic*'s plan for a new city against the background of that tradition, not as a lone thinker's dream about some impossibly perfect regime, but as one contribution among many to a living debate over the future of Greek society.

During the latter half of his life, Plato also became embroiled in politics in a more immediate and more unsatisfactory way, with his travels to the Greek city of Syracuse in Sicily. Our evidence for this biographical information comes from the *Seventh Letter*, and in light of that document's unreliability I will not make much of the events it recounts. (Plato wrote the letter, if it is genuine, to parties involved in Syracusan politics, who seem to have grown suspicious of his part in the events in question. So, even if he did write it, he had reason to slant his account of the events.) Suffice it to say that Plato visited Syracuse three times. The first time Dionysius the Elder was tyrant of the city; Plato met the tyrant's brother-in-law Dion, with whom he established an enduring friendship. When Dionysius died and his son, Dionysius the Younger, succeeded him, Dion wrote to Plato pleading with him to come again. Plato was sixty years old then. He had already written the *Republic*; Dion hoped that philosophers might influence the young, impressionable ruler at the helm of Syracuse into establishing an ideal city. Instead the young tyrant grew hostile and exiled Dion, and Plato fled back to Athens. A year later Dionysius wrote to Plato claiming to have had a change of heart; but although Plato went a third time to Syracuse, Dionysius remained unconverted, had Dion assassinated, and left Plato's sole experiment in establishing his city an undignified failure.

If that did happen, it would account for the striking disappearance of utopian thought from the political dialogues Plato wrote after the *Republic*. In the *Statesman* Plato's recommendations start from the premise that every city will decay, and plan a city that will do the least harm given the inevitability of that decay. The *Laws*, Plato's last work, aims at an ideal city, but works toward it by modifying the constitutions of Sparta and Crete. As in the *Republic*, Plato looks for a good society; but there is every difference between reforming something that already exists and developing a city out of theoretical truths about knowledge and human nature, as he does in the *Republic*.

Platonic dialogue

The reader first coming to Plato should not feel obtuse at the dialogues' frequent inconclusiveness, occasional vagueness, and regular hints that there are other subjects at stake, or other arguments the speakers might go into. Plato has long enjoyed a reputation for elusiveness. To a considerable extent his dialogues become clearer after repeated readings, and historical information can cast light on some obscure passages. But the dialogues' differences from one another, and their self-consciously literary form, leave even their most experienced readers tentative, at least at certain points, about what Plato himself is really saying. Attractive as they are to the inexperienced reader, the dialogues call for some advance preparation.

The dialogue form

If ancient anecdotes about Plato's life, however unreliable biographically, do inform us about his perennial reputation, then surely a telling anecdote must be the one that portrays him as a young poet. It is hard to imagine a more highly honored role in fifth-century Athens than that of the tragic playwright; and as a very young man, according to rumor, Plato aspired to become one. But after he showed his works to Socrates, and Socrates quizzed him about every line of verse, Plato burned his poetry and never wrote any more.

If such a confrontation had never taken place, it would have been necessary to invent one. For nothing less than stifled literary ambitions could account for the Platonic dialogues' skillful presentations of character, or for the subtle connections they draw between people's lives and the abstract theories those people espouse. The language remains grounded in ordinary speech, but it is ordinary speech made elegant and elastic. The conversations sometimes circle back to a single question, its every appearance deepened by the preceding discussion; more often the participants veer off into the tangents familiar to everyday conversation, except that in these dialogues the tangent has a way of leading back to the originating question. Given the dialogues' prosaic settings – a courtyard, a drinking party, a walk around the city – and characters drawn from daily life, the effect is one of bringing intellectual conversations up to the artistic level of high drama.

The dialogues provide ample evidence for Plato's consciousness of drama, and therefore of his status as a kind of dramatist. He frequently has his characters describe the conversations they find themselves in with vocabulary drawn from the stage. To mention only examples from the *Republic*, we have Socrates saying, "I choose [virtue and vice] like choruses" (580b), calling his account of women's place in the city "the female drama" (451c), and generally using the words "chorus" (490c, 560e), "tragic" (413b, 545e), and "tragic gear" (i.e. costume: 577b) to characterize the world of which his dialogue speaks.

Though all purport to record conversations, the dialogues vary in the extent and nature of their dramatic form. Some are highly developed dramas, while others allow only the most perfunctory interruptions to the main speaker's lecture. Some present only their characters' words; in others, one character narrates the entire conversation. Still others mix the two forms by enclosing the narrative in a dramatic frame. Socrates occupies pride of place in the dialogues, but in several – *Timaeus, Sophist, Statesman* – he yields the floor to another philosopher; he does not appear at all in the *Laws*. Most scholars consider these dialogues the last ones Plato wrote. Socrates' unimportance in them therefore serves as a sign that by the end of his life Plato had given up all pretense of representing his teacher's ideas.

This comment brings us to a further complication, the chronological arrangement of Plato's dialogues. They are commonly divided into four groups. The early or Socratic dialogues show Socrates interrogating complacent Athenians about their moral beliefs. These dialogues are short and inconclusive – the *Laches* and *Euthyphro* serve as classic examples – and may well represent the historical Socrates. Next come transitional or "early middle" works, the *Protagoras*, *Gorgias*, *Meno*, and *Euthydemus*, which in some respects resemble the first group, but with greater development of ethical theory by Socrates. After these are the middle dialogues, those most identified with Plato's fully developed metaphysical views: the *Phaedo*, *Symposium*, *Phaedrus*, and *Republic*, and perhaps the *Timaeus*. The Socrates of these works has all but forgotten his cross-examinations of the smugly ignorant. Rather than reduce his opponents to confusion, he builds complex theories *as if* by means of questions; but these questions so blatantly lead their respondents as to count as questions only by dint of their grammatical form.

The last group, most heterogeneous of the four, includes the *Laws*, *Theaetetus*, *Sophist*, and *Statesman*. The *Philebus* and *Parmenides* probably belong here as well; it is hard to say, because there are few characteristics common to all these dialogues. Some set forth theories, while others only criticize. In some Socrates performs his usual function and in others not.

Plato and Greek drama

It need not have been only a lament for his lost ambitions that led Plato to write dialogues after generations of other philosophers had chosen expository prose as the vehicle for their views. Those philosophers concerned themselves with the material nature of the universe, or the nature of existence, but only indirectly with moral and political issues. In Athens the acknowledged writers on ethical matters were held to be poets, and among these especially the playwrights, whose new dramatic genres were still developing in the first decades of Plato's life. The act of writing philosophy in dialogues therefore constituted a challenge to existing Athenian culture, an announcement that what had previously been done on the tragic stage amid great spectacle and verbal pyrotechnics would henceforth be the task of a new kind of writing, composed not by a poet but by someone who could reason abstractly about the issues. When Plato criticizes the literature of his own day, I think he has his own dialogues in mind as the form of writing that will supplant that literature.

Greek tragedy was the dramatic presentation of heroic or mythic tales, usually with a monarch at their center, and often depicting that character's death or downfall, whether complete or narrowly averted. But it is not the death or the unhappy ending that characterize tragedy so much as the inexorability of a tragic plot (which gives a play's events the look of being fated) and the genre's insistence on showing not only the path to a horrifying event, but also the wails, afterwards, of those who have witnessed it.

In developing his own dramatic genre, Plato positioned himself *against* Athenian tragedians, but *alongside* Aristophanes, the comic playwright. Plato had a high opinion of Aristophanes, who is made to speak more wisely in the *Symposium* than any other participant but Socrates himself. The dialogues are more reminiscent of comedy than of tragedy. Though death (witnessed, mentioned, or threatened) sometimes occurs in them, these works are more strikingly untragic for refusing to use any of the methods of tragedy. The dialogues don't show heroes delivering formal and foreign-sounding verse, but ordinary Athenians blurting out prose. There is seldom any plot or even incident, and what does happen follows not the stringent causal principles of narrative, but the meandering logic of conversation. Least of all does Plato let himself linger over tears: even when Socrates' friends weep at the sight of his execution (*Phaedo* 117c-d), the tears are mentioned, but the words of grief are not quoted. Socrates chastises anyone who cries, and the dialogue records much more laughter than crying. Plato's *Euthydemus* is plainly meant as a species of parody, as is much of the *Protagoras*. Plato constructs his dialogues as philosophical modifications of Aristophanic comedy, purged of Aristophanes' bawdy anti-intellectualism but carrying on his verbal wit, his critique of tragedy, his dream of a better political world, and most generally his hope for a resurrection out of the moral death that has thus far been human social existence.

Of all Plato's dialogues, the *Republic* best illustrates this last Aristophanic theme. No interpreter of the dialogue can ignore its recurrent metaphors of death and rebirth, especially birth out of a cave or some other underground place. The noble lie (414d–e), the Allegory of the Cave (esp. 514a, 516a, 516d), and the dialogue's closing myth of reincarnation (esp. 614d) are obvious examples of this narrative and metaphorical structure. Socrates' oddly insistent comments on infanticide (in which he reiterates that the wrong children will be left in "an unspeakable and unseen place": 460c), and for that matter the imagistic structure in Glaucon's tale of Gyges (esp. 359d), also equate death with enclosure, and cast successful narratives in terms of removal out of the earth's hidden spaces.

Now, Aristophanic comedy, if we may generalize from the eleven surviving examples of it, almost always tells stories of death and regeneration, often with particular attention to making sick or perverted human desires healthy again. Death and deathly states are evoked in language and settings of imprisonment, typically in a cave or other underground place. The comedy's progress takes its protagonist from that enclosure in the earth to a new life outside it. Since, as I claim, no narrative structure occurs as frequently in the *Republic* as does that of rebirth out of a cave, we have at least one literary reason to read Plato as an Aristophanic author.

A second reason comes from Aristophanes' favorite plot, in which the comic protagonist rejects the existing social order, establishes a new state, and fights off usurpers. The *Republic*'s first readers would have recognized, in *its* establishment of a new state out of disgust with existing civilization, clear echoes of an Aristophanic narrative. Those echoes alone would have shown the readers that instead of the inexorable march of a tragic plot, they could expect Plato to show them a more thorough escape from the present state of the world.

One Aristophanic play has a special relationship to the *Republic*. In the *Ecclesiazusae* (*Women in the Assembly*), written some fifteen years before the *Republic*, Aristophanes imagines a group of women taking over Athens' legislature and abolishing private property, the traditional family, and unequal gender roles. These reforms, in Aristophanes' hands an occasion for satire, comprise two of the three principal political changes that Socrates puts forward in earnest in Book 5. Minor parts of the satire, such as the absence of courts from the new city, and the establishment of common messes for all citizens, also find their way into Plato's political theory. Since Plato must have written about these subjects after Aristophanes did, we must conclude that the *Republic* recognizes a certain sort of debt to Aristophanic comedy. Plato's own comedy will assert the moral primacy of the self-sufficient individual; but now the interests and desires that comedy makes room for will not be the base bodily appetites so ubiquitous in Aristophanes, but the highest desires known to the human species.

The *Republic*

Probably more people alive today have read the *Republic* than any other single work of philosophy. It is the first, or the earliest surviving, systematic utopia in Europe's history. It also contains the first theory of psychology, the first examination of the origins of government, the first proposals for educational reform, and the first theoretical aesthetics.

But leave aside the "firsts", because that sort of praise can apply to fumbling efforts at an enterprise, as when we credit Hero of Alexandria with producing the whirling toy that we call, in retrospect, the first steam engine. Apart from any isolated insight or hypothesis, Plato retains his importance, and his attractiveness to a broad audience, first because of his thorough mistrust for the world of appearance, and secondly for his efforts, notwithstanding that mistrust, to show how the world he called real could affect the apparent one. The mistrust of appearance produces Plato the dualist, who had to construct changeless and perfectly intelligible Forms as compensation for the chaos of ordinary things. The effort to bridge the gap between these Forms and things gives us Plato the systematic philosopher, whose dialogues interweave questions of *value* – the definitions of moral terms, outlines of moral theories, political recommendations – with questions about the state of the universe – the nature of reality, the possibility and methodology of human knowledge. The works for which Plato is best known express his vision that dispassionate inquiry into the nature of reality will ultimately inform a human life. We may say, then, that his greatest importance to the history of philosophy (for better or worse) followed from his tireless effort to bring metaphysics into human existence.

The *Republic* is a classic Platonic dialogue. It contains the fullest expositions of the doctrines traditionally associated with his name: the theory of Forms, the parts of the soul, the condemnation of poetry, and, of course, the uncompromising recommendations for political change. But it also typifies the dialogues from this period of Plato's writings in the completeness with which it unifies metaphysical and ethical issues. The two kinds of questions are never completely divorced from one another in Plato. But in the early dialogues Socrates concerns himself far more with moral terms and moral theory than with questions of knowledge or being, which at best get treated in passing (*Euthyphro*, *Protagoras*). And although the dialogues from the last part of Plato's life form a harder group to generalize about, they may be said to divide the ethical issues from the metaphysical ones and investigate them in separate dialogues. (The *Philebus* is a notable exception to this pattern.) The *Statesman* and the *Laws*, the two dialogues after the *Republic* that discuss political matters, allow themselves little investigation into abstruse philosophical matters. Those dialogues need to be read by any serious student of the *Republic*, because of the light they shed on Plato's politics; but they lack the breadth of vision that the *Republic* provides, thanks to which it occupies its special place among Plato's works.

Characters and setting

As a whole, the *Republic* rewards a literary reading less than other dialogues do. Almost all its characterizations and historical allusions come in Book 1, and practically disappear thereafter. So the information here will scarcely apply to Books 2–10, whose characters are only Socrates, Glaucon, and Glaucon's brother Adeimantus.

The conversation in the *Republic* takes place in 422 BC, during the Peace of Nicias, that lull in the war that was to be ended by the Sicilian Expedition. Plato would have been five years old at the time of the conversation, which means that, even if some version of the *Republic*'s conversation had actually transpired, he could only have learned of it long after the fact, probably when most of the participants were dead. (The *Republic* was probably written around 375 BC, fifty years after the fact, which further suggests that the conversation has been fictionalized.) The *Symposium* and *Phaedo*, written about the same time as the *Republic*, similarly inform their readers that they cannot be factual accounts, as if Plato now wants to distance what he has to say from the historical figure of Socrates.

15

Plato knows as he writes that the conversation of the *Republic* cannot help being overshadowed by our knowledge of what will happen to its characters. Socrates, of course, will be executed as a threat to democracy; but, as if he had no sense of that danger, he cheerfully proposes a state run by committee, with no political participation for the majority of its citizens. At times his interlocutors warn him that the public will not take kindly to his ideas (e.g. 474a). These warnings let us know that this dialogue, like several others of Plato's most important, serves among other things as a defense of Socrates.

Polemarchus, one of the first characters to speak in the *Republic*, will also be executed on political charges, as will Niceratus, who is present (327c) but says nothing. The Thirty Tyrants will kill those two and force Lysias (328b), Polemarchus' brother, into exile, when the Piraeus, seaport of Athens, where Polemarchus and Lysias live with their father Cephalus, becomes the center of democratic opposition.

Cephalus, a wealthy businessman, appears early in the *Republic* (388b), though he quickly removes himself from the conversation. His conception of the good life centers around the comforts that his fortune has made possible; but we know, as Plato's original audience would have, that when the Thirty Tyrants come to power they will seize the family fortune. It is also noteworthy that Cephalus and his children are non-citizens and non-Athenians. Resident foreigners in Athens enjoyed some protection under the law, but could not own property, and only under the most unusual circumstances were they ever granted citizenship. As a result, Cephalus and Polemarchus will describe the good human life without mentioning politics, even though we know as readers that politics will render their conceptions of the good life irrelevant.

We may provisionally conclude that Plato wants the *Republic* to open with apolitical discussions of ethical theory to show how limited those discussions are bound to be. Even the third active participant in Book 1, the rhetorician Thrasymachus, comes from Chalcedon. Although he speaks of rules for life by appeal to a city's rulers, his idea of politics has the overly cynical tone, the attention only to naked power, that comes of living in a political system over which one has no control.

Thrasymachus is known to moderns mostly through his part in

Book 1. He and Callicles, from the *Gorgias*, mount the most critical, most unsentimental, and most competent opposition to morality in all of Plato's works. Thrasymachus outdoes Callicles in rudeness: he insults Socrates (337a, 340d, 343a), argues belligerently, sulks when Socrates defeats him. And yet this wild nihilist's challenge to morality takes Socrates the remainder of the *Republic* to answer. Thrasymachus understands more than he can defend in logical argument. He is after all one of the premier rhetorical stylists of his day. Plato acknowledges his skill in the *Phaedrus* (267c); Aristophanes takes the trouble to burlesque his oratory; Aristotle credits him with the invention of polished prose rhythm (*Rhetoric* 1404a14). Behind Book 1's unflattering description of a hot-tempered, arrogant, glib rhetorician, we should try to glimpse a man whom Plato respected enough to form into Socrates' most difficult opponent. We should bear in mind, too, all the rest of the way through the *Republic*, that Thrasymachus has stayed to listen to Socrates' reply; when he speaks up again in Book 5 (450a–b), it is to insist that Socrates say more about his political theories. With this interruption of the conversation Plato means to remind us that Thrasymachus is still present to hear and to test everything Socrates says.

For most of the *Republic* Socrates speaks to none of these men, but to the brothers Glaucon and Adeimantus, who are also Plato's half-brothers. Adeimantus tends to represent pragmatic resistance to Socrates' claims, while Glaucon seems readier to follow Socrates through difficult arguments, and to agree with him. But their personalities hardly emerge at all by comparison with those of Book 1. In this respect Books 2–10 belong among those later dialogues in which characters function as little more than names, whereas Book 1 harks back to the deft characterizations of the *Lysis*, *Protagoras*, or *Charmides*. What matters most about Plato's brothers becomes clear enough: they are morally upright and philosophically sincere, so that their argument against Socrates is posed as the work of devil's advocates.

The opening sentence

Knowing this much, we can get a sense of how Plato establishes the scene of the *Republic*. It is worth pausing over the dialogue's first sentence, not because we need to read the whole *Republic* with the same ponderous care, but because reading one sentence well can show that Plato's writing rewards the diligent reader:

> I went down to the Piraeus yesterday with Glaucon, son of Ariston, to pray to the goddess; and, at the same time, I wanted to observe how they would put on the festival, since they were now holding it for the first time. (327a)

"I went down" is in Greek a single word (*katebēn*), the first word of the *Republic*. Socrates descends from the plane of his intellectual existence to explain his views. As the dialogue's opening action makes clear, the threat of force will haunt the participants' high-minded talk of an ideal city: when Polemarchus sees Socrates and Glaucon at the festival, he jokingly threatens that they must remain in town as his guests, since he has more men on his side (327c). Socrates will never persuade him otherwise, he says, because "we won't listen." Through the *Republic*'s imaginings of the perfect city, Socrates faces the problem of how such a city could ever come into existence in this imperfect world; that he comes down to talk about the city, instead of working out its details among trained and sympathetic philosophers, shows that Plato intends to face the issue directly.

"I went down" also looks ahead to the most widely known image in Plato's dialogues, the Allegory of the Cave in Book 7 (514a–517a). Ordinary human existence resembles the fate of prisoners shackled in a sunless cave, while the philosopher is like someone who has escaped from the cave up to the brightly lit surface. After finishing his story Socrates makes its applications explicit: the philosopher must be chosen from among other people, educated, then compelled to return and rule the rest. In that passage Socrates repeatedly uses the same verb for "go down" or "descend," in explaining the philosopher's chore, that he used in the opening to the *Republic* to describe his own arrival at the scene of his discussions (516e, 519d, 520c). Plato wants us to realize that he will justify his city the hard way, not by beginning in consensus and clarifying the theory, but by beginning amid radical disagreement and nevertheless finding some common ground on which to build his argument.

"The Piraeus" was destined to become, not long after the dramatic date of the dialogue, the center of democratic forces in Athens. Again Plato seems to have made his own task as hard as possible, for Socrates will try to persuade this audience not only that a certain sort of dictatorship is better than democracy, but that democracy in fact weighs in as the second-worst of all political systems, preferable only to brutal tyranny.

More generally, the Piraeus was the port of Athens and contained a different community from the rest of the city. More than the usual number of itinerant merchants could be found there, as well as a high concentration of foreigners without citizen status, and more than a few criminals. To the extent that political rule implies order, the greater chaos of the Piraeus will again suggest the disorder that threatens a malfunctioning regime.

To these well-known meanings of the Piraeus, I would add a fact that has already come up, namely that the Piraeus was laid out by Hippodamus, whom Aristotle considers the first to inquire into the nature of the best city. This fact sheds more light on the dialogue's conversation. Plato places himself in the tradition of municipal reformers, but he also opposes himself to that tradition, as the first investigator to do the work properly. Thus we shall find him repeatedly digging deeper into the nature of the human soul, and into the nature of all moral value, to find the guiding principles for his political proposals. Anything less would amount only to politics as usual, patchwork reforms and opportunistic compromises.

"Yesterday" is all the *Republic* provides by way of a setting for its speaker. Socrates never indicates to whom he is recounting the previous night's conversation and, aside from this single "yesterday," seems in the course of the dialogue to forget that he is addressing an audience at all. (Later in Book 1 he comments that "it was summer" (350d), an odd thing to say when talking about the previous day.) The "yesterday" supplies no interesting context, then, only at best the reassurance that since this conversation took place so recently, Socrates might more plausibly remember it all.

"The goddess" to whom Socrates has come to pray, whose festival

Athens is celebrating "for the first time," is the Thracian moon goddess Bendis.

New gods came rarely into ancient cities, for public festivals were considered the city's endorsements of the worship of a god. The gods protected their chosen cities, so the cities had to take care in turn to protect their gods, especially by not permitting the observance of foreign deities. Only crises could bring a city to license the worship of new gods. Thus, during the fifth century BC, Athens only twice admitted significant new gods into its pantheon. The other was Asclepius, a Greek hero from the city of Epidaurus, first remembered there as a legendary doctor, then elevated to the status of god of medicine. Athens fully recognized him as a god in 420, but the first steps toward legal acceptance of his cult came in 430–429, the years of a great plague in Athens.

Asclepius at least was the local hero of a Greek city; Bendis would have struck Athenians as something much more exotic, and a competitor to the Greek Artemis. At least in the course of the fifth century, there was no other act comparable to the Athenian assembly's decree in 430 that Bendis now belonged with their traditional gods.

What accounts for this radical alteration to the public religion? Three years earlier, a group of Thracians had received permission to construct a private shrine to Bendis within the city walls. In that same year the king of Thrace had entered into an alliance with Athens. The Athenians had known from the beginning of the Peloponnesian War that success would depend on their naval superiority over Sparta. But fleets require timber, which Thrace possessed in abundance; so, after a few more years of war, Athens upgraded Bendis and even planned for her public festival.

This arrangement becomes ironic in light of the fact that in 399 Socrates' prosecutors would accuse *him* of introducing new gods into Athens. The mention of this first-time festival cannot help reminding Plato's audience that the city had introduced its share of new deities, and that for quite mercenary motives. (At *Phaedo* 118a, Socrates, on the verge of death, tells his friends to make an offering to Asclepius. I find it hard to read these mentions of both new deities as mere coincidence.) In part, then, this introductory reference to the festival exonerates Socrates from one charge against him.

How many of these implications and overtones did Plato mean to resonate in the *Republic*'s opening sentence? We do not need to quarrel about its details, as long as we remain conscious of Plato's careful construction of the *Republic*. Especially at certain passages, when we have to reconstruct arguments out of elliptical remarks and undefined terms, it will help to bear in mind that in Plato's hands even an innocuous aside may contain a crucial premise, or the gloss on another passage.

Outline of the dialogue

The *Republic*'s length and complexity can obscure its overarching structure. The reader needs to bear in mind that the *Republic* consists essentially of a single argument, with a foreword and afterword and a digression in its middle. The central argument comes in Books 2, 3, 4, 8, and 9, with Book 1 to introduce its issues and 10, almost an appendix, elaborating on specific points in the principal argument. These parts of the *Republic* make considerable sense even without the digression of Books 5-7, the political and metaphysical discussion which for the most serious reader forms the foundation of the dialogue.

The central argument I speak of sets itself the task of answering two questions, "What is justice?" and "Is justice profitable?" The English word "justice," while imperfect, captures two important features of the Greek *dikaiosunē*:

a) Both terms are primarily used of law-abiding behavior or institutions, especially when law-abidingness also implies regularity, predictability, and impartiality.

b) Both terms apply in contexts of relations among people. They are other-directed, as opposed to a virtue like courage, which need not involve anyone else, or honesty, which has natural applications both in solitary and social contexts.

But whereas these features exhaust the meaning of the English word, *dikaiosunē* goes beyond "justice" in implying a kind of *appropriateness*. In moral terms, this appropriateness means not wanting or taking more than one ought to have. (The English word approaches such connotations only in non-moral contexts: the adverb "just" can mean "exactly," and the printer's use of "justify" means the adjustment of lines of type to *equal* lengths.) Plato will exploit this implication of *dikaiosunē*; but though "justice" does not capture that overtone, I will use it as a translation. "Justice" works better than any other single word. "Right" is too vague, with too many unwanted overtones, to capture the meaning of *dikaiosunē*. "Fairness" is too weak and too specific. Moreover, at least some of the inexactness of the translation is the result of Plato's expansion and reinterpretation of the Greek word. Plato would never assume that we already know well enough what justice is. In that case, the failure of "justice" to fit Plato's usage may prove an advantage; for it will keep us conscious of the ways in which philosophers can reinvent the most ordinary words when they place those words in philosophical theories.

With that clarification in mind, we may schematize the *Republic*'s argument as shown in Figure 1.

Suggestions for further reading

For the life of Plato, see Paul Shorey, *What Plato Said* (Chicago, University of Chicago Press, 1933), pp. 1–57. On the life and thought of Socrates, two anthologies are useful: Vlastos, ed., *The Philosophy of Socrates* (South Bend, University of Notre Dame Press, 1971) and Benson, ed., *Essays on the Philosophy of Socrates* (Oxford, Oxford University Press, 1992).

On the nature of Platonic dialogue in general, see Hyland, "Why Plato wrote dialogues," *Philosophy and Rhetoric* 1 (1968): 38–50, Moors, "Plato's use of dialogue," *Classical World* 72 (1978): 77–93, and Patterson, "The Platonic art of comedy and tragedy," *Philosophy and Literature* 6 (1982): 76–93. For more information about Plato's use of dramatic language in his dialogues (as summarized on pp. 9–11), see Tarrant, "Plato as dramatist," *Journal of Hellenic Studies* 75 (1955): 82–9. On the relationship between the *Republic* and Aristophanes' *Ecclesiazusae*, see Adam, *The Republic of Plato* (2 vols., Cambridge, Cambridge University Press, 1963), volume I. And for differently conceived, extensively executed interpretations of the dialogue, see Brann, "The music of the *Republic*," *St. John's Review* 39 (1989–90): 1–103, and Ophir, *Plato's Invisible Cities* (Savage, Md., Barnes & Noble, 1991).

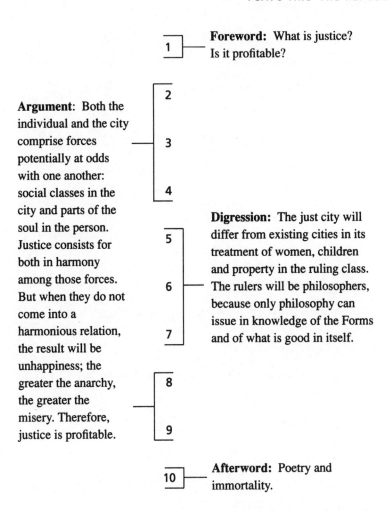

Foreword: What is justice? Is it profitable?

Argument: Both the individual and the city comprise forces potentially at odds with one another: social classes in the city and parts of the soul in the person. Justice consists for both in harmony among those forces. But when they do not come into a harmonious relation, the result will be unhappiness; the greater the anarchy, the greater the misery. Therefore, justice is profitable.

Digression: The just city will differ from existing cities in its treatment of women, children and property in the ruling class. The rulers will be philosophers, because only philosophy can issue in knowledge of the Forms and of what is good in itself.

Afterword: Poetry and immortality.

FIGURE 1   Outline of the *Republic*

Part two

The argument
of the *Republic*

Chapter 2

What is justice? (Book 1)

The peculiar nature of Book 1

Later ancient editors, not Plato himself, divided the *Republic* into ten parts, and the divisions are largely arbitrary. But in the case of Book 1, the editors were responding to a real feature of the text, for in every way Book 1 stands apart from the books that follow. Even the conclusions that Socrates reaches play only an indirect part in the rest of the *Republic*. The abrupt transition to Book 2 raises fundamental questions about the origin and purpose of Book 1, hence about the spirit in which its conclusions should be taken.

Differences from the rest of the Republic

Book 1 places Socrates in a highly realized setting, with characters who stand out as definite personalities; they sit, rise, gesticulate, sweat, and blush. Some speak elliptically and others hyperbolically, but each seems to say what he really thinks. Socrates treats each differently in

turn, starting with the interlocutor's claims about justice and tangling him in contradictions. He offers few doctrines of his own (see 336b–337e), and Book 1 closes with little in the way of fixed and satisfying conclusions.

In these respects, Book 1 resembles the dialogues of Plato's first period of writing. Even in the philosophical positions he implicitly holds, this Socrates is as much like the Socrates of those dialogues as the one in Books 2–10 is like the Socrates of the other dialogues from Plato's middle period. The early Socrates confines himself to moral issues, while the Platonic character (the middle-dialogue Socrates who is Plato's mouthpiece) develops theories of politics, metaphysics, religion, psychology, and education. In the early dialogues Socrates unceasingly compares ethical knowledge to human arts or crafts (see pp. 34–5); later he seems to regard mathematics as the best sort of knowledge. The early Socrates disavows all knowledge, conducting his investigations as jousts with adversaries, while the Socrates of the middle period didactically lays out his theories before placid respondents. The early dialogues make the people Socrates talks to psychologically vivid and historically concrete, so that their theoretical beliefs grow out of their personalities and circumstances. Later the interlocutors fade into little more than dramatic formalities. By every criterion Book 1 should count as an early dialogue.

These doctrinal and stylistic differences have led many commentators to believe that Book 1 was written much earlier than the rest of the *Republic*. Plato must then have found that dialogue inadequate to its aims and returned to it later, expanding it into the *Republic* as we know it.

The hypothesis of an earlier existence for Book 1 justifies the reader's frustration at having to trudge bootlessly through blind alleys of argumentation. If anything, the hypothesis justifies the reader's frustration too completely, in that it leaves us wondering why anyone should bother to read Book 1. Since Glaucon and Adeimantus will restate the problems of Book 1 in more philosophical form at the beginning of Book 2, why not skip ahead and begin reading the *Republic* there? Is there no way to acknowledge the unusual nature of Book 1 without casting it off as a failed youthful effort?

Book 1 as a preface

The hypothesis in question fails to do justice to the ways in which Book 1 introduces the themes of the rest of the *Republic*. Whether in passing or at length, Socrates and Thrasymachus speak of the species of human government (338d), the violence of tyrants (344b–c), the onerousness of rule (345e–346a), an ideal city run by good people (347d), the factiousness of injustice (351d–352a), the comparison between a city and an individual (352a), and the possession by everything of its proper task, which it alone is best equipped to carry out (352d–353a). Taken together, these mentions imply that Plato wants Book 1 to hint at the fundamental premises of his argument.

At a more general level, Book 1 may be read as a preparation for the *Republic*'s treatment of the virtues. The conversations of Book 1 constitute a progression away from conceptions of justice that look for that trait in some feature of the *actions* one performs, toward a view of justice as a characteristic of the *person* performing them. Hence ethics will concern itself not with commandments but with accounts of the virtues. This transformation is especially noticeable in Socrates' treatment of Thrasymachus (see pp. 42–7). So Book 1 effects a change in definitions of justice which must be gone through before the work of the *Republic* can begin in earnest. But in that case we have still more trouble with the hypothesis that Book 1 had been a separate dialogue; for only the oddest coincidence would permit an independently conceived work to pave the way for precisely the method of inquiry that the rest of the *Republic* will use.

If Book 1 was written together with the rest of the *Republic*, its evocation of the earlier dialogues would make it a deliberate pastiche of them. Rather than return to an unsuccessful early work, Plato began with the themes and topics of the *Republic* in mind, and composed a dialogue reminiscent of his Socratic works, into which he embedded those themes. But why should Plato have wanted to parrot his younger self at such length, then shift to the very different style and doctrines of his middle-period writings? Let me propose a speculation that might illuminate the *Republic*'s reassessment of Socrates: Plato wrote Book 1 after the manner of his early dialogues to emphasize that it would present the historical Socrates. Any inadequacy in Book 1's treatment of the nature of justice would therefore reveal the limitations of the Socratic method. The remainder of the *Republic*, as a sustained contrast to Book 1, could set off the merits of Plato's new philosophical methods, for those methods will, as Plato thinks, succeed where the others had failed.

This account requires Plato to have been a kind of ventriloquist, willing to write long stretches of his dialogues in someone else's voice (even if that someone else were his younger self). But he was. The speeches of Agathon and Eryximachus in the *Symposium*, the Lysian discourse recited in the *Phaedrus*, Socrates' long funeral oration in the *Menexenus*, perhaps even the whole of the *Apology*, are Platonic exercises in pastiche. For this writer, with this propensity for mimicry, to imitate himself, would have taken little effort.

Cephalus (328b–331d)

Cephalus instigates the conversation of the *Republic*, for he is the speaker who first uses the words "just" and "unjust" in his chat with Socrates about old age. Memories of unjust deeds, he says, make those on the threshold of death tremble for their fate in the next life. He feels lucky by comparison:

> The possession of money contributes a great deal to not having to cheat or lie . . . and moreover, to not having to depart for that other place frightened because one owes some sacrifices to a god or money to a human being. (331b)

Socrates takes the old man's remark to be a definition of justice, as if Cephalus had said, "Justice is identical with discharging all obligations." In reply, Socrates offers his counter-example of the friend gone mad, who returns to reclaim his weapons. Returning the borrowed weapons does count as delivering what is owed, but cannot count as the right or just action to perform. We would therefore call Cephalus' definition too broad, since it covers more cases than the thing it purports to define.

Cephalus' definition is blameworthy for scarcely being a definition at all. It identifies a few kinds of actions as just, without saying what property in them accounts for their justice. Suppose Cephalus had defined rain as water falling to the earth. Socrates would just as easily have dug up counter-examples – a waterfall, or laundry water emptied off a roof – that would have pointed up the definition's failure to capture a crucial feature of rain, namely that it falls as part of an atmospheric cycle. In the case at hand, the implicit identification of justice with some specific actions omits any mention of the character that gives rise to those actions.

We could not expect any such insights from Cephalus. He has absorbed his society's rules of good behavior to such an extent that he seems genuinely to feel happiest when acting rightly, but incapable of explaining why. He has enjoyed good fortune, reaching an age at which sexual desire no longer distracts him, and accumulating money enough to guard him from temptation. His life seems sober and prudent, and his unsentimental acceptance of old age has to count as the first stage of wisdom, at least. But he could have no advice for those differently situated, no hint of how to live justly without money. Our knowledge as readers that Cephalus' fortune will soon disappear shows us the inadequacy of this complacency amid good luck. When we hear him speak of following religious customs as if he were buying insurance, and quote Sophocles, Themistocles, and Pindar rather than think for himself, we yearn for something more substantial. No reader misses Cephalus after he goes off to make his sacrifices (331d); he in turn would not miss the discussion that follows, since it could only confuse him. Cephalus has kept himself so oblivious to philosophical investigations that, just at that time in his life when he should be evaluating himself and his values, and passing along guidance to his sons, he has nothing to say for himself but bromides, secondhand pieties, and the kinds of anecdotes that seem made to be overrepeated. In modern parlance, he is a bourgeois philistine.

Still, Cephalus plays a useful prefatory role in the *Republic*. His platitudes about the good life have touched on nearly all the ethical themes of the *Republic*:

a) bodily pleasures and one's liberation from them;
b) the importance to a good life of living in the right city;
c) fear of punishment in the afterlife;
d) the importance of living justly.

Cephalus has also initiated the activity of philosophy. Socrates is already at work, eliciting definitions of moral terms and finding counter-examples or inconsistencies that prove them inadequate – doing the work, in short, for which he is famous.

Polemarchus (331e–335e)

Polemarchus takes over his father's definition and improves on it a little, as Cephalus had improved on the inheritance his own father had left him. Polemarchus brings greater generality to his conception of justice, so that Socrates cannot simply demolish the definition with a counter-example. Instead Socrates deploys an extended refutation, showing that the proposed definition of justice, when taken together with other premises that Polemarchus accepts, leads to unacceptable conclusions.

A new definition (331e–332c)

Calling on the poet Simonides for his authority, Polemarchus defines justice as the act of giving to each "what is owed," which means doing good to friends and harm to enemies. Since doing good and doing harm are broader notions of action than the payment of money and performance of sacrifice that Cephalus had spoken of, this definition stands a better chance of telling us something essential about justice. Justice, we might equivalently say, consists in adhering to the obligations implicit in our social relationships.

It is striking that the Greek of this quote from Simonides may more naturally be read as if the poet were not *defining* justice but simply seeking to say something *about* it. "It is just to give to each what is owed" need not announce the identity of justice with the discharge of obligations, but may only have named one type of just action.

What could that matter? A philosophical definition, of the sort that Socrates looked for, is an unusual thing. Unlike the definitions found in dictionaries, it does not aim at clarifying the use of a word, but at unearthing new information about the concept. In a dictionary, the definition of "just" might include the word "right." As a clue to how to use the word that definition would be unobjectionable; to someone like Socrates, who wants the *properties* of justice, it would feel like a dodge, as if someone insisted on defining "automobile" by "car," without ever talking about engines and wheels.

The difference between philosophical and lexicographical definitions is clearest in the case of the disputable words of ethics. Any dictionary can explain how the words "good," "right," and "just" are used by speakers of English. Its information will keep us from linguistic gaffes ("Is the chicken justly done?"), but cannot help decide the truth of linguistically legitimate uses ("The UN embargo is just"). The philosophical definition presupposes the dictionary's information, but adds necessary and sufficient conditions to settle, in theory, all uncertainty about when to use disputable words.

In this century many philosophers have come to shy away from Socratic definitions. Wittgenstein's influence especially has engendered the position that philosophical definitions are neither possible nor even necessary. For example, in the European tradition of painting, the juxtaposition of colors on a canvas has been a central issue of critical evaluation. Some juxtapositions work better than others at producing effects of contrast, clarity, and spatial position. To some extent these relationships can be systematized: colors vary in hue and value, and can be compared in terms of both characteristics; in certain contexts, complementary colors produce the greatest contrast. But beyond the general rules, both critic and painter need to see countless examples of good and bad color-juxtapositions before they develop the knack of making reliable judgments. Not only does neither of them know how to state general principles that would capture all their uses of the phrase "good color," but no one else could systematize them either. Moreover, such a remarkable number of painters know how to put one color next to another, that one wonders what use one could ever find for the general principles.

I cannot lay this worry to rest in this book. But for the purposes of moving ahead with the argument of the *Republic*, I offer two considerations. First, most of Socrates' arguments could be salvaged against the objection about definitions. In the case of Polemarchus, it will turn out that Socrates' arguments depend only tangentially on this purported misunderstanding between Polemarchus' comment on justice and Socrates' treatment of that comment as a definition. Secondly, it is far from clear that Wittgensteinian criticisms apply to ethical terms in the direct way in which they apply to the terms of philosophical metaphysics. The project of clarifying the limits and nature of justice, by virtue of being more concrete than the project of clarifying human perception, say, is not threatened in the same way by critiques of philosophical method. In what follows, I will treat the problem of defining justice as if it were a legitimate question. As for Polemarchus, changing his definition to a comment about justice will not save him from Socrates' objections.

The work of justice (332c–333e)

The first objection forces Polemarchus to find what benefits friends and harms enemies in a number of specific contexts. Socrates finds the practitioners of specific skills likely to prove more useful than the just man. Farming is the skill most useful for producing food, shoemaking for making shoes, and so on. The use of justice must reside in some other sphere of human activity; so Polemarchus tells Socrates that sphere is the making of contracts, or the formation of partnerships.

Even here, Socrates finds his answer too broad. Depending on the activity in which one needs cooperation, any number of experts will probably be more useful than someone who is merely just. Finally Polemarchus admits that justice is useful only when money, or shields, or any other goods are lying useless and need to be guarded. Very quickly justice has gone from underwriting all social relationships to helping in the most useless work.

Polemarchean justice comes off as badly as it does in this passage because Socrates treats it as a *technē*. This word *technē*, which first appears at 332c, names a number of activities we tend not to group together in English, from medicine and navigation to horse-training, shipbuilding, shoemaking, and sculpture. All these require what we recognize as skill, and "skill" will do as a translation of *technē*, as long as we bear in mind that a *technē* was typically a person's occupation and livelihood. *Technē* figures prominently in the early dialogues as a paradigm for knowledge, which ethical knowledge must emulate if it is to deserve its name. So Socrates thought, and after him Plato. Hence, in the early dialogues, Socrates compares his interlocutors' clumsy allegations about virtue or poetry with a doctor's medical expertise, or a general's skill, or a cobbler's. A *technē* has a clearly defined domain or object (health, shoes), to every member of which it applies. The knowledge of the *technē* can be stated in general terms and taught. Once learned, this knowledge makes someone a practitioner of the skill in question: to know shipbuilding is to be a shipbuilder.

Putative moral knowledge fails all these tests, as Polemarchus' conception of justice does here. So long as Socrates is looking for a unique activity belonging to the just and to no one else, justice will seem to have nothing to do. One wants to object to Socrates that justice, unlike horse-trading, does not exist as a means to some other end, but as a characteristic of all human activities. When it comes to buying a horse, the point is not to compare the just person with the one who knows horses, since all the fairness and integrity in the world will not produce good advice if someone knows nothing. We should be comparing two horse experts, one just and one not; then it becomes obvious whom one would rather do business with. But this reply to Socrates is implicitly ruled out by the assumption that justice should have its own work to do, that it should resemble a specific skill. Just as there is medical practice unmixed with any other art, there should be a just practice also done alone, apart from the practice of any other skill. With this assumption at work in the argument, Polemarchus hardly stands a chance.

The moral ambiguity of justice (333e–334b)

Socrates then draws Polemarchus into agreeing that every skill implies both the greatest capacity for good and the greatest capacity for harm. No one can poison as effectively as a doctor; no one can lead a ship off course as smoothly and as skillfully as a trained navigator. If justice amounts to the capacity for guarding unused money, the just will also be the best at robbing it.

This argument seems so misguided that we are tempted to throw out any comparison between virtue and an occupational skill, or at least to reconsider the subject matter of which justice may be called a skill. Indeed, I believe that Plato himself draws this conclusion from

Socrates' arguments. However well they silence Polemarchus, they do not lead us toward greater understanding of moral knowledge. In the remainder of the *Republic* Socrates will speak much less frequently about *technē*. (The word occurs about 0.2 times per page in Books 2–10, as opposed to once per page in Book 1.) When he does propose a model for moral knowledge (Books 5–7), that model is not technical skill but the theoretical knowledge of the mathematician. *Technē*'s built-in assumption that human activities progress toward specific goals will keep it from illuminating the nature of justice, of which we might say that it is its own goal, or that it has for a goal not some distinct product, but an entire human life. I take the fruitlessness of this part of Book 1, then, to reflect Plato's belief that the traditional Socratic method, with its propensity to treat virtues as occupational skills, can only show the inadequacy of purported definitions of those virtues, not produce good definitions of its own.

Further objections (334b–335e)

Socrates has two additional criticisms of Polemarchus' approach to justice. First there is the unclarity of the words "friend" and "enemy." Because one may be mistaken about one's friends, justice on this definition might mean helping the wicked and harming the good (334b–335b). The point is well taken but easily answered: Polemarchus amends his definition to speak not simply of friends but of those who both seem to be and really are good, and, instead of enemies, those who are and seem to be bad.

Socrates' last point concerns the role of justice in harming anyone. Having circled around the other flaws in the definition, Socrates goes directly to its heart – or so it would seem. Unfortunately, his premise that one who is *harmed* becomes *worse* depends heavily on an ambiguity, almost a wordplay, without which the argument looks as weak as it is in fact. What is striking in this argument is Socrates' desire to conclude that justice cannot aim at anyone's misfortune. With this claim Socrates distinguishes his view from the traditional Greek conception of social relations, in which vengeance played a dominant role. Whatever justice turns out to mean for Socrates, he makes clear that it will not mean a purely contractual arrangement.

We may characterize Polemarchus as inadequate in two ways to the task of talking about justice to Socrates. In the first place, his ideas conform too patly to his culture's conception of virtue. Despite a sheen of sophistication, Polemarchus is very much his father's son, inheriting the old man's tendency to accept received opinions. Like his father, he appeals to a poet to substantiate his position, as Athenians often did in moral discourse. In Books 2 and 3 we will find Plato ejecting his culture's most highly prized poetry from the well-governed city, because it has functioned as a moral authority by dint of its charm, and left its audience adept at quoting nicely turned verses, but hapless at inquiring into the truth or falsehood that might underlie them. Polemarchus shows off his knowledge of Simonides, but turns out to have no arguments to support his sentiments. Under cross-examination he admits, "I no longer know what I did mean" (334b). Because he has not worked out the implications of his high-sounding but ultimately vacuous aphorism, Polemarchus really does not know what he is saying. To progress beyond this level of conversation, Socrates will need someone to talk to who can set prevailing wisdom aside.

Polemarchus fails in a second way as well. He has insisted on describing justice in terms of the actions it requires. Socrates' objections, taken as a whole, show how wrongheaded that conception of justice is bound to be. As long as Polemarchus tries to capture justice in a description, however general, of prescribed behavior, it will run the risk of looking like a minor skill, or a potentially dangerous one. The rest of Book 1 will change the terms of the discussion from this misdirected approach to a more productive one.

Suggestions for further reading

For a detailed treatment of Book 1, see above all Lycos, *Plato on Justice and Power* (Albany, SUNY Press, 1987), Joseph, "Plato's *Republic*: the argument with Polemarchus," in A. Sesonske, ed., *Plato's Republic* (Belmont, Calif., Wadsworth, 1966), pp. 6–16, and Sesonske, "Plato's apology: *Republic* I," *Phronesis* 6 (1961): 29–36, reprinted in Sesonske, ed., *Plato's Republic*, pp. 40–7. Cross and Woozley, *Plato's Republic* (New York, St Martin's Press, 1964) and Nettleship, *Lectures on the Republic of Plato* (2nd ed., London, Macmillan, 1901) are particularly helpful here as well.

For analyses of the historical Socrates' philosophical method, see Roochnik, "Socrates' use of the techne-analogy," *Journal of the History of Philosophy* 24 (1986): 295–310, Santas, *Socrates* (London: Routledge & Kegan Paul, 1979), Tiles, "Techne and moral expertise," *Philosophy* 59 (1984): 49–66, Vlastos, ed., *The Philosophy of Socrates* (South Bend, University of Notre Dame Press, 1971), and Vlastos, *Socrates: Ironist and Moral Philosopher* (Ithaca, Cornell University Press, 1991), "The Socratic elenchus," *Oxford Studies in Ancient Philosophy* 1 (1983): 27–58, and "Elenchus and mathematics," *American Journal of Philology* 109 (1988): 362–96.

Chapter 3

What good
is justice?
(Books 1–2)

Thrasymachus (336b–354c)

Thrasymachus violates the conviviality in which the
conversation has thus far proceeded, compelling
Socrates to put forward every argument he can muster
to stop the concern for justice from seeming like
naivety. Thrasymachus ends the fiction of a sociable
chat, exactly as his claims about justice purport to tear
away the self-deceit with which organized society
depicts its moral principles. So it is that Socrates
describes Thrasymachus with images of wildness and
vulgarity (336b, d; 344d), while Thrasymachus accuses
Socrates of mendacity (337a, 340d).

But anyone can be a boor. What sets Thrasymachus apart is the rhetorical skill for which he had
already become famous. Like most of the Sophists,
Thrasymachus was a non-Athenian who traveled among
the major cities of Greece teaching politically useful
skills, but especially rhetoric. He uses his rhetoric on this
occasion to threaten any talk of morality.

The advantage of the stronger (338c–339b)

The first form his attack takes is Thrasymachus' most famous statement about justice, that it is "nothing other than the advantage of
the stronger" (338c). This is not one more definition of justice.
Thrasymachus does not describe some characteristic of just people,
acts, or institutions that makes them just. Polemarchus had tried to give
a definition; but then, Polemarchus had thought that the adjective "just"
corresponded to a real property of things, and that the point of a definition was to capture that property. "The advantage of the stronger"
differs in using non-moral language to speak of a moral property.
Thrasymachus has warned Socrates not to define the just as "the need-
ful, or the helpful, or the profitable, or the gainful, or the advantageous"
(336c–d), on the grounds that such definitions stay within the conventional view of justice. His account, by contrast, claims to expose the
unnoticed origin of justice in the city's power structure: whatever group
rules a city passes laws to benefit itself. Since obedience to laws is
generally called just, that city's word "just" comes to refer to whatever
behavior benefits its ruling class. Hence "justice" corresponds to no
actual property of things or people, but is an attractive word with which
we cloak the naked exercise of power.

Such a statement rejects the very possibility of definitions.
Imagine that Socrates and Polemarchus had been trying to define
romantic love, say as the attraction to what one lacks, or the desire to
possess that which one resembles, or the craving after beauty. Now
suppose that Thrasymachus said, "Being in love is nothing but a chem-
ical state in the brain." He would mean that these other proposed
definitions had looked in the wrong place for an explanation of love,
that beyond identifying it with a state of the brain there was nothing to
say about it. In particular, the lover's belief that this feeling is somehow *about* the loved one – the belief that guided these false definitions
– is an illusion. In the same way, Thrasymachus claims that justice,
which looks at first like a characteristic of social relations, amounts to
nothing above and beyond whatever suits a given city's rulers. Given
the kinds of definition that have been entertained, this means that no
definition is possible.

We may therefore call Thrasymachus' definition a naturalistic
analysis of the concept of justice. It resembles a nihilistic rejection of

that concept in denying that justice exists. But Thrasymachus is not properly speaking a nihilist. To a nihilist, Socrates' talk of justice would be empty talk; Thrasymachus grants that Socrates is talking about something, but insists that it is not what Socrates *thinks* he's talking about.

The art of rule (339b–346e)

Socrates answers Thrasymachus with two objections to his claims. The first, in this section, attacks the idea of "the advantage of the stronger," and exploits Thrasymachus' comments about an ideal ruler to undercut his would-be Machiavellian cynicism. The second series of objections (348b–354c) more vaguely takes on his immoralist contention that injustice pays. I will concentrate my discussion on the latter arguments (see pp. 44–50), because their points of imprecision point ahead to the theory Plato will develop later in the *Republic*.

Rulers' errors (339b–340c)

The immediate weakness in the idea that justice is the advantage of the stronger is the capacity of the strong to make mistakes about their own advantage. If a city's rulers support a law that will in fact hurt them, then, on the Thrasymachean view, justice would have to consist in disobeying that law. But such an option robs the rulers of any sense of power, for it commits their subjects to deciding what will most help the rulers. The subjects will make the laws.

At this point Thrasymachus may add, as Cleitophon does, the qualifier that justice is the advantage of the stronger *as it appears to the stronger*; or he may deny that rulers make mistakes about what helps and harms them. The first option preserves the experience of power for the strong, since what they really want is obedience. But it leaves open the possibility that justice will benefit the weak. If a tyrant becomes mistakenly convinced that lower taxes suit his or her interests, when they actually serve the interests of the citizenry, then lower taxes in the city would be just according to Thrasymachus' own principles, without challenging the conventional understanding of justice.

So Thrasymachus takes the other option. Distinguishing the true or ideal practitioner of a *technē* from the one vulgarly called its practitioner, he claims to be speaking only of the former sort of ruler (340d–341a). The doctor who diagnoses incorrectly is not, in that moment, a true doctor; and rulers, in the moment of erring about their own advantage, are not properly to be called rulers. Hence justice is determined by the self-aggrandizing pronouncements of the ideal ruler.

Thrasymachus may have slipped out of one trap with this ploy, but only to find himself in a deadlier one. For by postulating an idealized form of the ruler, he has reintroduced the skill analogy, and with it all the same questions about skills that Polemarchus had been unable to answer. In particular, if justice or political rule are skills, what are their objects or goals?

The object of rule (341c–342e)

Socrates compares the skill of rule to those of medicine, piloting, and horse-training. The doctor rules over the human body, for it is the doctor who determines what the body ought to eat and drink, and what medical treatment it needs. This sort of rule, in contradistinction to the one Thrasymachus imagined, serves the interests of the thing it governs. Horse trainers, when properly so called, work for the good of the horses they rule. Pilots work for the benefit of sailors.

This point is structural, not psychological. Socrates does not believe that doctors and pilots are altruistic people. He means that medicine, considered as a body of knowledge, makes sense only as a way of treating the sick. To dispense pharmaceuticals with some other purpose is to be a poisoner or a drug dealer, not just a peculiar doctor. Then if political rule is a skill according to which one person governs others, it must resemble those other skills in *serving* those whom it *rules*. Thrasymachus is in trouble again, for if political rule serves the subjects of rule, the ruler's decrees will aim at the advantage of the subjects, and justice will be not the advantage of the politically stronger, but that of the weaker.

It is to Thrasymachus' credit that he still has a reply to make at this point. Against Socrates' appeal to the nature of a skill, Thrasymachus objects that this analogy fails in the case of political rule. Only from a limited perspective will power seem to work on behalf of its subjects. Sheep might imagine their shepherd to care about their welfare, but the goal of that care is only fatter sheep for slaughter. Therefore, political rule diverges critically from other skills, and cannot be illuminated by a comparison to them.

Socrates will try to save his analogy; but he can have no reply to the deep significance of Thrasymachus' objection. The problem is that skills presuppose a goal, and get their merit from their efficiency in reaching that goal. The goal may be a shoe, the state of bodily health, or music. In every case, a skill or craft directs itself to achieving its goal, not to determining which goal a situation calls for. Should Athens invest in stronger city walls or in more ships for its navy? Depending on the answer, shipbuilders or masons will be the artisans to help the city. But they are exactly the least appropriate ones to ask which goal the city should pursue; and *that* is the political question. So too, while shepherds are ideally suited to tending to sheep's health, their decisions about which sheep to slaughter, and when, will reflect not their skill as shepherds but their own purposes and personal desires. Socrates' analogy misses this point, because his attachment to occupational skills as models of knowledge has blinded him to their unsuitability to the task of discovering the ultimate ends of behavior.

The question of who is served by justice has begun to seem a quicksand from which neither Socrates nor Thrasymachus will escape to the solid ground of substantive claims about justice. Socrates hounds the issue a bit longer after Thrasymachus' latest diatribe, distinguishing the true work of any artisan from the wage-earning skill that makes that work profitable (345c–347d). But this distinction not only accomplishes nothing, it arrives too late. Thrasymachus has changed his position, as Socrates acknowledges, and they will have to move on to other issues:

> I can in no way agree with Thrasymachus that the just is the advantage of the stronger. But this we shall consider again at another time. What Thrasymachus now says is in my opinion a far bigger thing – he asserts that the life of the unjust man is stronger than that of the just man. (347d–e)

The profitability of justice (348b–352b)

In the course of pointing out that a shepherd's real concern is not for the sheep's welfare but for their sale as meat, Thrasymachus digressed to remind Socrates of a consequence of his original definition: justice profits not the just, but the unjust who take advantage of them (343c). This point seized his attention, and he directed the rest of his speech to illustrate the profitability of unjust behavior.

Clearly this is not the position he began with. In calling justice unprofitable, Thrasymachus is no longer redefining the term, but accepting its traditional *meaning* and denying its *value*. He represents immoralism now – the view that one ought to traduce moral principles – rather than the naturalistic perspective that had led him to call justice the advantage of the stronger. This does not mean that Thrasymachus has let himself be confused into misunderstanding his own position. Rather, he has seized on a single *implication* of his original definition. Assuming one is not in the position of governing, the immoralist view follows from the naturalistic description. (If one *is* the ruler, then by the original definition justice is profitable. Here Thrasymachus has changed his view, since he calls the tyrant unjust at 344a–c. But since the discussion is not focused on rulers, this change does not affect it.) Thrasymachus has decided to clarify and defend a single implication of his definition, because that alone will still let him unseat Socrates' simple-minded faith in the value of justice.

Now Socrates needs to address this threat to conventional morality. In a series of three arguments, he will try to show that justice deserves more praise than Thrasymachus has allowed. For the rest of the *Republic*, the Socratic question "What is justice?" will be tied to this new Thrasymachean question "Is justice profitable?"

Justice is knowledge (348b–350d)

Socrates first argues that in certain respects justice resembles knowledge and goodness, and therefore stands on the side of virtues, while injustice belongs among the vices.

The argument demonstrates that Thrasymachus still adheres to some traditional values. A real nihilist could shrug when Socrates concludes that the just person is good, since the word "good" need not correspond to real properties of things any more than the word "just" does. Thrasymachus agrees to Socrates' conclusions only reluctantly; he holds to some values, even if justice is not among them.

Otherwise the argument accomplishes little. Because Thrasymachus has refused to group justice with virtues and injustice with the vices, but calls the former innocence and the latter "good counsel" (348c–d), Socrates needs to begin by finding some characteristic of injustice that he and Thrasymachus can agree to. In Greek that characteristic is captured by the word *pleonexia*, which means the habit or trait of wanting and seizing more than one is entitled to. Justice, by contrast, is marked by the tendency to stay within proper bounds. Justice suppresses the spirit of unchecked competition for personal gain manifested in the unjust person's disregard for law and order. Socrates generalizes these characterizations in this way:

① The unjust try to get the better of all others, the just only to get the better of the unjust.[1] (349b–c)

Since Thrasymachus accepts ①, the restraint of the just must be a universally recognized characteristic of justice, perhaps a least common denominator of all theories of it. Socrates quickly generalizes from ① to the claim that the unjust try to get the better both of those like and those unlike themselves, while the just restrict themselves to outdoing only those unlike themselves (349c–d). Since the behavior of the just and the unjust, in this general sense, resembles that of the knowledgeable and the ignorant, respectively, and since those who know are wise and good, therefore the just resemble the wise and good, the unjust the ignorant and bad (350b–c). So the just are wise and good.

---

[1] Certain premises of arguments laid out in this book will be specially marked ① and numbered. These premises or assumptions either appear in later arguments, or function as assumptions throughout the *Republic*. They are listed separately in the appendix at the end of this book. I identify these assumptions to bring forward, among the welter of claims made in the *Republic*, those to which Plato is particularly attached, and on which he rests his conception of justice.

The greatest failing in this argument must be Socrates' sloppy use of the idea of "getting the better of." As applied to the unjust, that means cheating: the unjust get the better of others by, say, taking their money. In other contexts "getting the better" of others refers to competition. The non-musician tries to be better at making music than the musician is. These two senses of the phrase have nothing in common: competition may be honest. The apparent similarity between the just and the knowledgeable fails to show that the just resemble the good, since the equivocal use of "getting the better of" someone prevents the two premises from talking about the same thing.

The argument has other problems. There is no justification for the transition from a similarity of features between the just and the good to the identity of the two. We would first have to know how essential those features are to the just and the good. Logically aware readers may also spot ambiguities in the implicit quantifiers of the argument's premises, which must be sorted out before we can assess the argument's validity.

But we will get more from evaluating the argument's purposes in the larger discussion. It has afforded Socrates the opportunity of presenting a general conception of justice as restraint (①). In the terms of the present argument, ① has done no useful work; but once Socrates decides to define justice in terms of the state of one's soul, the principle will guide him to look for restraint within the soul, in the tendency of each human motivation to stay in its place.

Justice is cooperation (350e–352b)

For now that goal still lies far off. Socrates wants to show directly how justice can be profitable, so he spells out one consequence of his last conclusion: justice means cooperation, injustice factiousness. Any human activity that calls for a group to act together requires at least some cooperation, hence at least the etiolated justice that we call "honor among thieves." So justice benefits the just.

This argument depends on the preceding argument's conclusion (see 351c), and therefore can be no more reliable than that one was. And it ignores the obvious objection that, while a little justice mixed in among injustice yields better results than unadulterated injustice, that mix of virtue and vice might also prove more efficacious than justice by itself. Socrates could complicate his position to make it stronger – arguing that a mixture of justice and injustice collapses into total injustice, or that the profits of injustice are merely apparent – but he leaves it as it is, ignoring so much about social organizations that it is best left alone.

In one respect the argument moves Socrates further forward, toward a very new approach to justice. "When injustice comes into being" in a group, he says, it divides the group's members (351d); then he goes on: "If . . . injustice should come into being within one man . . ." (351e). Injustice sounds like a force abiding within a group or a person, "possessing a power" to bring about discord (351e). Socrates has begun to speak as if he assumed that

②   Injustice is a force, with the power of promoting disunion, that can exist within an individual or a society.

Socrates will spend little time, in the remainder of the *Republic*, looking for a justice or injustice that inheres in the set of acts called just or unjust; from now on justice and injustice will be forces inhering in persons and societies and *giving rise to* those acts. In short, Socrates has already changed the subject of this conversation, from just and unjust actions to just and unjust agents. The ethical system of the *Republic* will not specify which behavior is right, but will instead analyze the just person and the just city. The superiority of justice over injustice will not lie in the profitability of particular actions, but in the profitability of being a certain kind of person, or organized in a certain social pattern.

Justice and happiness (352d–354c)

We have arrived at the last and best argument of Book 1. Although it can be broken down into more detail, its outline is simple:

1. ③ Everything has a work (*ergon*) that it alone can do, or that it does better than anything else can. (352d–353a)
2. The excellence or virtue of a thing is that which makes it perform its work well. (353b–d)

("Virtue" translates *aretē*, which, like many Greek words of praise and blame, combines a number of unexpected connotations. Apparently related to "Ares," the name of the war god, *aretē* at first referred especially to manly prowess in battle and nobility. Its meaning spread to include every sort of excellence: as a moral term, *aretē* meant "virtue" or moral excellence, but outside the moral domain it made ordinary sense as a term of praise for animals, property, or anything else. Thus what may seem the strangest comment in the argument, that eyes and ears have virtues, is uncontroversial in the original.)

3. The work of the soul is living. (353d)
∴ 4. From (2) and (3), the virtue of the soul makes it live well. (353e)
5. ④ Justice is the virtue of the soul. (353e)
∴ 6. From (4) and (5), the just live well. (353e)
∴ 7. The just are happy. (354a)

There is a sense of legerdemain about this argument, as if it moved to its conclusion by an unexpected path. Perhaps the biggest surprise is Socrates' sudden introduction of the soul, which had appeared only incidentally before now. The premises that speak of the soul are too vague to be called true or false. In what sense is life the work of the soul? Because dead things have no souls? But then the soul might be an effect of life, not its cause. As for (5), Socrates may have shown justice to be a virtue; but for (5) to work in this argument, justice must be not only *one* virtue of the soul (among many), but its characteristic or defining virtue. For a virtue to make a thing do its work well, it must correspond to that thing's function, as sharpness does to cutting and keensightedness to seeing. If a thing possesses more than a single function, it may have more than one virtue, each making different work possible. We may think of a fork as having two tasks: it spears food on the plate, and also carries it to the mouth. To spear well the fork must have sharp tines, and to carry food well it needs a sturdy handle. The two virtues cannot make up for one another. A sturdy fork with its tines blunt will not spear food well, however much we feel moved to praise its sturdiness; and a flimsy plastic fork, even though its tines cut deep into meat, may buckle *en route* to the mouth. So, even if one thing the soul does is live, and even if justice is one of its virtues, we have no grounds for attributing good living to that virtue. Here again the argument fails through its ambiguity, and through silence where the context calls for more explanation.

Other crucial terms in the argument have been left unexplained. "Happy" and "living well" are as vague in Plato's Greek as in modern English, and, depending on how they are defined, the step from (6) to (7) ranges from obvious implication to obscurantist sophistry. But I began by calling this Book 1's best argument, and it is time to see its merits. First, ③ brings to the fore an assumption that will prove important later in the *Republic*. The word *ergon* by itself can be indeterminate. Literally "work" or "deed," it applies to anything that requires work – my business, the fruits of my labor – or even, very broadly, any act. But one's *ergon* often refers to the occupation that is *proper* to the person, and Plato will rely on this sense of the word, first specified in ③, when he later says that each inhabitant of his city will perform a single task (⑥, 370a–b).

Secondly, this argument anticipates the strategy of Books 2–4 in linking morality to happiness. Rather than link the two directly, Plato will argue that both moral behavior and genuine happiness issue from a single source, namely the soul in a certain state. Once in that state, which Plato conceives of as a balance or harmony, the soul will automatically produce just behavior; because that state is somehow enjoyable to possess, the one whose soul is in the state will be happy.

Redirecting attention to the soul will let Plato answer radical attacks on morality. Whether they take the nihilistic form that there is no moral truth, or the cynical form that it is not worth paying attention to, such attacks say that morality corresponds to nothing natural. Plato will argue that morality and its effects are truths of psychology, therefore truths that we might call scientific. The closing argument of Book 1 fails to reach a foundation this secure, not because its approach is misguided, but because the pivotal term it introduces, "soul," appears in the argument without definition or elucidation. Before proving justice profitable Plato will have to say what the soul is. We might say of Book 1's last argument, then, that it goes as far toward proving the profitability of justice as Plato can go without any ancillary investigation.

How can these flawed arguments have silenced Thrasymachus? Assuming we do not want to accuse Plato of either blindness to his arguments' flaws, or dishonesty in making them victorious, we must conclude that he takes them as first sketches for a successful account and defense of justice. Because they are no more than sketches, they slide past crucial points with equivocal words and ad hoc premises. But because the arguments point the way to a better account, those equivocations and assumptions provide opportunities for discovering deeper philosophical ideas. In short, the arguments work against Thrasymachus, despite their obvious faults, precisely because those faults betray the overcompression of deep truths. The remaining nine books will correct the faults of this one, not by turning the discussion in a new direction, but by doing with a political, metaphysical, and educational theory what the Socrates of Book 1 (as I claim, the historical figure) has been content to accomplish with scattered intuitions.

Glaucon and Adeimantus

The brothers

Thrasymachus represented an advance over Socrates' other interlocutors. He detached himself from received wisdom enough to propose a genuine analysis of justice; he displayed his argumentative skill by keeping Socrates from easy victories. But in the remaining nine books of the *Republic* he will say almost nothing: Glaucon and Adeimantus speak up at the start of Book 2, and continue talking to Socrates until the dialogue's conclusion. What makes them better than Thrasymachus?

One sign of the limitation of Thrasymachus as an interlocutor is that Socrates takes their discussion to be done when he has silenced him, even though the originating question about justice dropped out of their conversation unanswered, and though the matter of justice's profitability got only a hasty treatment. Faced with such a belligerent opponent, Socrates can only refute his position or let it stand, not develop it into a constructive analysis of justice. Thrasymachus lacks the flexibility to see where their argument might lead, because in his cynical way he really believes his critique of justice.

In that case, the ideal person for Socrates to talk to would share Thrasymachus' independence from popular opinion, but not his attachment to immoralism. It would be better still if that interlocutor resembled Cephalus in managing to behave appropriately even without a theory of justice. The best interlocutor would also retain some of Polemarchus' respect for received opinion – not enough to obey traditional society unthinkingly, but enough to recognize that any proposal of a new society must speak to those who live in the old one.

When Glaucon and Adeimantus open Book 2 with their elaboration of the Thrasymachean position, they prove themselves to be such interlocutors. They want a defense of the just life (358c, 361e, 367b, 368a), but have enough intellectual integrity to know that Socrates has not provided one (357a, 358b, 358d). They would willingly question or reject many details of traditional Greek morality (e.g. 362e–367a); at the same time, they expect a satisfactory answer to Thrasymachus to preserve some version of the values they have grown up believing in.

The most noticeable difference between Thrasymachus and Plato's brothers is their docility toward Socrates. With the transition to Book 2 the *Republic* settles into a long Socratic lecture sometimes interspersed with questions from Glaucon and Adeimantus, but more often broken only by the sounds of their agreement. More Socrates' audience than his opponents, they can remain as restrained as they do because they do not believe their own speeches against justice, because they have given up the partisanship that so often characterizes Socrates' interlocutors. Most of Plato's later works contain interlocutors as passive as Adeimantus and Glaucon, as if Plato had come to fear that the pricklier sort, despite their ability to inspire an exciting conversation, lacked the curiosity and the discipline to follow a sustained exposition. If anything, an interlocutor's prejudices, however colorful dramatically, would get in the way of thoughtful inquiry. Plato needs Glaucon and Adeimantus now because he has a new theory to lay out.

The challenge to Socrates (357a–367e)

The argument

Socrates must show that justice, considered by itself, is preferable to injustice. "Justice by itself" will be justice understood in isolation from its social effects; for if its benefits lie in those effects, it may remain a merely conventional social relation.

Glaucon distinguishes three ways of valuing an object, activity, or experience (357b–d). It may be valued for its own sake, as pleasure is, or merely for its consequences, or for both the intrinsic experience of it and for its consequences. Glaucon and Socrates rank the things so valued:

1. Good in itself and for its consequences;
2. Good in itself;
3. Good only for its consequences.

The second of these will not enter into the discussion, since everyone agrees that if justice is good at all it is at least good because of its consequences; so it must fall under either (1) or (3). Glaucon fears, and argues to Socrates, that justice belongs to the lowest class of good things, because

1. The rules of justice arise in social situations, out of agreements made by people pursuing their own interests. (358e–359b)
2. No one who could get away with cheating would abide by the rules of justice – i.e. people value justice only for its consequences. (359b–360d)
3. The life of the unjust is better than the life of the just. (360e–362c)

This organization of the three claims builds rhetorically from the most neutral, the account of the social origin of justice, to (3), which most uncompromisingly criticizes the worth of justice. Their *logical* order, though, is (1)–(3)–(2). *Because* justice is a social compromise, its pursuit disadvantages the just when they are deprived of the social rewards for their behavior. And because everyone has come to realize this, people ignore the demands of justice when they can. From the point of view of its logical importance to the argument, therefore, (2) is secondary. Universal reluctance to obey the rule of justice, however unappealing a characteristic of humanity, is only a symptom of the deeper problem, that there is in fact no good reason to obey those rules. The core argument that Socrates will have to answer may be stripped down to this:

1'. The rules of justice have arisen only within organized society, as a means of preserving that society's members.
3'. When the society's sanctions are left out of consideration, injustice pays better than justice does.

If Socrates wants to deny (3'), he will have to argue either that (1') is false, or that (3') does not follow from (1'). He has no need to address (2), for if (3') is false, all the people who resent the strictures of justice will simply be mistaken about it.

So I will not dwell on (2) here, or on Glaucon's story about Gyges and the ring, which illustrates it. The point of the story is that since most people would exploit a ring of invisibility, they must already believe that they have no reason to act justly in the absence of social sanctions. Thus the tale may illustrate the pull of a temptation away from morality, but it adds nothing to Glaucon's argument.

The origins of justice (358e–359c)

What we call by the name of justice, as if it were a natural force in the world, actually describes an arrangement made within human society. Everyone would like to enjoy the fruits of unrestrained domination over everyone else, but no one wants to end up dominated and exploited. So everyone agrees to ban the behavior called unjust, giving up the benefits of exploitation in order to avoid being victimized. The result is the social contract or convention that we call justice.

On this view, every legal or moral principle has the status of those laws we recognize as purely conventional. We accept the conventions of traffic law, not as embodiments of moral goodness, but as necessary rules of the game called traffic. According to Glaucon's story of justice, our prescriptions against murder, burglary, and contract violation work in exactly the same way. Hence justice is a convenience, not an intrinsically valuable state of character.

Glaucon's speculative history of morality invokes the distinction between *nomos* and *physis* (359c) that in Plato's Athens had come to be used as a critique of all moral standards. The latter term denoted nature and the former anything that developed out of human social organizations, hence anything not natural. (This distinction means, in particular, that "the natural" was not opposed, as it often is today, to "the artificial," i.e. to anything touched by human hands, but more narrowly to the customs and laws of human communities. For other uses of this distinction in Plato, see *Gorgias* 482e and 492a–c, *Theaetetus* 172b, and *Laws* 888e–890a.) If justice is a social arrangement, its benefits cannot exceed whatever benefits the society is able to grant to the just.

Now we begin to see what Glaucon meant by opposing "good in itself and for its consequences" to "good only for its consequences." These phrases may be misunderstood if we take the consequences of an activity to include *all* its possible effects. For then Glaucon would be seen as taking sides in the modern debate between deontological and consequentialist conceptions of value. For the deontologist, consequences are irrelevant to the evaluation of an action. Telling the truth is right and lying wrong, not because of their effects, but because of the kinds of actions they are. Consequentialism claims, on the contrary, that an action is right if and only if it produces good consequences. Glaucon would therefore seem to be a deontologist. He asks Socrates to dismiss the "wages" of justice and injustice, and "whatever comes of" them (358b). The remaining constituent of the value of justice would then have to be evaluated deontologically.

But Plato is using subtle language here. In the first place, Glaucon asks Socrates to defend justice by revealing the "power" (*dunamis*) that it has in the human soul (358b). *Dunamis* refers to the capacity to perform in a certain way, so justice must be in the soul to *do* something, and its doing that thing, its effects, must be what makes it worth possessing. Secondly, when Glaucon describes the three kinds of good, his language refers to the acts of liking, welcoming, and choosing those things. To value them is not to esteem them in an impersonal manner, but to want the things for oneself, to *profit* from having them. Finally, Glaucon's examples of things that are good in themselves include pleasure, joy, good health, and the power of sight. Whatever these states have in common, it is no abstractly conceived value. One *enjoys* them.

So the distinction between deontological and consequential value misses Glaucon's point. The consequences he speaks of do not include all the effects that modern consequentialism considers. In his story of the social nature of justice, Glaucon has in mind as consequences only those consequences it produces *in a society*. Since Glaucon has opposed society to nature, he must mean to distinguish those social consequences from consequences of justice that we would acknowledge as natural. A thing is then both good in itself and productive of good consequences if both its natural and social effects are good.

Lives of the just and unjust (360e–362c)

This reading is borne out by the last part of Glaucon's argument, in which he contrasts the life of the just man who is universally considered unjust with that of an unjust man with an unearned reputation for justice (360e–362c). Glaucon spells out the penalties that will fall upon the misunderstood just man, and lavishes every benefit on the craftily unjust. His point is clear: any advantages that we may think belong to one who lives justly are merely the advantages of a just reputation.

The social consequences of justice and injustice need to be set aside because they follow less reliably, or less immediately, than the natural effects of the two states. For instance, the natural effect of physical strength would be an enhanced sense of vigor, while its social consequence might be steady work at heavy labor. Because employment requires more than strength alone, that social consequence is at best an indirect effect of the strength. But heightened vigor always comes with bodily strength. Glaucon wants Socrates to identify a natural effect of justice that similarly follows straight from the person's just disposition without the aid of social sanctions.

Adeimantus (362d–367e)

Where Glaucon bemoaned the bad reputation of justice, Adeimantus speaks just as despairingly of the praise people give it. As a society grows aware that its prescriptions are artificial, its moral rhetoric communicates a cynical attitude toward virtuous behavior. When fathers exhort their sons to be just, they praise not justice itself but the good reputation it leads to (363a). Even promises of otherworldly rewards for justice implicitly call it a burden, by suggesting that in the next life no one bothers to practice virtue (363c). Moreover, once the just life has been posed as a mere intermediary to something else, people will look for a shortcut to that other goal. Look at religious rituals: if the gods mete out rewards and punishments after death, then supplications, sacrifices, and initiations into mystery cults can bring about bliss after death without the bother of virtuous living (365e–366b).

Adeimantus focuses on existing society: he lacks Glaucon's capacity to imagine the origins of justice. But his speech does underscore two important points. First, Adeimantus makes clear – as Glaucon had with his tale of Gyges' ring – why purely conventional justice is bad for a society. When the advantages of justice are taken to inhere in the rewards that society bestows on the just, people become more cynical, and more apt to evade the call of justice when they can. Secondly, Adeimantus echoes one of Glaucon's assumptions about justice when he complains that no moral teacher has yet argued "what each [justice and injustice] itself does with its own power when it is in the soul of a man who possesses it" (366e). Glaucon has already expressed the wish to know "what each is and what power it has all alone by itself when it is in the soul" (358b). In using this language to talk about justice, both brothers are accepting ② and ④, assumptions that Socrates had slipped into his arguments against Thrasymachus. ② had spoken of injustice (hence justice too) as something in a person that exercised certain powers; ④ located justice within the soul. Socrates has already succeeded in changing the subject of their conversation from justice as a characteristic of human actions to justice conceived as a trait of the human soul.

It is not yet clear what this distinction amounts to. When we attribute the virtue of honesty to someone's character, we generally mean that the person tells the truth. Character traits might be understood simply as shorthand for telling what a person has done. Glaucon and Adeimantus want more. By "justice by itself in the soul" they must mean some features of the soul that cause one to act justly, as neurosis may cause me to lose my temper, though neurosis is not the same thing as anger. They want Socrates to show that the features of the soul that produce just behavior also lead, by some natural process, to more happiness than do the features that produce unjust behavior. The argument from here to the end of Book 4, which is taken up again in Books 8 and 9, will aim at establishing this conclusion.

Suggestions for further reading

For information about the historical figure of Thrasymachus, see Gotoff, 'Thrasymachus of Calchedon and Ciceronian style,' *Classical Philology* 75 (1980): 297–311. Lycos, *Plato on Justice and Power* (Albany, SUNY Press, 1987) and Cross and Woozley, *Plato's Republic* (New York, St Martin's Press, 1964) are particularly helpful on this last part of Book 1, as are Bambrough, "Plato's political analogies," in P. Laslett, ed. *Philosophy, Politics, and Society* (Oxford, Blackwell, 1956), pp. 98–115, and Thayer, "Plato: the theory and language of function," in A. Sesonske, ed., *Plato's Republic* (Belmont, Calif., Wadsworth, 1966), pp. 21–39.

Annas, *An Introduction to Plato's Republic* (Oxford, Oxford University Press, 1981), Nettleship, *Lectures on the Republic of Plato* (2nd ed. London, Macmillan, 1901), and White, *A Companion to Plato's Republic* (Oxford, Blackwell, 1979) are useful in explaining the challenge posed by Glaucon and Adeimantus. See also the relevant sections of Crombie, *An Examination of Plato's Doctrines* (2 vols., London, Routledge & Kegan Paul, 1962), Murphy, *The Interpretation of Plato's Republic* (Oxford, Oxford University Press, 1951), and Taylor, *Plato: The Man and his Work* (London, Methuen, 1926).

Chapter 4

Justice
in the city
(Books 2–4)

To show how justice may naturally produce good effects, Socrates sets himself a broader task than the brothers assigned him. He will make his subject not merely justice as it exists in the soul, but also the justice of an entire city. Whether Plato conceives this larger project as a pretext for addressing political issues, or seriously thinks he needs the discussion of justice in the city to prove the worth of psychological justice, from this point on the *Republic* concerns itself with politics. At times, in fact – so much does Plato warm to the subject – the individual's justice is eclipsed by the question of how to produce and sustain a just city.

The city and the soul (368b–369b)

Since justice exists in both souls and cities, Socrates says, it should prove easier to study in the latter. Hence he will begin by asking how justice arises in a city, and only then apply what he has learned to the smaller matter of the soul.

59

Socrates offers no argument for his analogy, but asserts that because both cities and souls can be just, they must contain an identical characteristic called justice. He will argue in Book 4 that the analogy does hold, that what his inquiries have revealed about cities will hold true of individuals. Despite the surprising sound of this assumption, then, we should not regard it as a surreptitious move in the argument, but as a hypothesis: Plato will work out his picture of the city and then look to see how well it applies to the soul.

Already we can see that the analogy will predispose the *Republic* toward the conception of individual justice that Book 1 worked to introduce. In a just city, justice takes the form of just institutions and laws, and just relations among the city's residents. Its legal systems will not discriminate unfairly among citizens; nor will a small wealthy class enjoy disproportionate power. The justice of the city will consist in *internal relations*, whether between two individuals or between one individual and the city understood as a whole. Socrates will have little to say about a city's relations toward other communities, almost none of it concerned with just behavior (422e–423a, 469b–471b). So for the analogy between soul and city to work, the just soul will similarly have to be, not the soul of one who behaves justly toward other people, but a soul that is internally constituted in some particular way. This will mean, among other things, that the human soul contains internal divisions or "parts," corresponding either to the city's individual citizens or to collections of them.

Socrates' picture of the soul (Book 4) will follow out these implications of the city–soul comparison. The *Republic*'s political theory, for its part, will also be shaped by the comparison; for if a city resembles a soul, it should be thought of as a unity. The good of the citizenry ought to defer to the good of the city taken as a whole, since in the case of the soul only the good of the whole matters. Furthermore, in the case of the soul unanimity benefits the individual so much more than discord does, that the comparison predisposes us to prefer unanimity in the city over any manner of dissent. We shall therefore have to remain on our guard, as we follow the details both of the theory of the soul and of the theory of the city, to distinguish between those claims that follow from explicit arguments, and those that creep into the theory, unjustified and often unstated, thanks to the work of the analogy on Plato's imagination.

The first and second cities (369b–373e)

The primitive paradise (369b–372e)

Beginning with the needs for food, shelter, and clothing, Socrates describes the growth of a minimal community. Justice and injustice will reside somewhere in the relations this community makes possible, for if it is a real community it will contain both just and unjust behavior. Since this first city has been conjured up in the simplest terms, it will contain none of the aged institutions, bureaucracies, and power relations that complicate our study of existing political organizations. The seat of justice and injustice will come more readily into view.

It is hard to imagine a plainer community than this first city Socrates describes, though he is practical enough not to make the city *too* stark (369b–372e). It will have farmers, builders, and weavers, but also every variety of craftworker, even merchants and a currency. The city owes its remarkable simplicity to its having been derived, as if mathematically, from two principles:

1. ⑤ Humans taken individually are not self-sufficient. (369b)
2. ⑥ People are naturally disposed to perform different tasks. (370a–b)

The city comes into existence in the first place because of ⑤; it takes the form it has because of ⑥. To ⑤ the city owes, in particular, its characteristic of being a unity formed out of the multiplicity of its inhabitants. When Plato returns, through the *Republic*, to his emphasis on preserving the city's unity, he can claim to be returning to one of human society's guiding principles.

Given that a city must exist, and that it exists to satisfy human needs, the only remaining question is how those needs might be most efficiently met. Plato introduces ⑥, the principle of the division of labor, to explain why societies tend to be heterogeneous rather than homogeneous. Nothing could guarantee efficiency better than a social arrangement in which all work was done by those best suited to it.

A few comments about ⑥. First, the division of labor has a natural origin. Socrates repeatedly uses words for "nature" and "natural" in defending ⑥ (370a, b; 374e). Secondly, the principle should not be mistaken for praise of individuality: Plato wants nothing to do with a society that encourages experimentation in ways of life, as his description of democracy will make clear enough (557c–558c). ⑥ defends a political organization with the power to impose the different social roles on its citizens. Finally, ⑥ will have far-reaching implications. In this chapter alone, we shall find it justifying both the existence of a standing army and the censorship of dramatic poetry. Plato has been preparing for this principle's appearance with the proposition ③ that everything has its special work. ⑥ merely applies that principle to human beings.

The first city complete, Socrates asks where its justice and injustice may be found. Adeimantus suggests that they arose "somewhere in some need these men have of one another" (372a). ⑤ and ⑥ together entail that every city requires cooperation. Since justice is the essential social virtue, it must amount to cooperation. (① and especially ② are also reflected in Adeimantus's suggestion.) Plato cannot rest with this analysis, since he is about to turn to far more complex societies, whose justice and injustice call for more complex definitions. But the definition he finally reaches (433a) will resemble this initial account in finding justice in the cooperation among social groups with different functions.

Apart from wanting a model of the city, Plato has an ulterior motive in describing this primitive community. Glaucon looked back to the birth of human society as evidence for a conventional interpretation of justice. The history of an institution can often make what had been taken for granted suddenly look contingent or even arbitrary. If the concept of justice arose at a particular time in human societies, it is not an inevitable fact about such societies. Plato counters this skeptical use of history with his own story of the origins of society. By basing his first city entirely on ⑥ and ⑤, both of which he claims to be natural facts, he is arguing that human society is natural. Because justice arises in that one social relationship essential to every city, justice in turn becomes a natural concomitant to every city.

The second city (372e–373e)

Now Glaucon objects that Socrates has described "a city of pigs" (372d). The hardy hamlet strikes Glaucon as too unlike any civilized community that he might want to live in. To keep his society close to the demands of nature, Socrates has permitted its inhabitants only the desires required by nature; Glaucon, who has grown accustomed to more rarefied tastes, wants the city he imagines to provide for those tastes as well. So Socrates agrees to expand his initial account to produce what he calls a "feverish" and "luxurious" city, as opposed to the true or healthy city of his own fantasy (372e).

If the point of the political discussion had been to describe the best city possible, why look at a worse variety? Since Socrates never returns to his first city, the entire *Republic* might seem a betrayal of the political organization that Plato really wants. Some interpreters have suggested that the city of pigs was never Plato's ideal, because it has no place in it for the philosophical activity that Plato so highly values, and in general holds out no promise for the kind of self-awareness or reflection needed for the cultivation of genuine virtues like justice. Socrates never challenges Glaucon's description of this town as a city of pigs, so he may tacitly agree that life so simply described falls short of human society.

And yet Socrates clings to the thought that the first city is the true or healthy one. So it may be instead that, while that city does contain the best human lives, it is the wrong entity to study from the point of view of developing a political philosophy. The very perfection of the first city, which leaves it lacking any irrational or expansive elements of the sort that call for social constraint, may make it an unilluminating case study for a theory that will see justice as a network of restrictions. Perhaps justice will not appear as clearly unless it has the opportunity to contrast itself with the injustice possible in a more complex city. However desirable in itself, the city of pigs is not an apt subject for philosophical inquiry.

I lean toward this account, partly because Plato is fond of rural life (*Statesman* 271d–272b, *Laws* 739), but mainly because this passage is a warning against misreading the *Republic* as naked fantasy. To the extent that utopias describe the best communities possible, the *Republic* acknowledges and resists the temptation to utopia; it would be sweet to daydream about the perfect community, but Glaucon's grumble about that community's austerity shows that such daydreams would never bear fruit. Plato wants to produce a political philosophy not only rigorous in its theory, but also imaginable in practice. He will compromise enough with the world as he has found it to make his theory desirable to more than just a few ascetics. This does not mean that Plato concedes everything to popular tastes. Even though Socrates begins by listing every luxury an Athenian of his time could have wanted – from furniture and perfume to dramatic poetry – he will eventually purge this city of its dangerous excesses (399c). Not every taste will find satisfaction in the city, since some (especially the taste for poetry) are by their very natures conducive to immorality, while others (e.g. for jewelry) are tolerable only in moderation. But Socrates never again suggests trimming the city back down to its porcine first incarnation.

The guardians (373e–412b)

A standing army (373e–376c)

A luxurious city, however, will go to war (373d–e). (Here too, the philosopher we think of as a dreamy idealist shows how well he understands the material realities of politics.) Now ⑥ comes into play again: just as a city functions more efficiently when the natural cobbler and the natural merchant perform their tasks and no others, it will also function better if its warring is conducted by specialists, that is if it has a standing army (374), which Plato calls an army of guardians.

Plato now finds himself in a difficult position. Without ⑥ he would have no organizing principle to justify his city's politics, and his commitment to ⑥ forces him to accept the existence of a permanent professional army. At the same time, he has seen enough of politics to fear that a permanent class of warriors might impose a self-serving dictatorship on the defenseless citizenry. In such a city there could be no question of justice.

The army of Plato's city may call to mind ancient Sparta, which Plato admired in spite of his own city's war. He appreciated the discipline and stability of Spartan society; he appreciated, as every Athenian would (in an era before underdogs became attractive), the merits of a society that could win so many wars. But he also knew that in Sparta the class structure meant tyranny and civil war. The Spartans had originally settled their city by conquering a native population, the Helots, whom they forced into the subservient position of performing all productive labor. The warriors had to keep the Helots docile with the constant threat of force, and even so they sometimes rose up in protracted rebellions. If Plato wrote the *Republic* around 375 BC, as many suppose, he would have known of the latest revolt by the Helots, which by 370 had won them a substantial measure of independence. Rule by force was therefore both distasteful and, in the long run, inexpedient.

Thus, keeping the guardians loyal to the other citizens' best interests becomes Plato's next obstacle. He trusts the guardians' education to solve the problem. Like other radical reformers, he is a pessimist about the possibility of a good society, given human nature as it exists, and an optimist about the power of education to change human nature. But educational reform, as he conceives it, is no small matter of tinkering with reading lists or overhauling the city's systems of formal schooling. Plato's educational reform will transform the entire society. From this point to nearly the end of Book 3, Plato details what activities the young guardians may engage in, what sorts of poetry they will read, even what sorts of music they may listen to, in order that they might be made simultaneously fierce in war and gentle at home (375b–c).

The guardians' education (375b-412b)

Socrates calls music and gymnastics the two elements of the guardians' education. "Music" (*mousikē*) means all the activities sponsored by the Muses: poetry of every stripe, dance, astronomy, history – roughly what we call in English "the liberal arts." Of these, Socrates enters into the greatest detail on the subject of poetry; only in this case do his remarks about education become part of a larger critique of Greek culture.

Poetry (376c-398b)

From his earliest dialogues to the last one, Plato returns to the subject of poetry, almost always with the aim of distinguishing between one's irrational experience of poetry and the more reliable and virtuous participation in philosophy. In Book 10 of the *Republic* he speaks of an "ancient" quarrel between philosophy and poetry (607b), a quarrel which in his philosophical city must result in the expulsion of the latter. In the *Ion* and (more ambiguously) the *Phaedrus*, poetry becomes a species of madness; in scattered comments elsewhere (*Apology*, *Protagoras*, *Sophist*, *Laws*), Plato identifies poetry with ignorance, fraud, and intellectual confusion.

In Books 2 and 3 Plato's attack mostly focuses on the role of poetry in the guardians' education. First Socrates forbids the young guardians' exposure to those tales that depict the gods initiating evil, promoting unwarranted suffering, changing their shapes, or lying. Such myths misrepresent the gods and provide the wrong role models to the young. Nor should stories about gods or human heroes show them as weak or undignified, for the guardians ought to have no share in such traits. The protagonists especially should not fear death or lament it, and should master their ignoble appetites rather than yield to them.

It is too early in the game, Socrates says, to legislate the content of stories about human beings. That will have to wait until we have shown in argument what sort of life is in fact best (392c). Here Socrates seems to be saying that the regulation of poetry brings it into agreement with what we know to be true. This principle echoes Socrates' first criticism of tales about the gods, that they are lies that do not resemble, even allegorically, what we can demonstrate to be true about gods (377d–e, 379a). Since the poems of Homer and Hesiod accounted for nearly all of a young Athenian's reading, Plato wants to correct their errors. His censorship therefore seems to work only against falsehood, and only with an eye to audiences too young and gullible to read these pieces critically.

Justified in such terms, Plato's censorship may sound inoffensive, as if he only wanted to weed outdated textbooks from local schools, as we regularly discard books about astronomy, physics, and biology that contain superseded theories. Of course, Plato is speaking of falsehoods about the gods rather than about the motions of the planets. But even overlooking the important differences between these subjects, we cannot excuse this section so easily. How pernicious

Plato's censorship is depends on the answers to two questions: to what extent does the censorship in fact trim popular tales and poems in accord with the truth of the matter? And how far into the community will Plato reach to suppress false or insidious poetry?

In the beginning, Plato's goal would seem to be the avoidance of falsehood at all costs. But a few lines after the beginning of his critique, Socrates expresses his willingness to ban stories about Cronus "even if they were true" (378a). By the time he has gone on to Homeric heroes, Socrates' references to what must be true dwindle beside his more pressing concern over what effect the stories might have on the guardians (386c; 387b, c; 388a, d; 391e). Any history book can supply stories of tyrants who live into successful old age, dubious moral examples for all the verity of their existence. Plato would never praise such tales merely on account of their truth. Nor does he object to his rulers' lying to the young (382c–d). When a lie would benefit the city it is positively called for (389b–c; also 414–415, 458b–460b). But this greater importance of psychological effect over factual truth implies that the truth of Plato's sanitized myths is a happy accident, not an integral part of the argument. If he had reason to believe that the gods are indeed deceptive and malicious, he would still advocate censoring those stories about them. His educational plan aims above all else at inculcating the right kinds of behavior in his young soldiers.

Even if the *Republic* considers more than simple falsehood relevant, the fact that this is a plan for education might still make the charge of censorship sound premature. School libraries today avoid exposing children to blatantly offensive books. Controversial cases aside, no one advocates stocking the shelves with pornography or racist tracts.

Still, Plato's position is more radical than any advocated today. Contemporary book-bannings, at their worst, concentrate on books written for juveniles. Plato wants to bowdlerize Homer's *Iliad* and *Odyssey*, and the works of Hesiod and Aeschylus. Homer's poems stood at the heart of a cultural education, and together with Hesiod's poetry transmitted the essential elements of Greek religion. The tragedians were considered moral teachers to the city. In subjecting his civilization's morally most prestigious poetry to such stern scrutiny, Plato is advocating a censorship far more extensive than any familiar to contemporary democracies.

One more apology is possible. Children can be easily confused, especially by exciting stories. Near the end of the film *Birth of a Nation*, a mob of emancipated slaves besieges the cabin that holds an innocent white family of former slave-owners. The little cabin shakes before the crazed and bloodthirsty mob. At last the brave warriors of the Ku Klux Klan, tall and chaste in their white hoods and robes, ride over the hill to preserve justice. Here the artistic elements combine so powerfully to depict the Klansmen as heroes as to mislead young viewers into a despicable moral belief. It would be simpler not to let children watch the film until they are old enough to detach themselves from its narrative strategies. Why not let Plato do the same for the young guardians and Homer?

The problem, often overlooked, is that everyone in the city will be affected by the censorship. As long as anyone at all has heard the objectionable tales, eventually the children will hear them as well. Socrates comes quickly to specify that "as few as possible" should know that Cronus castrated his father (378a), that no one, "younger or older," may hear it said that a god causes evil (380b–c), and that mothers remain ignorant of stories about the gods changing shape, so that they do not pass them along to their children (381e). In order to protect the young guardians, the entire city will have to change its uses of poetry.

In Book 10 Plato will make clear that even virtuous adults risk moral corruption from the poets. For now this implication remains latent, since his topic is the education of the young. He tips his hand when Socrates says that the city will "not provide a chorus" (that is, not offer the public funding on which dramatic performances depended) to any tragedy that slanders the gods (383c), or says that certain things "should not be heard, from childhood on" (386a; see 387b). "[W]e'll not let our men believe" that Achilles was illiberal with money, or disdainful of the gods (391b). It is worth bearing this greater implication in mind, to lessen the shock of Book 10 when it comes. The plain fact is that this first criticism of poetry already takes us far beyond care for children's minds and into the realm of state control over the arts. One might agree with Plato's recommendations; but one may not believe them to be mild.

From the content of poetry, Socrates turns to its formal characteristics (392c–398b). Any poem's story can be cast in either narrative or dramatic form, depending on whether the author makes the characters speak for themselves. Drama tells its stories exclusively through dialogue; most historical narrative, as we know it, contains none; modern fiction, like the Homeric epics, combines dialogue and narrative. With few exceptions, Socrates proposes purging poetry of its dialogue. The *Iliad* and *Odyssey* will therefore become plot synopses of their former selves, while tragedy and comedy disappear entirely.

This passage commands special attention by virtue of being Plato's first discussion of the concept of *mimēsis*. Sometimes translated as "imitation," *mimēsis* began shortly before Plato's time to function as a technical term of aesthetics. Plato built on earlier mentions of the term, constructing a theory of the fine arts around the relationship between a thing or person and its representation in poetry and painting. In Book 3 his attention is more narrowly focused on the representation of character. Since the Platonic city was founded on the assumption that each citizen would perform only a single task ((6)), writing and performing a character's part become perversions of citizenship, since they give a single person more than one nature to live out (397d–398a). Even apart from that abstract objection, mimicry leads the young into bad habits, coarse language, and inappropriate responses to crises (395c–d). So the young guardians should at most dramatize the lives and acts of their most virtuous role models (396b–e).

Apart from its ambiguous use of *mimēsis* – Socrates sometimes seems to be thinking about acting, sometimes about playwriting — this stretch of argument is remarkably prosaic. It works only against the practice of reciting parts in a play, or the dialogue from an epic, and understands that practice in the crudest possible way. Finally, the implications of the argument are limited by Socrates' focus on the one who is acting out a part; since a fraction of any city would actually write for or perform in a dramatic festival, the argument blames mimetic literature for damage to what could only be a few citizens. In Book 10 Socrates will expand *mimēsis* into a more complex phenomenon, and overtly bar all poetry from the city.

Music and gymnastics (398b–412b)

Most of the remainder of Book 3 prescribes more details of the guardians' education. These call for little explanation: the modes and rhythms of music, and the guardians' physical training, all aim at producing tough soldiers, experienced enough in intellectual culture not to treat the unarmed citizens savagely, but not so softened by sweet food and music as to become incapable of fighting the city's enemies. Education unites their aesthetic taste with their conscience.

By now it should have become evident that Plato's attention has drifted from the inhabitants of his city as a whole to the army that defends them. After introducing the guardians, he hardly goes back to the huge class of merchants, farmers, artisans, and wage-laborers, except occasionally to say that they should know their place. *Their* children's education remains unexamined; the pattern of their daily life apparently deserves no comment, though Plato will soon specify the dining and sexual practices of his guardians. It has become a commonplace to accuse Plato the aristocrat of keeping himself haughtily unaware of ordinary people's lives. Whatever truth it contains, that accusation suggests that the large productive class is a class of thuggish, unskilled workers. In fact, Plato conceives of this class as equivalent to an entire Athens: some of its members make shoes, but others are doctors, and others wealthy traders. Plato says little about them because their lives remain unchanged.

More importantly, Plato addresses only the class of guardians because only they *need* special attention. The members of the productive class find sufficient incentive for their labors in the profit they earn. Their motives are purely and comprehensibly economic. But the standing army cannot be permitted economic motives, since its power within the city would soon lead the soldiers to loot the citizens. The good city may only exist if political power remains divorced from economic power. (Plato saw as clearly as Marx that in the usual course of events all power rests on wealth.) Without the chance to share in the city's riches, the guardians need another incentive; their education provides it, by molding them into obedient patriots.

Class relations and the justice of a city (412b–434c)

The complete political plan (412b–427c)

With two of the city's classes specified, Plato turns to the matter of who "will rule and who be ruled" (412b). For that task Socrates selects the best and oldest guardians. In one sense this act does not define a third class, since the rulers come from the ranks of the guardians. But because the work of the two groups will differ, Socrates gives them two different titles, "complete guardian" for the ruler and "auxiliary" for the one ruled (414b). Just as he stopped referring to the city's productive class after introducing the standing army, so too Socrates will increasingly ignore the army from this point on, as he examines the nature and nurture of the city's administrators. We see as soon as they are described, for instance, how much of the potential rulers' lives will be marked by tests above and beyond the military discipline they grow up with (412e–414a). If the concentration of arms in the class of soldiers had made Socrates eager to provide for their civic loyalty, the greater concentration of legislative, executive, and judicial power into the hands of the guardians makes him double his efforts to exclude inappropriate citizens from this rank. His stress on the subject betrays Plato's worry that the good city will never work *without* a concentration of power, but that *given* a concentration of power it will be kept only by superhuman effort from sliding into corruption.

We immediately come upon one of these superhuman efforts in the *noble lie* that Socrates proposes to tell the citizens (414b–415d). Their memories of childhood and education had been a dream, for in fact, the story will go, all the citizens sprang fully grown out of the earth. As they are children of the earth, it is not surprising that some (the guardians) have gold mixed into their souls, others (the auxiliaries) silver, the rest bronze and iron. Hence their place in the city reflects their true nature as crafted by gods, not the historical accident that separates the citizens of other societies.

Again we find Socrates seeking a natural basis for social phenomena. He takes his story to be an allegory of ⑥; the lie is "noble" (*kalon*) because it resembles the truth, as poets' lies about the gods do not (see 382d). As any effective propagandist has to, he

71

fashions this myth of the state out of elements that the Greek audience would have found familiar. The tale is "Phoenician" (414c) because it recalls the mythical birth of all Thebans out of the earth in which Cadmus, a Phoenician, sowed a serpent's teeth. The differentiation of people by metal, meanwhile, recalls Hesiod's five ages of humanity. Ultimately conservative about religion – he regularly defers to the Delphic oracle as the highest religious authority (427b–c, 461e, 540c) – Plato uses traditional mythology to justify political power, as European monarchs, once their legitimacy was threatened, began to speak of the divine right of kings.

The myth is meant to generate blind loyalty: it implies that the city is its citizens' mother (414e), and that nothing matters more than each citizen's assignment to the right class (415b–c). ⑥, the principle of the division of labor, has by now taken precedence over any question of what the citizens prefer, or how they want to live. This might be the first point in the *Republic*, therefore, at which its readers accuse Plato of totalitarian politics. Not only has he separated a society into castes, but he wants the people to accept a myth of the state that justifies their own positions. Although Plato is no democrat, one might defend him from the harshest political criticisms by pointing out how his classes are supposed to function. Since the class differences in his city separate economic power from political power, a higher status does not translate into wealth or enjoyment. Indeed, we will find Adeimantus complaining of the rulers' unhappiness (419a; also 519d–521a), because ruling this city promises no benefits to the rulers.

Furthermore, Plato wants to base class distinctions on ability instead of wealth or birth. The noble lie implies that a guardian's child will pass to the lower class if its soul is iron or bronze, but also that a talented child of farmers or laborers can become a guardian (415b–c). Socrates makes this promise explicit at 423c–d, and at 468a provides for the demotion of cowardly guardians. It is a nice promise, even if we may be permitted a healthy skepticism about it. Plato expects gold and silver children to turn up only very rarely among bronze parents; so the *Republic* identifies no perspicuous, workable mechanism for examining children of the productive class for signs of talent. Without some such examinations, they can never be moved up. Plato means what he says, but he does not care enough about social mobility.

It would be such an injustice, on his terms and on ours, to deny gifted children the place that they are most suited to, that anyone who seems to be establishing a caste system but promises that mobility is possible had better say exactly *how* it will be possible. Anything vaguer is an insult to the people in question, however sincere Plato may have been, in the same way that modern politicians' slogans about poverty, however heartfelt, demean the poor if the slogans are not developed into programs.

With the social structure of his city in place, Plato begins to describe its workings. As before, the greatest issue is the potential corruption of the guardians. Although the fully radical proposals for avoiding that corruption will wait until Book 5, already we can see how unusually the guardians will live. The rulers and auxiliaries will share their meals. No one will own more than essential personal property; no one will have a private room (416d–e). No guardian or soldier may ever touch gold or silver, or even be under the same roof with it (417a). In a sense the soldiers' education never ends, for this discipline is intended to stave off any temptation they might feel to seize more worldly power.

Socrates will expand on the guardians' lives later, and especially on one comment made only in passing here, concerning the community of women and children (423e). He says enough already to make clear why the auxiliaries and rulers are permitted nothing we would recognize as private. Even to consider private benefits for this class would be to give its members an allegiance distinct from their allegiance to the city. The rulers would divide into factions, and the city as a whole would lose its opportunity for happiness.

One typical version of this Platonic emphasis on the whole city comes at 420b–421c, when Socrates answers Adeimantus' complaint that the guardians will not be happy. Another occurs in a discussion of war: every city but the ideal one, Socrates says, "is very many cities but not a city . . . There are two, in any case, warring with each other, one of the poor, the other of the rich" (422e–423a). This passage, as revealing as it is typical, names Plato's greatest fear, civil unrest, and identifies its cause in competition over money. Plato imagines a solution not in terms of an equitable balance among competing interests, but in the eradication of that competition. For Plato all civil discord is a sign of political failure – not because he venerates order for its own sake, but because he refuses to see discord as the clash between genuinely opposed philosophical views. Like Marx, he locates all conflict in economic conflict; hence it always indicates that members of the city are putting their immediate needs above the good of all. Civil unrest represents an abandonment of the enterprise that the city makes possible.

Justice and the other virtues (427c-434c)

Finally Socrates returns to one originating question of the conversation, "What is justice?" The participants have characterized a city in enough detail to assure themselves of its goodness; now they can use it as the large-scale model of justice they needed. Socrates lays out the strategy for finding justice:

1. The city we have described is perfectly good.
∴ 2. It is wise, courageous, moderate, and just.
∴ 3. If we set aside those defining characteristics of the city responsible for its wisdom, courage, and moderation, whatever characteristics remain will define its justice. (427e–428a)

Although this argument may point to a fruitful *strategy* for identifying justice, we should not expect too much from it as a *proof*. Even granting the truth of (1), the argument cannot reach (3) without two unstated assumptions. First, (2) will not follow from (1) unless we assume

1′. If a thing is good, then it is wise, courageous, moderate, and just.

Goodness must include at least these virtues for (2) to follow. All four were indeed accepted by most of Plato's contemporaries as virtues, though not in any systematic way. But even if we accept (1′), we also need

2′. If a thing is good, then it is wise, courageous, moderate, and just, *and nothing besides*.

For Plato to know that once moderation, wisdom, and courage have been accounted for, "what's left over" must be justice, he first needs to demonstrate that the four virtues exhaust goodness, that besides them no other virtues exist. In some intuitive sense, of course, the four may add up to a moral life. Together they allow for both action and reflection, both self-regarding constraint and consideration of others. The problem is that, as Plato lays out this section, he makes the site of justice appear to depend on its being the only virtue not accounted for when the other three have been assigned to their places in the city. He turns an unexamined casual belief into a technical claim, much as if an astronomer were to pronounce the cause of supernovas to be a mineral, on the grounds that it is neither animal nor vegetable. Obvious counterexamples come to mind: if generosity should turn out to be a virtue just like these others, then separating out the first three virtues of the city might leave us with some characteristics that constitute its generosity, instead of its justice. The suppressed premise (2′) will probably seem all the less convincing to those modern readers who, under the influence of Christian ethics, might want to include humility or love in the list. But even someone of Plato's time and place might object that the list is incomplete. In other dialogues Plato treats piety as a virtue (*Laches* 199d, *Meno* 78d, *Protagoras* 329c, *Gorgias* 507b); by the time he writes the *Republic* it has disappeared from his list. Why?

The problems do not end there. How will we know what to count as "characteristics" of the good city relevant to its virtues? Once we have named three of the city's features, how clear will it be that something else is "left over"? Taken by itself, the argument can dissolve into metaphors. As a method for inquiry it works much better, prodding Socrates to discover where the city's virtues lie, and therefore to specify the general nature of a community's virtue.

Socrates and Glaucon easily conclude that the city owes its wisdom to the rulers (428d). They are not the only citizens with knowledge of their work, but they are the only ones whose wisdom makes the city wise. (Plato cannot say at this point that wisdom essentially involves commanding, because he has not yet analyzed the nature of wisdom: that will come in Books 5–7.) A city's wisdom manifests itself in the city's treatment of its citizens and of other cities (428c–d). But that wisdom is nothing but wise rule, and rule is the work of the guardians. To be a wise city is therefore to have wise guardians (428a–429a).

Why does Plato rule out the expertise of other citizens so quickly? He would answer that only the guardians' knowledge concerns benefits to the city *as a whole* (428d). This is not a matter of the producers' motives; Plato cannot justifiably claim that a doctor or shipbuilder never considers the good of someone else. One may pursue money and still think about other people from time to time. The limitation of the productive class follows instead from the kind of work they do. A farmer may know best how to maximize the city's production of wheat. But political questions about farming, which the city will answer either wisely or unwisely, concern tariffs on imported food, embargoes on exports, and state support for foods otherwise too expensive to produce. In such cases the general benefit of food production needs to be weighed against other benefits to the city. Even supposing farmers look altruistically beyond their interests, the narrowness of their expertise would still leave them incapable of subsuming their farming knowledge under a more general question about the city. Farming knowledge is, *ex hypothesi*, the only expertise they have. (Modern proponents of free enterprise may object that a society functions best when all its producers aim at their own profit. But even if that is true, the decision to make enterprise free in the city can only be made by the rulers. Even advocates of the free market would not call a society wise just because it contains profitable businesses, but only if its government permits those businesses to seek profit without hindrance.)

Plato's point here is not to glorify the guardians, but to analyze the concept of "a wise city," in a way that will yield him a strategy for defining justice. A city's virtues can seem vague and disembodied entities. Plato points a way out of the vagueness by locating wisdom in the individual wisdom of the members of a class.

Unsurprisingly, courage then turns out to mean the courage of the city's soldiers, since only their courage makes the city brave (429a–430c). Moderation likewise inheres in the city's classes, though this virtue calls for a more complicated analysis (430d–432b). *Sophrosunē*, the subject of Plato's early dialogue *Charmides*, means in the first place a habit of restrained, even deferential behavior, self-control that expresses itself in society as modesty. But it also implies self-knowledge: one becomes gentle by virtue of being conscious of one's shortcomings. Now that the simpler virtues have brought Socrates to look for virtues in the city's class structure, he can define self-mastery as the harmonious domination of one class over the rest. Because their domination is harmoniously achieved, the classes ruled by the guardians accept their rule willingly.

Only justice remains to be defined. But rather than look for the social structure his analysis has left out, Socrates announces that justice in the finished city is the principle according to which he and his interlocutors had constructed the city, namely the principle that everyone has a single job to do and ought only to do that one job (432e–433a). This definition deviates in one respect from ⑥, for Socrates is no longer interested in the division of occupations into farming, shoe-making, and so on. The effect of carpenters making shoes poses little threat to a city's well-being, compared to the effect of either carpenters or shoemakers trying to rule (434a–b). The city's three classes correspond to the three major kinds of work a person may do for their society, and it is these three labors that must remain distinct for a city to be just.

Socrates justifies his definition with a blend of common-sense and theoretical arguments. First, he identifies his definition with the proverbial injunction "not to be a busybody" (433a). Then he claims that it satisfies the argument with which he began looking for virtues. Justice is "left over" in the city after the other three virtues have been defined, presumably by being a virtue not identical with any of those three. Its status is higher than the others' because, when the members of each class do what they ought to, the rulers will rule (wisely), the soldiers will preserve the city (bravely), and the farmers and laborers will get their private work done and leave the rest to the guardians. In short, if everyone in the city is politically just, the city as a whole will be wise, courageous, and moderate. Justice includes all the other virtues, though it is not *identical* to the sum of the others, because it has a distinct description.

It is clear now that Plato has not relied illegitimately on the argument that introduced this section. The virtues other than justice can be assigned to their classes of the city whether or not they add up to goodness; as for justice, Plato's essential point about it here may be lifted off the argument to stand meaningfully by itself: justice cannot be accounted for by the operations of any one class, institution, or social body in a community. Analytical approaches to justice will always fail to explain its origins, as long as the inquirer looks at something less than the whole community, i.e. looks at some social action that is less than the cooperation of all parts of the community. The point works just as well if there are three or thirty virtues; Plato has confined himself to four to make his point clearer.

But now it seems as if the irreducibility of justice to any one class in the city makes the whole class structure irrelevant. Why paint a picture of the stratified society if its stratifications are expressly unrelated to the city's most important virtue? Here Plato has a plain answer. Justice may not reduce to the functioning of any single part of the city, but its cooperative work requires parts of the city if it is to be defined. The cooperation occurs among discretely identified groups in the city. So the purpose behind Plato's theoretical division of the city had been all along to show how the classes come harmoniously back together.

Socrates concludes this passage with two more arguments for his definition of justice, which try to accommodate his theoretical account to common conceptions of justice. First he points out that justly decided court cases are those that assign the appropriate reward to each person. That appropriateness of reward is nothing but an example of his definition (433e–434a). Next he argues that, since the movement between classes destroys a city, and since the greatest evil one can commit against a city is injustice, social mobility must constitute injustice. Social stasis therefore is the essence of justice (434a–c). A crucial premise of this brisk little argument is the assumption that injustice is the greatest evil one can commit against a city; I take that to be a popularly held belief. In the end, common sense remains for Plato a touchstone for political theory. This does not mean he is out to justify the prejudices of his fellow Athenians; nor could anyone accuse him of having erected the theoretical structure of the *Republic* only to reassure his contemporaries that all their beliefs were right. But a philosopher bent on examining ethical and political concepts is not free simply to redefine them. However alien justice might first appear when Plato has defined it, it must bear some relationship to justice as commonly conceived, or Socrates' interlocutors will rightly complain that this condition of the city may be useful and stable, but not in any way *just*.

Plato continues the balancing act that he began in Book 1. He wants to challenge and change his readers' *conception* of justice in order to produce a better world, but he also wants to preserve their *allegiance* to justice enough not to destroy the world as it stands. In this sense his political and ethical theories need to be both radical and conservative.

Suggestions for further reading

Crombie, *An Examination of Plato's Doctrines* (2 vols., London, Routledge & Kegan Paul, 1962), and Guthrie, *A History of Greek Philosophy*, vol. IV: *Plato* (Cambridge, Cambridge University Press, 1975) are both useful for understanding this section of reading. On the critique of poetry see Belfiore, "'Lies unlike the truth,'" *Transactions of the American Philological Association* 115 (1985): 45–57, Havelock, "Plato on poetry," in A. Sesonske, ed., *Plato's Republic* (Belmont, Calif., Wadsworth, 1966), pp. 116–35, and Tate, "Plato, Socrates and the myths," *Classical Quarterly* 30 (1936): 142–5. Annas, *Introduction to Plato's Republic* (Oxford, Oxford University Press, 1981) and Nettleship, *Lectures on the Republic of Plato* (2nd ed., London, Macmillan, 1901) are particularly illuminating on the definitions of the virtues and the relations among the virtues.

By this point in the *Republic*, most readers will have begun to grow suspicious of Plato's dictatorial tendencies. No one has pressed this accusation more forcefully than Popper, *The Open Society and Its Enemies* (London, Routledge & Kegan Paul, 1945), which calls Plato the predecessor to modern totalitarian states. For responses to Popper, see Bambrough, ed., *Plato, Popper, and Politics* (Cambridge, Heffer, 1967) and Robinson, "Dr. Popper's defence of democracy," in *Essays in Greek Philosophy* (Oxford, Clarendon Press, 1969).

Chapter 5

Justice
in the soul
(Book 4)

.

The last eleven pages of Book 4 (434d–445e) bring
Socrates back from his musings about a well-designed
city to the subject that Glaucon and Adeimantus had
challenged him to explain, justice as it arises in the
soul. This section begins to deliver answers to the
dialogue's initiating questions, though often with hints
of further, unanticipated questions.

Justice in the soul (434d–445e)

Here, as at a number of points in the *Republic*, the
dialogue's double argument can be disorienting. At
times Socrates' language suggests that justice in the
city serves only to illuminate justice in the individual
soul; at other times he speaks as though the city had
been his subject all along. This dual approach is in fact
one of the *Republic*'s virtues, for it shows that Plato
takes both subjects seriously. If the dialogue were only
an extended argument from analogy, then at this point
we would find Plato mechanically transferring what he

says about the city to the individual soul. Instead, he emphasizes that the political analysis will have to work for the soul on solid psychological grounds. If it does not, Socrates says, they will go back to the city and revise their account of *its* virtues (434d–435a). At least in theory, the analogy to the city works only to suggest how to look for justice in the soul.

Socrates claims to be justified in reading city politics back into soul politics, because the city owes its virtues to its citizens' virtues (435b–d). The rulers' wisdom makes the city wise; this must mean that the city's wisdom will resemble the human wisdom that produced it. (This passage suggests, more than any other, that for Plato the individual virtues are more fundamental than the political ones.) But if any virtue of the city is to share more than a name with a person's virtue, the two examples of the virtue must also bear some deeper structural resemblance to one another. We need something in the soul that corresponds to the city's divisions – not to the individual citizens, since they scarcely enter into Socrates' description of justice, but to the classes whose interaction makes a city function badly or well. The stretch of argument that follows (436b–441c) aims at showing that the soul is complex enough to support the analogy.

Parts of the soul (436b–441c)

The core argument of this section lays out a psychological theory according to which the soul has three parts, or faculties, or types of motivation. Any word would be imprecise here. Of course a soul cannot have parts in the way that a piece of land or a stretch of time does. But "part" is vague enough not to presuppose such a literal interpretation. For his part, Plato seems remarkably unconcerned about what sorts of divisions these parts of the soul might be; in this respect he resembles Freud, who in most of his own explications of the soul's topography says nothing about what or where the superego is. If the reader wants a sense of "part" that will make Plato's theory more intelligible, it might do to think of the parts of the soul as analogous to the parts of a car, namely as elements that must work together to make the greater unity work. Or they are like the parts in a play, parts for the actors who perform it. In any case, the soul itself is a wholly hazy entity, especially in modern secular societies, and imprecision might be the best approach. It may help to substitute "personality" or "character," which despite certain unwanted connotations are broad enough to serve. "Personality" also saves us from thinking of the soul as immortal. Although Plato believes that it is, he does not need immortality for his psychological theory.

The argument begins with the observation that souls contain conflict:

1. Conflict in the soul implies different parts that are opposed to each other. (436b–438a)
2. Desire is opposed by the calculating part of the soul. (438a–439d)
3. Spirit is different from both desire and the calculating part. (439e–441c)
∴ 4. From (1), (2), and (3), the parts of the soul are identical in number and function with the parts of the city. (441c)
∴ 5. Virtue in the individual person will be structured the same way as virtue in the city. (441c–442d)

Like Freud, Plato sees inner conflict as both the most intrinsically important fact about human existence, and the phenomenon that most reveals the structure of the personality. What Plato calls injustice, approximately what Freud calls neurosis – what both consider the greatest misery – is the debilitating loss of control that results when one feels inclined at once to accept and refuse, to love and reject (437b). Hence the phenomenon needs to be studied. And both Plato and Freud look at malfunctioning souls to learn how the mechanism ought to work.

Plato begins with the premise that when one thing performs two different acts at once, the thing must contain more than one part (436b–437a). The soul performs two different acts when it moves toward an object at the same time that it keeps itself from it (437a–438a). Socrates argues at length (438a–439a) that desires by themselves are blind impulses, not the sorts of drives that regulate themselves in any way. Therefore, a thirsty person's urge not to drink, as when the water supply needs to be rationed, cannot be a desire just like the desire to drink. It must be the faculty of reason that counsels against drink when one's thirst is clamoring for it (439c–d). The dieter's debate over whether to take another helping, the night guard's battle to stay awake, and the celibate's struggle with lust, all exemplify the conflict between reason and desire. Reason sometimes holds back desire out of what we call moral motives (as, perhaps, in the case of the celibate), sometimes (as in the dieter's case) out of prudential ones. But always reason seems to be that part of the soul best suited, and most inclined, to look after the welfare of the entire person. It is not one more impulse among many, but the part of the soul by virtue of which I *decide* between two desires, instead of being simply *buffeted about* by them. Plato is not looking simply at cases of accepting and rejecting an object, but at cases in which the two motivations are qualitatively different.

Into this simplified picture of conflict, Plato introduces what he calls "spirit" (*thumos*), distinct from both reason and desire, though more sympathetic to the former. Socrates' examples of *thumos* (440a, c) make sense if we construe it as anger, as long as we stretch anger to encompass such complex feelings as ambition and competitiveness, and such moral emotions as indignation and the thirst for revenge. These emotions entail a judgment, over and above the raw feeling of anger. I cannot feel indignant without believing that someone has got away with doing something wrong: in the absence of that belief the feeling is not indignation, but a flush in my face. Being angry means doing some thinking. So spirit shows traits of both the other parts of the soul. It can support reason, because anger and competitiveness can make one more apt to act as reason commands. My cool judgment that someone is being mistreated will not always goad me into intervening, especially if I worry about the risk to myself. But if I get angry at the malefactor, I may well forget the danger and butt in.

Some variety of shame also has its roots in this part of the soul. To feel ashamed of having lapsed back into smoking after two months' abstinence is to feel angry at oneself for the weakness. Thus the inclination toward anger, if properly trained, can serve as a powerful motivational force in the ethical life. By introducing spirit into what would otherwise be a simple dualism between reason and desire, Plato offers the rational impulse a strategy for good behavior. Once trained, anger can enforce the moral law within the individual's soul, because it matches the appetites in strength.

Platonic justice and ordinary justice (441c–445e)

Given this much similarity between the class structure of an ideal city and the motivational structure of a soul, Socrates claims justification for applying the definitions of virtue from one domain to the other. A soul is wise when its reason rules, and courageous when its spirited part acts bravely (441c–e), moderate when all three parts accept the rule of one's faculty of calculation (442c–d). Justice, as the supreme or all-inclusive virtue, therefore consists in each part performing its appropriate task (441d–e). Its essence is unity: justice makes one "[become] entirely one from many" (443e). Socrates was right, after all, to have called justice *the* virtue of the soul ((4)) in his battle with Thrasymachus. He was also right to have seen in justice the spirit of restraint ((1)) and cooperation ((2)), though Thrasymachus mocked the very ideas.

If the soul is as Plato has described it, it will function smoothly only through the rule of its calculating function and the well-trained expression of its spirited part. Anyone who has experienced inner conflict will agree that existence is more desirable without it. And since it is the calculating part that recognizes the demands of morality, its rule within the soul will produce actions most in accord with the strictures of ethics. Thus the soul that functions best by nature will also be the best-behaved: the just soul is the happy soul. Scientific facts about human psychology will have provided the foundation for morality.

To this point (442d) Socrates has argued that the well-organized soul, which he calls just by analogy with the just city, is the healthy soul. But when Glaucon and Adeimantus originally challenged Socrates to show that the just man could be happy despite his misfortunes, they meant one who was just in the ordinary sense of the word, one who performed actions conventionally regarded as just. The justice that has emerged from Socrates' process of definition consists in a balance of power among parts of the soul. Even supposing that someone with a soul in that condition will enjoy life more than anyone in psychic disarray, what good does that do to the one who obeys legal and moral rules?

Socrates first plays up the similarities between the justice he has defined and the one the brothers asked about, to reassure them that he has answered their challenge. Immediately after offering this reassurance, he switches to the opposite tack and emphasizes the *difference* between justice in its everyday description and the new justice he has defined. Merely because existing society has myopically stumbled on some truths about how to live, does not mean that it has understood the significance of those truths.

Socrates moves the two conceptions of justice closer together when he tests the new definition, as he says, "in the light of the vulgar standards" (442e). The just-souled will be the least likely people to embezzle money, rob temples, betray friends, break oaths, or commit any impiety, adultery, or filial negligence (442e–443a). These deeds are committed by those with their souls in some less orderly pattern (442e, 443a). Therefore, the cause of conventionally just behavior is the political arrangement in the soul (443b). Socrates has not, after all, changed the subject.

At the same time, he has not left things as they were. Justice in the good city, Socrates says, now appears in its true light as "a phantom of justice" (443c), an approximation to the genuine article. True justice applies the injunction to stay in place to "what is within," to the parts of the soul (443c–e). Those with just souls, when they behave according to conventional rules of justice, do so not out of blind adherence to the rules, but because that behavior helps to preserve the order in their souls.

Socrates insists on this last claim (444a–e). Just actions are both *symptoms* and contributing *causes* of justice in the soul, unjust ones both symptoms and causes of injustice. Someone with the riotous internal constitution of the unjust will give in to every impulse and carry out every shameful misdeed, and those misdeeds will, through habit, encourage the unruly elements of the soul and leave reason still more powerless. Just and unjust actions of the sorts that Glaucon and Adeimantus asked about are therefore still relevant to this discussion of justice, but in the secondary way that symptoms are relevant to the discussion of a disease: they betray the existence of a deeper problem and can exacerbate it, but they are not identical with it. (See pp. 94–8 for more on this issue.)

Having defined justice and injustice, Socrates needs to address the second part of the brothers' challenge, namely to show that justice by itself, even without its social rewards, will benefit the just (444e–445a). To prove the superiority of justice, Socrates will examine all the species of injustice available to souls and cities, and argue in each case that the vices lead naturally to misery, or at least to less happiness than virtue does (445a–c). The end of Book 4 (445c–e) finds Socrates poised to go through his list of five political regimes and the five corresponding souls, from the one best form of each through the categories of badness, down to the worst souls and cities.

Further discussion

Plato's psychology gains familiarity from its *prima facie* resemblance to Freud's; it is also the picture of the soul we expect from Plato, with reason, philosophers' perennially favorite faculty, disciplining the more pedestrian desires. But since this section contains the kernel of Socrates' answer to Glaucon and Adeimantus, it is worth puzzling at greater length over a few of the steps in these pages that have most exercised scholars and students.

What is desire?

This part of the soul probably strikes the reader as transparent enough, since everyone has experienced desire. The problem is that once we get away from the examples of hunger and lust, which crowd out their competitors in philosophical discussions of the desires, we become less sure about what counts as one. Once that grows more obscure, it becomes harder to spot the defining characteristics of desire. If Plato makes this part of the soul too complex, he cannot draw the sharp distinction he needs between a desire and the calculation that it should be curbed. If, on the other hand, he makes the third part of the soul too simple, if desire comes to look too bestial, then the word "desire" will only work to describe hunger and thirst, not also all the other desires that need to fit into that commodious category.

The problem arises in the first place because of Plato's use of inner conflict to demonstrate the complexity of the soul. Suppose that instead of the examples he chose, Socrates had described someone who was simultaneously thirsty and libidinous. In such a person the appetites would stretch out (as Plato might put it) in two directions at once. Since pursuing and drinking cool water is ordinarily incompatible with pursuing sexual gratification, it may be said to imply the negation of the latter pursuit. Then we have a conflict in this sexually excited thirsty person between wanting and not-wanting, embracing and denying, just the sort of ambivalence that Socrates takes to characterize ethically relevant conflicts. But if the conflict between thirst and sexual desire is a legitimate conflict, it calls for a further division within the conflicted person's soul. In that case, the rag-bag of "desire" divides up into a mob of more specific appetites, each corresponding to a part of the soul, and the soul looks something like this:

> reason
> spirit
> hunger
> thirst
> sexual desire
> sleepiness
> greed (580e)
> morbid fascination

(I take this last desire from the story of Leontius at 440a. That the corpses and the executioner remain outside the city walls suggests a taboo surrounding the execution of criminals; so Leontius' urge to look has the morbid quality of violations of death taboos.) "Desire" begins to look like a lazy thinker's umbrella term for several other motivations, any two of which may come into conflict.

Plato recognizes the multiplicity of desires. In Book 9 he calls the appetites a "crowd" and a "swarm," and the soul in which they run free "anarchic" (see 573e–575a). He hints that the complete psychological theory may be more complicated than his analysis has shown, when Socrates mentions that there might be "some other parts in between" the three he has unearthed (443d). And yet this multiplication of psychic entities threatens to destroy Plato's theory. The analogy between city and soul gets lost; worse, the primary conclusion of this section fails to follow. For if all these conflicts occur at once, there is nothing special about the conflict between reason and any appetite.

The demands of reason take their place alongside the demands of hunger. The soul resembles a democracy with no elected officials, in which politics has become a competition among all impulses to gain the upper hand.

Eager to show that the soul's many desires share some essential property, and also to distinguish their demands from the voice of reason, Socrates argues that they lack any means to qualify themselves, aside from their choice of object:

> [T]hirsting itself will never be a desire for anything other than that of which it naturally is a desire – for drink alone – and, similarly, hungering will be a desire for food. (437e)

> So a particular sort of thirst is for a particular kind of drink, but thirst itself is neither for much nor little, good nor bad, nor, in a word, for any particular kind, but thirst itself is naturally only for drink. (439a)

If thirst by itself could discriminate between the drinks that will quench it and those that only bring the thirst back with a vengeance, or between a quantity of drink that will satisfy the body and a quantity that sends it into cramps, then thirst could curb itself. Needless to say, reason would have no work to do – we would lose any sense of a conflict between reason and thirst. To make that conflict clear, Socrates strips thirst of any powers of judgment or deliberation. Then when reason conflicts with an appetite, it conflicts in a way that two appetites cannot conflict with one another. If I have to choose between the contingently incompatible desires for eating and sleeping, then I directly follow my stronger wish. The philosophical example of Buridan's ass, equiposed between its water and hay and paralyzed by indecision, describes a case of incompatible desires, but not two desires that directly attack each other. But if I choose between eating and hewing to my diet, I am caught between two kinds of motivation, one of which considers factors that the other, because of its non-deliberative nature, is incapable of understanding.

The Platonic city offers a helpful comparison. Although the rulers and auxiliaries each have a single job to do, the large class that Socrates calls "the ruled" accounts for a multiplicity of skills. These shipbuilders, farmers, musicians, barbers, and doctors hardly perform the same tasks. We can only specify the nature of this third estate's work by identifying what it does *not* do: the members of this class work toward private, *non*-political goals. So too in the soul: disparate though the appetites may be, they resemble one another in their unconcern for the whole person. They are not necessarily more stupid than reason so much as they are heedless of reason's concerns. Reason deserves to rule because "it is wise and has forethought about all of the soul" (441e); as such, only it even entertains the question of how a given desire, or its satisfaction, will affect the person. Appetites no more know how to rule the soul than doctors know how to set public policy. All desires, therefore, however blunt or specific, natural or perverse, join together in their unconcern for the good of the person. To desire an object is not simply to go after it, but to go *gropingly*.

This picture of the "lower" drives is familiar enough. Too familiar, in fact. For if Plato's account of the soul opens itself up to an interpretation of desire too contemptuous toward that kind of human motivation, the account threatens to fail as a psychological theory. Normally Plato does not think of all appetite as dirty, bad, and bodily. Sometimes he comes close to it, though. And oversimplifying desire in this way has two bad consequences. First, it makes a mystery of Plato's preference for harmony in the soul, a preference on which his ethical theory relies. Secondly, it excludes too many other motives, which find themselves without a place in the soul.

At 431a–b, when examining the virtues of the city, Socrates speaks of moderation as a kind of self-mastery: "The phrase 'stronger than himself' is used when that which is better by nature is master over that which is worse." This "something worse" refers to the person's desires (see 431c–d), even though Socrates has not yet mapped out his psychological theory. Now, it is striking that, on the whole, Book 4 refrains from calling the appetites a worse part of the soul. They form the *lowest* part, to be sure (443d), the part that ought to be reason's slave (444b), but not a part with intrinsically immoral aims. Immorality arises not from the existence of desires, since many of them are necessary to life, but from their usurpation of the rule that belongs to reason (443d, 444b).

This is Plato's considered view. But sometimes his language

betrays a more condemnatory attitude toward the appetites. In the passage just quoted Socrates calls them *worse* than the other parts. In that case, the good life would require not that the three parts of the soul harmonize with one another, as individually valuable impulses coordinated to produce a greater good (443d–e; cf. 589a–b), but that the worst of the parts suffer constant and unyielding suppression. Though Plato does not want to embrace this idea, he does not always take pains to distance himself from it.

A bestial interpretation of desire also threatens the plausibility of Plato's theory. Consider examples of conflict that Socrates never describes. Friendship may conflict with anger; it conflicts with reason when a friend has broken some serious law, and one feels simultaneously pressed to report the friend and bound by loyalty. Where does friendship belong in the soul? Pity makes a still more insistent example, since it is repeatedly recognized in the *Republic*: sometimes Socrates speaks of it as of an appropriate motive with good effects (516c, 518b, 589e), but at other times he calls for its suppression (415c, 606b–c). Pity must therefore be a genuine human impulse. It too can conflict with reason, as when one pities the suffering patient who has to undergo painful treatment; it can conflict with spirit on the battlefield. Thus friendship and pity belong in neither reason nor spirit, and must be desires.

In itself this is no accusation against the theory. But recall how brutish desire had to become to stand clearly apart from reason and spirit. An appetite gropes after its object. How well does such a description characterize pity (even if we leave aside the more complex case of friendship)? There may be self-indulgence in much pity; certainly it ignores the good of the pitier. Still, the mechanisms of thirst and drowsiness hardly accommodate a feeling like pity, which promises no personal gain, and which does not rowdily threaten to take over rule of the soul.

It is telling that for Plato friendship and compassion have to join the grubby ranks of hunger and lechery. It would be a far greater criticism of his theory if there were no room for these motives at all. Without them the theory fails as a description of human behavior; with them the meaning of "desire" is stretched to the verge of vacuousness.

Does Platonic justice have ethical content, or is it merely a formal characteristic of souls?

One great advantage of rule-oriented ethics is the clarity of its content. "Do not steal" and "Pay back your debts," however pedestrian, at least prescribe a way of life different from its alternative. To what extent can we say the same of Platonic ethics? Does the ethical view developed in this passage give its readers guides for living, or only high-sounding phrases that can justify any actions at all?

We have learned from Socrates' argument that justice means the cooperative functioning of all the parts of the soul. This has an almost amoral sound to it; to say that reason rules is to say little more than that the person decides what to do and then does it. To be sure, plenty of people are incapable of that much. But even if Socrates' definition of justice leaves us with a small number of "just" people, it tells us next to nothing about how they will behave. Does Plato's system end up incapable of distinguishing between right and wrong?

The answer will depend on what exactly reason does when it rules in a just soul. How does the calculating part of the soul deliberate about what is just? If it faces no constraints besides the definition of justice we have already seen, then we might seem to face an absurd conclusion. If I am Platonically just by virtue of my soul's non-rational parts serving my reason, then anything I decide to do will *ipso facto* be a just action. What makes it just is the way my spirit and appetites fall into place and do as they are told, *no matter what my deliberations lead me to do*. Justice, on this account, seems to be a function of what happens *after* I have deliberated. We are left uninformed about what my deliberations themselves look like.

This way of putting the problem already shows that there is some content to Platonic justice. For the soul not only has to remain orderly after reason hands down its commands, but must remain orderly *by virtue of* those commands. Because reason is the part that thinks on behalf of the entire soul, and because it wants to maintain its authority, it must weigh possible actions, habits, and occupations with an eye to determining which will best preserve the soul's balance. Although indulging once in tobacco is not wrong, I would want to abstain if I suspected that a single indulgence might make me crave more, that my appetites might subsequently yelp more loudly for a second cigarette and then a third, until at last reason had lost control. The just act would be the act of denial, because that act best maintains the soul's order. Similarly, if my temper is provoked, my calculating faculty has to decide whether giving vent to the anger is the wisest course of action. If I always suppress my anger, I run the risk of dampening that emotion until it no longer helps me. If I lose my temper at the slightest provocation, I run the risk of coming unduly under its influence. My reason has the task of deciding how much anger, and when, best suits my soul's orderliness. Therefore, not anything it decides to do will be a just decision. Platonic justice implies a level of self-regulation that not every life will manifest. This is not a matter of having no emotions or appetites, but rather of keeping them from overpowering one's capacity to reach sane decisions.

But reason still lacks a mandate that might narrow down its choices of action further. As gatekeeper to the other psychic motivations, reason may, if it likes, give a bigger role to the appetites, or abstemiously deny them altogether, as long as it maintains its control over the soul. In one way this is a congenial view: it accepts all human motivations as legitimate, and instructs us to consider their long-term effects on the person. But someone who wants a defined course of action may be frustrated by the formal theory. (And everyone may suspect that Plato is not really as open-minded as he lets on.) Here is the real problem: Plato's depiction of the just life remains empty because it pins all the work of ethics on the soul's administrator without giving that administrator any other goal but administration. Intrinsically empty, reason conducts the traffic of the other motivations in the soul, but lacks aims of its own that it will privilege above all other claims on its attention.

We shall see later that this is not the only view of reason put forward in the *Republic*. It emerges that reason not only rules the soul, by virtue of its awareness of the whole soul, but also has its own desires, which will turn out, not surprisingly, to be directed toward philosophical truth. As the city's guardians turn out in Book 5 to be philosophers, their time divided between governance and metaphysical inquiry, so too reason, that class's analogue in the soul, will play two different roles in the good person's life. On the view offered in

Book 4, reason evaluates and ranks the options available to a person. On the view still to make its appearance, reason contemplates the truth, and organizes the soul in such a way as to make contemplation available to the person. The second view identifies the good life with the life of the philosopher, the first with no specific kind of life at all. Plato is holding his full plan for living in abeyance, until he can first explain in greater detail what reason does. The ethics of Book 4 look empty not by accident, but because the dialogue has not yet reached the point at which it can reveal the work of reason.

How closely does Platonic justice resemble justice as commonly conceived?

The *Republic*'s argument to this point has yielded a definition of justice, or rather of what we may call "P-justice," as a reminder that Plato has not yet shown the state *he* calls justice to produce the behavior commonly called just:

1. P-justice is the good organization of the soul.

If Socrates can show that

2. the well-organized soul is the happiest possible soul,

he will be able to conclude that

3. ⑧ the P-just soul is the happiest possible soul,

and answer the challenge posed in Book 2.

The argument for (2) will have to wait until Books 8 and 9, when Socrates compares the just life to all the varieties of unjust lives. But already we can see that, welcome as ⑧ may be, it will not work as an answer to Glaucon and Adeimantus, who wanted Socrates to show that

4. justice, by itself in the soul, makes the just happier than the unjust.

The trouble arises over Glaucon's conception of "the just man." Though this man's justice may be rooted in his soul, he can be identified for what he is by virtue of the acts he does and does not perform (see 360b–362c). So Glaucon wants Socrates to show that

5. the soul of one who performs O-just deeds is happy,

where "O-justice" refers to some conception of justice recognizably like an ordinary conception. For (5) to follow from ⑧, it must be the case that

6. ⑦ the P-just soul = the soul of one who is more likely than anyone else to perform O-just deeds.

⑦ requires the P-just soul to find itself, at all times, in a person who regularly, predictably does O-just deeds.

Why should this be a problem? The "vulgar standards" to which Socrates subjects his nascent definition are intended, after all, to connect P-justice to O-justice (442e–443b). He lists cases in which the person with a P-just soul will refrain from acts of O-injustice. Examples are not arguments – still less so are bald assertions – but Socrates has a compelling reason for his claims. P-justice most of all entails self-control, and the more self-control people enjoy, the less likely they are to succumb to the temptations of their desires. Most ordinary misdeeds may be traced back to such temptations, so the P-just soul will probably find itself suited to avoiding them.

The problems begin, as modern critics have stressed, when we look back to Glaucon's performer of O-just acts. Socrates has argued that

7. P-justice in the soul brings about regular, predictable, habitual O-just action.

A comforting thought. If P-just souls should ever come into existence, they will serve as inspirational examples of performers of O-just acts who also – assuming Socrates can prove (2) – enjoy great happiness. But this will not quite satisfy Glaucon's request, which was that Socrates show not that *some*, but *all* performers of O-just acts lead happy lives. To reach that, Socrates needs the additional premise

8. the regular practice of O-just action implies a P-just soul.

The identity stated in ⑦ is the conjunction of (7) and (8). According to some of Plato's critics, he not only never shows (8) to be true, but even seems not to realize that he needs it. Without (8) Socrates never answers Glaucon's challenge; for what drives Glaucon to anxiety about justice is precisely that justice, *as he conceives it*, might not benefit the doer of just deeds. If Socrates does not speak to precisely that anxiety, he will have committed the fallacy of irrelevance.

(8) is a difficult statement to prove. Worse, it has a most un-Platonic air, for it asserts that all diligent servants of society's laws can claim to have, even without knowing it, the arrangement of their souls' parts that the philosopher labored through four books of the *Republic* to discover. It would make more sense, given Plato's aloofness from ordinary practices, to deny his interest in arguing for (8). He may be better off claiming, not that everyone popularly considered just is just, but that those normally considered just have made substantial though incomplete progress toward genuine justice. If Glaucon remains depressed after learning this, so much the worse for him. He needs to get better at accepting revaluations of his moral values.

While certainly a plausible account of what Plato might believe, this does not seem to me to be Plato's response. I think he is willing to grant that any person who predominantly performs O-just acts – a more reliable Cephalus, say, who did not have to wait until old age to worry about the state of his soul – does have a P-just soul. After all, Socrates has not suggested (yet) that P-justice belongs only to philosophers. And if anyone is to enjoy the benefits of P-justice, why shouldn't it be the steady workers of O-just deeds?

Indeed, Socrates says that they do, in an argument that meets the challenge Plato's critics have posed. When applying vulgar standards to his definition of justice, Socrates concentrates on the question of what the P-just will or will not do. But he also attributes to the P-*un*just some of the O-unjust acts from which the P-just will refrain:

> [In the case of embezzlement,] do you suppose anyone would suppose that he would be the man to do it *and not rather those who are not such as he is*? (442e–443a; emphasis added)

> Further, adultery, neglect of parents, and failure to care for the gods *are more characteristic of every other kind of man than this* one. (443a; emphasis added)

Besides arguing for (7), Socrates is also saying that

9. if one does not have a P-just soul, one is more likely to do O-unjust acts.

Let us identify being unjust with not being just, as Plato does. Then we may infer from (9) that

10. if one does not have a P-just soul, one is not the most likely person to do O-just acts,

which implies that

11. if one is the most likely to do O-just acts, one has a P-just soul.

(11) is only a restatement of (8). So Socrates has indirectly argued that the performer of O-just acts does possess a P-just soul.

Socrates asserts (8) outright only a page later, while explaining how P-justice is produced:

> Doesn't doing just things also produce justice and unjust ones injustice? . . . Isn't to produce justice to establish the parts of the soul in a relation of mastering, and being mastered by, one another that is according to nature? (444c–d)

He says as much again later in the *Republic* (588e–591e). So the regular practice of O-just action *does* imply that one's soul is P-just, perhaps because dutiful (even if unphilosophical) adherence to socially mandated behavior promotes the rule of reason. Far from despising the common conception of justice, Plato wants to show its close relationship to true justice. If what he has said about P-justice baffles his readers, that is because we are unaccustomed to a philosophical analysis of justice, not because the justice of our daily lives is a fraud. Naturally, without the philosophical analysis we are doomed to misunderstand the nature of justice, and to deliberate about it clumsily. Let no one accuse Plato of congratulating the unphilosophical on their grasp of moral issues. But none of his praise of philosophy means that a conscientious moral life is aimed in the wrong direction.

It is fair to complain that Plato has not proved all his claims about justice. He never explains how O-just actions could affect the deep structure of the personality. Without an account of that change, he cannot show that the justice defined in Book 4 is identical with the conception of justice with which Socrates' interlocutors began the conversation. But since he responds to this problem, even if only with unsupported claims, he cannot be accused of ignoring it.

Suggestions for further reading

For general discussions of the psychological theory, see Nettleship, *Lectures on the Republic of Plato* (2nd ed., London, Macmillan, 1901) and Cross and Woozley, *Plato's Republic* (New York, St Martin's Press, 1964). Murphy's analysis, *The Interpretation of Plato's Republic* (Oxford, Oxford University Press, 1951) raises problems with the theory that are not easily laid to rest.

On desire (pp. 87–91), see Murphy and N. White, *A Companion to Plato's Republic* (Oxford, Blackwell, 1979). On the formal conception of justice in Book 4 (pp. 92–4) see Irwin, *Plato's Moral Theory* (Oxford, Clarendon Press, 1977), and Nussbaum, "The *Republic*: true value and the standpoint of perfection," in *The Fragility of Goodness* (Cambridge, Cambridge University Press, 1986), pp. 136–64. On the relationship between Platonic justice and ordinary just actions (pp. 94–8), see above all Sachs, "A fallacy in Plato's *Republic*," *Philosophical Review* 72 (1963): 141–58, which has inspired this debate, and, among other responses to Sachs, Annas, *An Introduction to Plato's Republic* (Oxford, Oxford University Press, 1981), Demos, "A fallacy in Plato's *Republic*?," *Philosophical Review* 73 (1964): 395–8, Mabbott, "Is Plato's *Republic* utilitarian?," in G. Vlastos, ed. *Plato* (2 vols., Garden City, Doubleday, 1971), vol. II, pp. 57–65, and Vlastos, "Justice and happiness in the *Republic*," in the same volume, pp. 66–75.

Chapter 6

Radical politics
(Books 5–7)

Now that we have the apparatus for describing justice
and injustice, the defense of justice ought to proceed
predictably. In fact, when Socrates does get around to
finishing his argument in Books 8 and 9, it contains few
surprises. The surprise is rather that he takes as long as
he does to take that next step. For between the definition of justice and the proof of its desirability lies the
long digression of Books 5–7.

Without this digression the *Republic* would be a
complete and tighter argument. By the end of Book 6
the first-time reader will wonder what Plato's theory
of knowledge could contribute to a study of justice.
But the *Republic* would be much less important
philosophically without Books 5–7. For, in the guise
of a digression about the ideal city, Plato outlines both
the most revolutionary political reforms he seeks to
make, and the classic form of his metaphysical theory,
which in turn includes two strands, the new theory of
philosophical method (dialectic) and the entities that
method makes possible (the Forms). Whatever their

part in the *Republic*'s argument, these discussions are no minor things, but the heart of Platonic philosophy.

For the sake of clarity I will leave the metaphysical issues until the next chapter; this one addresses the politics of Books 5–7. This is not to say that Plato would have conceived the subjects as separate concerns, only to recognize that these three books make more sense if the reader takes up one of their topics at a time.

The digression

The opening of Book 5 signals its new beginning with dramatic cues, all the more remarkable for the undramatic style that the dialogue has settled into. Socrates prepares to itemize the four types of vice in the individual and in the city. Then we learn that Polemarchus, silent since Book 1, has been listening closely all along from his seat close to Adeimantus (449b). He grabs Adeimantus by the cloak (449b) and asks, "Shall we let it go" – meaning the communistic life of the guardians, which Socrates has been content to mention in passing (423e–424a). At the beginning of the *Republic*, Polemarchus had sent a slave to grab Socrates by the cloak (327b), and refused to "let [him] go" back up to Athens (327c). Now he wants to initiate the discussion all over. No wonder Socrates speaks of moving back to "the beginning" (450a).

Socrates' interlocutors want him to suspend the analogy between city and soul. The city may have come into their conversation to illuminate justice in the individual, but in the three books to come Socrates will drop even the pretext of erecting a city parallel to the soul. Plato wants the freedom to talk about the good city without the encumbrance of its analogy to the soul. Besides, he sees the figure of the philosopher, who will emerge in Book 5, as an opportunity to pursue more abstract issues. The opening of Book 5 calls to mind the opening of the dialogue in order to heighten the contrast between the historically specific Socrates who had wandered down to Piraeus and this speaker, Plato's mouthpiece, who promises to climb down into the cave of vulgar human affairs, the insights of philosophy in hand.

Two waves of paradox (451c–471b)

Glaucon, again appointing himself spokesman to the group, charges Socrates with describing the community of women and children among the guardians. Socrates demurs, on the grounds that the city he describes might prove either impossible or bad (450c). Glaucon eggs him on as if uninterested in those questions (450c–451c), though soon enough (471c) he will be pressing Socrates to answer them. The good city's possibility, until now beside the point, will begin to nag at Socrates' friends as soon as they talk about the city without regard for the city–soul analogy: for if the city is worth discussing as a political being, it must be a political possibility.

Women (451c–457c)

Socrates begins with the equality of the sexes. At most, women differ from men in degree but not in kind. Therefore they should share in men's work and education. Everything Socrates has said about the young guardians' training will apply equally to those guardians who happen to be girls. And when the guardians go to war, they will fight as a mixed group of men and women (452a). The two sexes should, in short, do everything together, without regard for unenlightened public opinion. Even though the sight of naked old women wrestling with naked old men would "look ridiculous in the present state of things" (452a–b), Socrates maintains his scorn for "what is habitual" (452a). In the matter of gender relations, he disavows any concern for considerations of how people actually live or what they value. Indeed, Socrates hardly shows greater contempt for public opinion in the *Republic* than here.

What does give him pause is the political principle that underlay his description of the good city, namely (⑥) that each citizen is naturally best suited to a single task. ⑥ would apparently define a separate civic role for women, for since they bear children and men do not, their natures must be different from men's, hence also their tasks in the city (453b–c). This is a familiar argument, even today, against women's participation in government or the professions. It is a problem for Plato because, while respectful of women's abilities, he cannot abandon ⑥. If women give birth, they should not also take on the work of running a city.

Socrates responds by distinguishing (454b–c) between those characteristics that define a person's nature and those that do not. Only traits that affect the performance of a task should determine what tasks the citizens are set (454c–d). So women's childbearing should have nothing to do with the political question of their civic duties.

Socrates' analogy to bald and hairy-headed cobblers should raise a red flag. Does the difference between the sexes amount to no more than that between a bald man and one with a full head of hair? Even if women's reproductive organs have no effect on their physical or intellectual abilities, still one might argue that childbearing links women naturally to the care of children, whereas men's hair commits them to no additional activity beyond combing. If those who bear children also take responsibility for rearing them, then this difference between male and female natures implies great differences in their activities.

Socrates patches up his analogy with an argument (454c–456b) that specifies the meaning of "nature" in ⑥.

1. "Nature," as used politically, means the aptitude for one kind of work rather than another. (455b)
2. Aptitudes are distributed without regard for sex, as shown by men's ability to do everything that women do. (455c–e)
∴ 3. There are no differences in nature between men and women relevant to the role each should play in the city. (456a)

Notice that (2), on which the argument depends, is true only if childbearing ceases to count as a task. Since we cannot exclude it on the grounds of the unimportance of childbearing as a human activity, the reason must be that it takes too little time or effort to merit more attention. If we accept traditional conceptions of the family, that assumption sounds far-fetched. Depending on the number of pregnancies a woman guardian goes through (a subject Plato never addresses), and the complications she encounters, we *might* be willing to discount pregnancy alone as a full-time job. But if the one who gives birth to children also shoulders the work of caring for them, childbearing turns into a demanding occupation. So Socrates must be assuming that women do not take responsibility for child care. His argument assumes a divorce between bearing and rearing children, i.e. assumes a very different social system of child care.

This is why Socrates moves so quickly to his next point. The additional premise he needs to justify women's participation in government, namely that childbearing may be separated from child care, and therefore in itself does not affect the division of labor, requires the abolition of the family.

Marriage and children (457c–461e)

Children and parents will not know each other in the upper classes (457d). But even that change is more imaginable than the next one Socrates names, that wives and husbands will not know each other – or rather, that men and women will not share any relation comparable to that now holding between husbands and wives.

The coexistence of men and women in the guardians' camp will lead to sexual activity. This needs to be regulated (458d). Since the rulers must meddle in these sexual relations in one way or another, they should use the relations to help the city, arranging marriages so that the best young male and female guardians breed together. When Socrates speaks of these "marriages" among the guardians, he means temporary procreative couplings. At special times of the year the rulers announce which pairs may breed. To ward off the soldiers' resentment at this control over their lives, the rulers will use a fraudulent lottery that makes the pairings seem random (460a). The children born to the best couples will be reared as a group by specialists, while their parents return to their own communal lives. Infants born to unheroic guardians will not be reared, nor will any other children born outside approved "marriages."

Plato is elusive about what happens to the inappropriate children. In the case of those born to older guardians he recommends abortion (461c), while babies of the worse guardians and those born deformed apparently are to be exposed in a cave (460c). At other times he speaks of not rearing certain children (459d–e, 461c), probably with reference to their demotion to a lower class. It is becoming clear that the rulers will exercise more power over the guardians than Books 2–4 had indicated. They "will have to use a throng of lies and deceptions for the benefit of the ruled," Socrates says, equanimously enough (459c–d). But at least now he can say that women's reproductive capacities have been severed from the usual work of motherhood (460d), and it makes greater sense, in retrospect, for Socrates to have shrugged off childbearing as incidental to women's natures.

Plato's feminism

Book 5 argues for a remarkable degree of sexual equality. Conscious of women's potential, Plato calls for their participation in the governance of his city, and insists that they be educated alongside his most talented young men. The *Republic* also contains what must be the earliest request for gender-neutral language. As Book 7 draws to a close, Glaucon compliments Socrates, "You have produced ruling men who are wholly fair" (540c). Glaucon uses the word *archōn*, the masculine participle of *archō*, "to rule." Socrates corrects him: "And ruling women [*archousas*], too, Glaucon ... Don't suppose that what I have said applies any more to men than to women" (540c). With his insistence on including the feminine participle, Socrates is not only reminding Glaucon of their agreements, but also warning him that the use of masculine language to apply to all people may lead one to forget about the place of women among men.

Plato deserves still more credit for his proposals when we realize how misogynistic his society was. By ancient Roman standards, for instance, the Greeks treated their women with unusual harshness; among the Greeks, the Athenians of Plato's day stood out for their sexism. Women of the middle class were married off by their early or middle teens to men twice their age; when they did not die in childbirth, they could look forward to a life enclosed in the house, supervising the kitchen and spinning or weaving cloth. Plato recognizes the waste of human resources in this social system, and opposes it pitilessly.

Still, the worry about his feminism persists, because many interpreters have objected to what I have just said as misleadingly simple. Some claim that Plato's apparent empowerment of women has nothing to do with genuine feminism, others that in spite of his good intentions Plato continued to share in the misogyny of his time.

It would be easy to sink into a morass over determining whether or not Plato is a feminist. Feminism today comprises a cluster of beliefs and methods, and has subjected itself to searching scrutiny over what it does or does not mean; it does not even commit itself to a single account of its own history, so that we could look to the origins of feminism to determine whether or not it matches Plato's treatment of women. But we can say, tentatively, that if modern feminism cannot recognize itself in Plato's proposals, this is because modern feminists want to uphold women's rights, or help women fulfill their desires, while Plato gives no perceptible thought to either matter. It has struck him that a more efficient city would make its women fight in wars and write laws. Women might feel more fulfilled under such a political arrangement, but Plato's argument works just as well if they do not. No one expects Plato to agree with every tenet of today's feminist theory, but so palpable a disregard for what women want, or how they might benefit, seems to exclude Plato from consideration as a feminist.

Whether or not this argument works depends on how essential we deem rights to be in political philosophy. If every acceptable political theory must recognize the rights of the individual, it follows that every *feminist* political theory must recognize the rights of women. If, on the other hand, a political theory may legitimately make light of the individual's rights, then its claims about the appropriate place of women, while they *can* be true or false, wise or foolish, ought not to be rejected for pursuing other goals besides women's rights. This objection to Book 5 is too strong, because it rules out every political utterance in the *Republic*, where rights have no place at all. The guardians get no right to happiness in their work (420b, 421b), nor any right to privacy (416d). The other citizens have no right to govern themselves (432a, 434a–b). And no one should have rights in the sense of enjoying personal liberties (557b). Since no one's rights matter to Plato, his inattention to women's rights is no sign of his failure as a feminist. If we only take as a necessary principle of feminist theories the proposition that women have been wrongly denied equality of opportunity, then Plato counts as a feminist, so long as "equality of opportunity" refers to the society's right to exploit its citizens' talents, rather than the citizens' rights to pursue their dreams.

We are left with the problem of misogyny. Several of Plato's dialogues speak disparagingly of women. In the *Apology*, Socrates calls those who plead for their lives in court "no better than women" (35b); in the *Phaedo* he speaks of the distractions of womanly lamentations (117d). The *Timaeus* warns men that if they live immorally they will be reincarnated as women (42b–c; cf. 76d–e). The *Republic* contains a number of such passing comments (387e, 395d–e, 398e, 431b–c, 469d), evidence of nothing so much as of contempt toward women. Even Socrates' words for his bold new proposal, "the community (*koinōnia*) of women" (e.g. 464a), suggest that the women are to be "held in common" by the men. He never hints that the men might be held in common by the women, even after we realize that a woman can have as many as twenty breeding-relations, perhaps all with different men. Plato cannot shake the idea that women belong to men; Socrates twice refers to the "possession" (*ktēsis*) of women by men (423e, 451c). And there is no mention of an expanded role for women in the city's large lower class.

We also have to explain Socrates' insistence that men surpass women at any task that both sexes attempt (455c, 456a), and his comment in Book 8 that one sign of democracy's moral failure is the sexual equality it promotes (563b). We cannot blame these statements on carelessness; they follow from a deep-seated belief that women do not equal men. To say this is not to reject Plato's recommendations, but to recognize his vulnerability to the prejudices of his age. He becomes something less of a feminist by virtue of these persistently misogynistic beliefs, even though his considered proposals remain as revolutionary as they had first appeared.

The big family at home and at war (462a–471b)

With the dissolution of the family, Socrates completes his picture of the good city. The present section, which furnishes the most vivid glimpse at the good city in action, also gives a clear sense of how different Plato's city will look from any society that his readers ever inhabited.

First Socrates defends his proposals about the family, arguing that unity offers the greatest good a city can possess (462a–464b), then informally listing the immediately appreciable benefits to the city. This double strategy should be familiar by now: after every significant political or ethical claim in the *Republic*, Plato first puts forward the theoretical defense for his position, then renews his attachment to conventional morality with a defense that requires no theory.

By abolishing families, Socrates has turned the city, or at least its governing class, into a single family. That "or" of course glides over an important question, which is hard to answer on the basis of textual evidence: is Plato imagining unanimity and fraternity to arise among all the citizens of his town, or only among the guardians, since the family reforms apply only to them? His language sometimes implies the former (462b, e; 463e; cf. 432a) and sometimes the latter (463c; 464a, b). In all likelihood he is forgetting the productive class, and therefore thinking of unity among the guardians as sufficient for unity among the citizens at large. In any case, Socrates argues that the unity improves the city:

1. The greatest good for a city is that which unifies it; the greatest evil, that which divides it. (462a–b)
2. When all citizens share in the same pleasures and pains, the city is unified; when they have private pleasures and pains, it is divided. (462b)
3. The city in which women and children are held in common enjoys the greatest unanimity in matters of pain and pleasure. (463e)
∴ 4. The community of women and children among the auxiliaries brings the greatest good to the city. (464b)

The argument is valid. Are its premises true? It is hard to say about (3). That the Platonic city will contain total harmony is unlikely, for people may split into groups even without families or property to fight over. Plato gives little thought to the possibility of intellectual disagreement among the rulers and auxiliaries, but that kind of disagreement can divide a community. And even though the guardians have no money or land, they enjoy lesser and greater honor within the city. Surely a desire to be the city's bravest warrior could bring two guardians into unhealthy competition.

Nevertheless, Plato is right to place special blame for civil unrest on the family. More than any other institution, the family engenders loyalties of the same sort and same intensity as loyalty to the state. Families function, as Aristotle observes, as microcosms of the state, with their own rule, their own economies, and their own sanctions for behavior (*Politics* II.7 and 13). But whereas Aristotle will use this parallel between family and city to justify government, Plato interprets it as a threat to organized society, since loyalty to the family may undermine one's loyalty to the state. Moreover, Plato seems to think that the feelings produced within a family reach a level of irrationality unmatched by the feelings that the guardians will share with the members of their class. Among the ills to be found in traditional cities, Socrates includes "private pleasures and griefs of things that are private" (464d). Although any guardian's death in the good city will pain all the others (462b), that pain will not equal the pain of private mourning. Within a family the relationships are simply more intense.

The problems do not end there, because if the guardians' sentiments are so diffused they will simply not be present in any form, as Aristotle observed: intense feelings may be replaced by no feelings at all, and the guardians will lack personal loyalties altogether. But it is premise (1) of this argument that really sounds an alarm, because it shows how far Plato takes the implications of his fundamental premises. As his definitions of civic and psychic justice in Book 4 showed, Plato identifies the greatest threats to the good life as internal conflict, whether that be civil war in the city or ambivalence in the soul. Book 1 prepared the way for this position by identifying injustice first with unbridled competition (①), then with whatever force dissolves the unity of a social group (②). The present premise (1) replaces "injustice" with "the greatest evil that can befall a society," and hence follows directly from those premises. Again, the establishment of a city in Book 2 began with the assumption (⑤) that human beings require a community in order to lead recognizably human lives. This principle implies that whatever erodes the bonds of that community will threaten its citizens' capacity to lead acceptable lives; therefore, (1) may also be said to follow from ⑤.

If (1) builds on assumptions about justice that have so deeply informed the *Republic*'s argument to this point, it can be discarded only at risk to the greater argument. But the present context shows that (1) leads to dangerous extremes in social control. The abolition of the family is only one example. As long as unity takes precedence over every other value, then Plato's city may justify any concentration of power, any violation of what we consider inalienable rights of free speech and religion, or due process for the accused, or of control over one's own home and body. The present argument warns that unity demands sacrifices from the individual. (See pp. 195–200, for more remarks on Platonic dictatorship.)

After the argument comes the list of mundane benefits (464c–466d). The city in which women and children are held in common will free itself of lawsuits, factions, assault, and the ignominies that accompany household poverty. If anything, Socrates is belaboring the point, when he should face the question of whether such a city could ever come to exist. Since the matter of the city's possibility has already arisen twice in Book 5 (450c, 457d), this would be the logical time for Socrates to address it directly. Instead he postpones the discussion a third time, until Glaucon's protest at 471c–472b. Seldom does Plato build his reader's anticipation so deliberately: this last delay should tip us off conclusively about the importance and difficulty of that remaining issue.

In the meantime, Socrates describes the city at war (466d–471b). The passage from 469b to 471b deserves special notice. Socrates distinguishes between the city's practices in wars against barbarians and its practices when fighting other Greek cities. The limitations he prescribes in the latter case are an early recognition that even the state of war may retain some civilizing restraint, an anticipation of such modern international codes as the Geneva Convention. But even as he asks his guardians, and implicitly his contemporaries, to transcend their traditional allegiances to the home city, Plato reveals his own attachment to the prejudices of his time and place. Like most Greeks, he draws a sharp line between those who share his language and culture and everyone else (see 452c). Later, Socrates will hint that the good city might be born in a barbarian land (499c), but the hint comes and goes by far more quickly than the present condemnation of barbarians does. We may take Plato's inconsistency here, as in his treatment of women, as an example of the extent to which even thinkers determined to escape popular opinion can still be tempted into accepting its pettiest beliefs. It is, however, noteworthy that the *Statesman*, written later, digresses to reject arbitrary divisions of humanity into Greeks and barbarians (262c–e). See also Plato's acknowledgment of the non-Greek origins of many Greek words in the *Cratylus* (409d–e, 425e), and his respect for Egypt in the *Laws* (e.g. 656d–657b; 819b–d) and *Timaeus* (22b–23b).

Philosopher-rulers (471c–502c)

The possibility of the city (471c–473c)

Socrates tries every maneuver he knows to escape the question of whether this fine city will be possible. He even resorts to the disclaimer, overfamiliar by now, that he has only talked about the just city in order to discover the nature of justice in the soul (472c; cf. 592a–b). But the city has come to life too much to have its existence ignored.

What follows, to the end of Book 7, is the statement and defense of the *Republic*'s most radical political idea, that either philosophers become kings or existing kings learn philosophy. Since a defense of this proposal presupposes a conception of what philosophy does, much of the ensuing discussion will venture into accounts of knowledge, and of the methods available for attaining it. I will save discussion of those accounts for the next chapter; the rest of this one will take up the overtly political issues from here to the end of Book 7. Those pages cover the two parts of Socrates' defense of rule by philosophers:

1. why philosophers make good rulers, and why rule by philosophers is possible (473c–502c);
2. how to prepare the guardians for rule as philosophers, given their existence in the Platonic city; or, how a city we can recognize as good may be maintained in existence (502c–541b).

The following pages will cover the first of these topics, and pp. 116–23 the second.

Knowledge, belief, and the philosopher (473c–487a)

Once he agrees to speak on the city's practicability, Socrates proposes that philosophy and political power "coincide in the same place, while the many natures now making their way to [the practice of] either apart from the other are by necessity excluded" (473d). Though neither small nor easily accomplished, this single political change *is* possible, he says (473c). It follows that the good city is possible as well.

From this point to 502c, Socrates argues that the good city might come to exist. Very broadly stated, the argument ascribes every excellence to philosophers and therefore justifies their dominance:

1. The good city is possible if and only if virtuous and expert rule by its leaders is possible. (484d)
2. ⑨ Virtuous and expert rule is possible if and only if the rulers may be philosophers.
3. Rule by philosophers is possible. (502a–b)
∴ 4. The good city is possible.

Neither (1) nor (3) invite much comment. It is ⑨ that occupies Socrates' attention in this part of the argument, as he tries to show that the specific characteristics of genuine philosophers also make for virtuous and effective political rule. He will separate ⑨ into claims about virtue and knowledge, then claim that both are found in philosophers and in no one else. Thus the present passage (474c–487a) argues for the truth of ⑨, on the basis of philosophers' attachment to learning:

1. Philosophers love every kind of learning. (474c–475c)
2. No one else loves every kind of learning. (475c–480a)
3. ⑩ The love of every kind of learning produces knowledge of ethical matters.
4. The love of every kind of learning produces virtue. (485a–486e)
∴ 5. By (3) and (4), the love of every kind of learning makes one a virtuous and expert ruler.
∴ 6. ⑨ By (1), (2), and (5), one is a virtuous and expert ruler if and only if one is a philosopher.

If this argument works, it will defend Plato's political theory. It will also turn politics into an intellectual pursuit, instead of the very practical pursuit we are accustomed to – or rather, it will force us to re-evaluate what we mean by "intellectual pursuits."

Premise (2), which rules out governance by non-philosophers, comes into this argument for a concrete reason, as we realize when Glaucon warns Socrates that a mob will seize and punish him for his proposal (473e–474a). Plato's dialogues often foreshadow the trial and execution of Socrates – the *Republic* in particular alludes to his life and fate at 494d–e, 516e–517a, and 539a–d – but *this* foreshadowing especially resonates, because the discussion of rule by philosophers would have reminded every Athenian of the contempt with which Socrates' associates had treated democracy. Recall that the climactic Athenian loss during the Peloponnesian War had come in the botched Sicilian Expedition, which could not have been executed without the influence of Socrates' young friend Alcibiades; recall that after the war Critias and Charmides instigated the worst antidemocratic excesses of the Thirty Tyrants. And here we find a conversation, set in more innocent days, in the course of which Socrates proposes rule by philosophers. The challenge for Plato is to distinguish these philosophers from their imitators, which is to say, from the dictators who seize power armed only with false confidence in their own superior wisdom.

So Socrates moves immediately to define the philosopher, lest that figure be mistaken for a Critias or Charmides. He calls the philosopher a lover of every kind of learning, but Glaucon points out that lovers of sights and sounds (which include, most of all, the sound of political speeches) also want to learn (475d–e). Socrates therefore draws a sharp line between the philosophers and their rivals.

Two arguments follow, a quick one to explain this distinction to Glaucon (475e–476d), and a more elaborate one to explain to non-philosophers why their "knowledge" is really only opinion by comparison with the genuine knowledge of philosophers (476d–480a). The details of this argument belong in the next chapter; for the moment I will suppose Socrates' conclusion to be true. The question remains nevertheless: what has he shown of relevance to the political rule of philosophers? If the argument is to justify their rule, it must demonstrate not only that philosophers alone know something, but further that what they know will make them the best rulers. They must possess knowledge of ethical matters (⑩), of a sort that can lead a city.

Among the objects of a philosopher's knowledge, both parts of the argument include justice (476a; 479a, e). Nor is that a trick on Plato's part. Moral terms, as I shall explain, fit especially well into this critique of the dilettante's opinions. The critique remains inconclusive, however, because it directs itself to saying why the dilettante *lacks* knowledge, not to why the philosopher *possesses* it. As a strategy for excluding pretenders to political expertise it works much better than as a justification for ⑩. This passage is vague about what these Forms are that philosophers know, and how they can be said to know them. In this sense the argument is a promissory note on arguments to come, beginning at 502d and continuing into Book 7. So far Plato has not shown that the theoretical knowledge associated with philosophy can promise any practical knowledge of the kind that rulers need.

If it seems impossible to imagine practical and theoretical knowledge going together, that is no accident, nor a minor issue, but in my opinion the most important problem facing the *Republic*. Remember that ⑥ asserts, and that the *Republic*'s argument has reiterated, that every person is by nature best suited to a single task. Now Socrates proposes that political rule, which depends on practical expertise, and philosophy, whose expertise is highly abstract, be yoked together. How can this proposal fail to violate the division of labor? If Plato gives up ⑥ his political system will collapse. If ⑥ stands, the conjunction of philosophy and rule is unnatural; but since the good city depends on that conjunction, it is unnatural, too, and can never exist. Either way, Plato must surrender his hopes for a good city, unless he can show that philosophy inherently entails ethical knowledge.

For the moment, Socrates leaves that issue aside and turns to the remaining necessary premise of this section's argument:

4. The love of every kind of learning produces virtue.

If he can show that philosophers "will be able to possess these two distinct sets of qualities" (485a), knowledge and virtue, then his argument will be complete.

Socrates argues (485a–487a) that virtue always accompanies the practice of philosophy, thanks to the passion for wisdom found in every philosopher, a passion that reduces one's other passions (485d).

Freed from mundane concerns by their love for wisdom, philosophers grow moderate (485e), courageous (486b), and just (486b).

This argument claims an overriding passion for philosophers that may never have existed so strongly in anyone. It ignores the possibility that a passion so strong could lead to new vices unknown to slaves of the bodily appetites. On top of that, the argument ignores the massive evidence that people absorbed in cerebral pursuits can still prove themselves as susceptible as anyone else to lust and greed. But the argument is noteworthy for introducing an idea that will have far-reaching implications later in the *Republic*. Socrates supports his claim of the philosopher's virtue by emphasizing the erotic nature of the philosopher's affection for learning. Philosophers are "in love with" a kind of learning (*erōsin*, 485b), their attachment to it is a desire (*epithumia*, 485d; cf. 475b). We may attribute to Plato the premise that

⑪ The rational part of the soul has desires of its own.

No such desire was evident in Book 4's discussion of reason. Book 4's silence about the desires of reason is, in fact, why its ethical theory seemed purely formal (see pp. 92–4). If reason has desires, justice will amount to more than a balance of human passions; as we shall see in Book 9, the good life will privilege the activity of philosophizing.

Moreover, if reason can simultaneously perform its practical governance of the soul and its theoretical pursuit of truth, then the philosopher (whose reason is better developed than anyone else's) is simultaneously, naturally, and without contradiction both a practical master of the city and a theoretical hunter for truth. Then ⑥ will not prevent the philosopher's rule but demand it.

Philosophers in existing society (487b–502c)

But before he can fill out his theory of philosophocracy, as we may call rule by philosophers, Socrates has to face the untheoretical person of Adeimantus. This flattering portrait of the philosopher is all well and good, he says, and Socrates has drawn Glaucon into it through his famously tendentious questions, but no one could believe it (487a–d). Experience shows that most adults who pursue philosophy become eccentric – "not to say completely vicious" – while the few decent ones are useless to the community (487c–d).

Plato needs to confront this accusation if his political philosophy is to speak to the realities of politics. As before, he follows the abstract argument with one acknowledging the importance of popular perceptions. This time it is a parable: the city is like a ship and its public the ship's owner, a powerful but deaf and myopic man with scant knowledge of seafaring. Politicians resemble sailors who vie for the ship's captaincy, scheming against their competitors for the owner's approval, all of them hostile toward someone with real knowledge of navigation. They call the true captain's study of the stars and wind stargazing; in their eyes, every attempt at navigation is useless (488a–489a).

This image owes more than a little to Aristophanes' *Knights*, a political allegory in which a befuddled old man named Demos ("the people" or "the commons") has to be protected from wily merchants; Plato simply transfers the comic situation to a ship. If we take the parable as an argument it begs the question, since it presupposes the philosopher's knowledge of statecraft, and so far Plato has not shown that there is any such knowledge. (The image also fails in falling back on the comparison of moral knowledge to a skill. I noted the weakness of that comparison when Socrates made heavy use of it in Book 1; see pp. 34–6) But Socrates is not merely explaining why philosophers *seem* useless in existing societies, but why they really *are* useless (489b). Given how political power unfortunately operates in the world, knowledge of the best policy for a state to pursue has nothing to do with the execution of that policy.

When Socrates turns to the subject of vicious philosophers, he agrees again with Adeimantus, and again turns the criticism back against the society that has corrupted the philosophers. The public corrupts young intellectuals by forcing them to court popular favor rather than pursue the truth (489d–495b). It persecutes anyone who tries to educate them, thus diverting that teacher's talents to the undignified practice of political intrigue. (At 494c–495b especially, Plato wants the reader to think of Socrates and Alcibiades.) As for the perversion of philosophy that Adeimantus has overlooked, the pretense to wisdom of showy philosophers *manqués* (495c–496a), that too happens only because human society has refused to honor the insights of philosophy. In this world an uncorrupted philosopher can hope only to lead a virtuous private life – not a bad goal, Socrates says, but far from the best (496a–497a). (Here too Plato is thinking of the historical Socrates, regretting the political realities that stopped him from doing the true philosopher's work.) Philosophers belong in the good city, where their talents can improve everyone's life. In every other city Adeimantus' objections will be true (497a–c).

Adeimantus has seen something important about the volatile relationship between philosophers and politics. Even in the good city, its rulers will have to mind the potential for corruption latent in talented intellects (497c–498c). It is not only that philosophers, being human, remain vulnerable to corruption; rather, something about their natures leaves them unusually susceptible to the blandishments of wealth and glory. Significantly, this passage marks the first overt statement in the *Republic* of the need to preserve and test philosopher-rulers in the light of their fragility. Still, despite these concessions to Adeimantus, Socrates has not answered him. He has offered an alternative account of the phenomena Adeimantus describes: rather than proving the intrinsic badness of philosophers, their failure in society condemns the society's divorce of power from knowledge. But an alternative account has to have its own plausibility if we are to consider it as closer to the truth than the usual story, and the plausibility of Socrates' account rests on his claim that philosophers have knowledge that would make them the better rulers. Plato needs to show that what philosophers naturally do is directed toward politically valuable insight; he needs to prove the truth of ⑩ .

Philosophers in the good city (502c–541b)

We have reached the heart of the *Republic*. At first Socrates defines the purpose of this section narrowly: assuming the birth of the good city, how can it maintain itself? What system of education will protect the philosophers from corruption? But the answer to this question will also have to explain how a philosophical education prepares a guardian for political power. To solve *that* problem, Socrates will have to investigate the ultimate purpose of philosophical activity. So he digresses again to sketch the highest goal of philosophy. We may therefore divide this section into two, the sketch of the Form or Idea[1] of the Good (502c–521b) and the pedagogical system of the city (521c–541b).

The Form of the Good (502c–521b)

Still pretending to be speaking only of the philosophers' education, Socrates mentions exposing them to "the greatest study" (503e, 504d). Pressed to explain it, he uses a series of images to suggest the Form of the Good, the pinnacle of philosophical inquiry. The Form of the Good is like the sun (507c–509c); the relations among the Form of the Good, all other Forms, and the objects of the visible world may be mapped out along a divided line (509d–511e); human beings' relationship to the Form of the Good resembles the relationship of prisoners in a cave to the sun (514a–517c).

As the highest principle for both ethics and metaphysics – at once the *best* thing in the world and the *most real* – the Form of the Good promises to justify rule by philosophers (506a). One who masters the philosophical practice of looking for the most general principles behind a phenomenon will eventually come to this entity, which explains what the goodness of everything else consists in. Without knowledge of this Form one can never think coherently about moral issues, and certainly not plan a moral pattern for human life (505a–b).

The cost of this all-inclusive theory of reality and the good life is that it degrades the value of ethical behavior when practiced without philosophy. In terms of the *Republic*'s argument, this means that the Form of the Good replaces justice as the object of ethical inquiry. It also means that ⑦, which equates Platonic justice with ordinary just behavior, and which Socrates worked to demonstrate in Book 4, will prove not to be the last word about ethics. Book 4 defined justice

[1] This is one of the very few points at which I depart from the terminology of Bloom's translation. Bloom uses "idea" to translate the Greek *idea*; I will use the somewhat more customary word "Form."

as the pre-eminent virtue and foundation of all morality. Now all eyes turn to the Form of the Good. Socrates not only calls that Form "greater than justice" (504d), but claims that "it's by availing oneself of [the Form of the Good] along with just things and the rest, that they become useful and beneficial" (505a). He had warned his interlocutors in Book 4 that their definition of justice would be a second-best accomplishment, inferior to the true understanding of moral principles (430c, 435d). We have now taken the longer route and reached that understanding. From this vantage point, "the other virtues of a soul" lose their luster, amounting to no more than "habits and exercises" (518d–e).

Does this falsify the theory of Book 4? It would be more accurate to call that theory *partial*. It fails specifically in offering no explanation of the nature of reason. A complete ethical theory will add to Book 4's account a more active role for philosophical reason.

The Allegory of the Cave brings politics back into this discussion of the Form of the Good. Human life, says Socrates, may be depicted as the state of prisoners in a cave, shackled in rows with their backs to the cave's opening, unable even to turn their heads away from the shadow theater that plays on the cave wall in front of them (514a–b). These are not the shadows of real objects, nor are they cast by the light of the sun, for that light cannot penetrate into the cave. Instead, there is a fire behind the prisoners, with men walking back and forth holding up models of real objects. The prisoners watch the shadows of those objects and take themselves to be viewing reality (515b).

In this allegory, learning philosophy becomes the process of being unshackled and forcibly brought to see first the fire, then the mouth of the cave, and at last the sunlit world outside. Once out there, the initiates have to accustom themselves to the much brighter light by first looking at the shadows and reflections of humans and other things, then at those things themselves, and finally at the source of all light, the sun (515c–516b). It is no wonder that anyone who returns to the cave and tries to disabuse the remaining prisoners of their ludicrous opinions about reality should be scorned and scoffed at: ignorant of the greater light behind them, the prisoners take the disorientation of one who comes from light into darkness for the superficially similar confusion of someone going from darkness into light (516e–517a; 518a–b).

Although the prisoners' derision for the philosopher brings Socrates to mind again, Plato wants to do more than defend his friend's memory. The focus of the allegory shifts from the society to the philosopher, from the mistreatment philosophers face in the world as we have found it to the duty they shoulder in a well-run world. Anyone who reaches the Form of the Good will prefer not to return to the petty affairs of humans (517d–e, 519c), but in the Platonic city philosophers will be compelled to enter politics (519d).

Glaucon protests that this compulsion would do the philosophers an injustice (519d). Socrates' answer, substantially the same one he gave Adeimantus about the guardians' happiness (420b–421c), is that the city does not exist to subsidize any one class of its citizens, but to produce a harmonious whole (519e–520a). Furthermore, the guardians have enjoyed subsidy enough from their city, for unlike philosophers who manage to spring up on the stony places that are existing cities, these owe their contemplative happiness to the city's institutions (520a–c). And only they have what their city needs: rule by these philosophers benefits the city more than any other rule would, because it is the only example of power wielded reluctantly. Only philosophers know a happier life than that of ruling; hence only they will rule without falling into factions (520d–521b; cf. 345e).

While the *Republic*'s relentless denial of individuals' right to run their lives should bother any reader, this passage is not the worst manifestation of that attitude. But in another sense the discussion threatens Plato's political theory more fundamentally, for it implies that the philosophers have something better to do than rule the city. If the philosophical activities of ruling and contemplating are so different from one another – different enough for Socrates to deny that the former is "fine" (540b) – then the unity of philosophy and politics becomes questionable. Though not denying philosophers' aptitude for rule, this passage gives them two quite distinct tasks to perform. So ⑥, which the Form of the Good was supposed to accommodate to philosophocracy, appears still at odds with the political organization of the city. The union of theoretical and practical knowledge remains a problem for Plato.

The education of the best guardians (521c–541b)

Socrates finally returns to the originating question of this digression within a digression: what steps will turn the city's governors into philosophers, attentive not to the changeable sights of the world but to the eternal truths of the intelligible realm? The remainder of Book 7 suggests a curriculum to effect the conversion. To music and gymnastics, which had made up the guardians' education in Books 2 and 3, Socrates adds mathematics (522c–e; 525b–526c): this includes arithmetic, plane and solid geometry, astronomy, and harmonics. After the end of that period of education the guardians undergo two or three years of gymnastics (537b). From twenty to thirty they pass through a synoptic study of all subjects (537b–c), after which, from the ages of thirty to thirty-five, they get their first introduction to dialectic (537c–d; see 532d–534c for a description of education in dialectic). They next serve the city for fifteen years in military and civil posts, as soldiers, police, and lower administrators (539e–540a). Only at the age of fifty are they brought to a vision of the Form of the Good, and once they have seen *that* they divide their time between philosophy of the highest order and government at the highest rank (540a–c).

Plato's educational theory

As an educator, Plato combines progressive recommendations with the most repressive and militaristic ones. His most general proposal here has grown into an attitude so common that the reader may overlook its significance. Plato denies that schooling consists in packing knowledge into the soul (518b); it is rather a conversion in which the soul "turns around" (518c, d) and directs its attention to new objects (521c–d). Book 3's list of banned books may have suited the earlier education of the guardians, which aimed only at moral training; the more ambitious enterprise at hand, the production of philosophers, calls for the development of a particular kind of ability. Pure and applied mathematics enhance that ability, providing the city's educators keep their approach to those subjects philosophical (526e, 529a, 531c). Such comments make it abundantly clear that Plato (probably the first to do so in European history) is advocating an education centered on methods of analysis rather than on facts. He envisions the process as a natural growth, at least for talented students (535c): this is why their learning can begin as games (536d–537a).

Plato joins these visionary comments to stuffy conservative ones. Though he wants mathematical studies to draw the soul upward to being, he also recommends them to military strategists (522d–e, 525b, 526d). He is motivated by the desire to show that a single curriculum will serve both warriors and philosophers (525b), hence that the guardians can naturally fulfill both roles at once. But this motive does not make up for the objectionable sound of Socrates' arguments; he repeats his earlier point about children watching battles (537a), as if to stress the parity of war and philosophy in the guardians' lives. If we should not generalize from these mentions of war to call Plato a militarist, we just as clearly should not forget that the class of guardians began as the city's standing army, that for all his hopes about the perfectibility of human beings Plato is always prepared to exercise force on those who remain unperfected.

The threat of dialectic

The process of education outlined here bears little resemblance to the process by which the historical Socrates brought his friends into philosophy. If we may trust the portrayal given in Plato's dialogues, Socrates took to his investigations after realizing that his peers and political superiors had only inconsistent, undefended, and often anecdotal things to say about vital issues (*Apology* 21c–22d). The early dialogues that most probably reflect Socrates' instructional method (*Charmides*, *Euthyphro*, *Gorgias*, *Laches*, and *Lysis*) show him making his interlocutors aware that their high-sounding moral theories fail to cover even the most obvious phenomena, and that their talk of ethical matters is therefore meaningless.

Plato has chosen to substitute a formal curriculum in mathematics for his teacher's cross-examination of Athenians' moral claims. It is not too much to conclude that he mistrusts the Socratic method of teaching. Socrates warns Glaucon that the philosophical examination of moral principles must not be revealed to the young (537c–539d). The young students of dialectic are "filled full with lawlessness"

(537e), trained at refuting tradition (539b) but not stable enough to remain good people in the face of moral uncertainty (539d). These warnings against exposing the young to dialectic can only mean that Plato has come to share – however qualifiedly, however provisionally – the Athenians' judgment that Socrates corrupted the youth. Plato would rather populate his ideal city with obedient citizens who never interrogate the received wisdom as Socrates had; at the same time, he cannot gainsay the value of that interrogation for the production of moral theories. He hopes that his propaedeutic of arithmetic and geometry will inspire the same fervor toward abstraction that Socrates had wakened, without bringing the same skepticism to these future rulers.

The young guardians' weakness in the face of the corrosive power of dialectic recalls Socrates' explanation to Adeimantus that the philosophical nature is especially open to corruption (491d–492a; cf. 518e–519a). The warning against dialectic intensifies our sense of the philosophers' vulnerability. Even what makes them can unmake them, for those elements of one's character that produce philosophical ability – a quick mind, the love of argument – may easily also produce a cunning demagogue or a tyrant's apologist. No wonder Books 6 and 7 harp on the need to test the city's guardians (503a, e; 539e), to compel them to labor in their education (504d), to watch constantly for the bad ones (536a). The philosophers' sureness of knowledge is matched by their corruptibility.

Plato's sensitivity to the weakness of the philosophical temperament becomes a problem when we remember how much power these rulers wield. They make the laws and decide on the manner of their enforcement; they keep the army in houses where no one escapes a master's scrutiny; they move their citizens' children up and down across class lines. Such absolute power finds its warrant in the infallibility of the philosophers' knowledge. But now one must ask how infallible that knowledge can be when held by people so susceptible to moral decay. Perhaps such a nature can be trained into incorruptibility; but that degree of perfection, on which Plato's investment of power in his guardians depends, makes a mystery of the inevitable decay of the city in Book 8, a decay that Plato blames on the guardians' fallibility (546a–547a). One wonders why Plato's awareness of human fallibility did not bring him to see the virtues of democracy, whose inefficiency, ideological confusion, and constant sense of compromise, though they make democracy the least likely government to pursue a systematic public policy, also leave it the most resistant to tyranny. Given that we live in a world in which the best people err both morally and intellectually, perhaps we should provide for a system that will offer not the best way of life imaginable, but the best under the circumstances, the best at avoiding some worse state. In the *Statesman* Plato will reason this way, concluding that when human society cannot depend on the stable rule of fixed laws, democracy is the most desirable form of government (303a–b). In the *Republic* he only selectively acknowledges, and cannot seem to bear in mind, that we live in what Christians call a fallen world.

Suggestions for further reading

On Plato's proposals for the city, see first of all Aristotle, *Politics* II.1–6; also Barker, "Communism in Plato's *Republic*," in A. Sesonske, ed., *Plato's Republic* (Belmont, Calif., Wadsworth, 1966), pp. 82–97, Brann, "The music of the *Republic*," *St. John's Review* 39 (1989–90): 1–103, Rankin, *Plato and the Individual* (London, Methuen, 1964). White, *A Companion to Plato's Republic* (Oxford, Blackwell, 1979) and Nettleship, *Lectures on the Republic of Plato* (2nd ed., London, Macmillan, 1901) are both excellent on these topics. Bambrough, "Plato's political analogies," in P. Laslett, ed., *Philosophy, Politics, and Society* (Oxford, Blackwell, 1956), pp. 98–115, begins with the ship of state and expands its discussion to analyze Plato's conception of political knowledge. On the guardians' education and the Form of the Good, see Cooper, "The psychology of justice in Plato," *American Philosophical Quarterly* 14 (1977): 151–7, and Ross, "The Sun and the Idea of Good," in *Plato's Theory of Ideas* (Oxford, Oxford University Press, 1953), pp. 39–44.

On women in the Platonic city, see Bluestone, *Women and the Ideal Society* (Amherst, University of Massachusetts Press, 1987), which addresses both the reforms of Book 5 and the history of their reception; also Calvert, "Plato and the equality of women," *Phoenix* 29 (1975): 231–43, Lesser, "Plato's feminism," *Philosophy* 54 (1979): 113–17, and Pierce, "Equality: *Republic* V," *The Monist* 57 (1973): 10–11. Irigaray, "Plato's *hystera*," in *Speculum of the Other Woman*

(Ithaca, Cornell University Press, 1985), pp. 243–364, represents a radical critique of Plato's view of women. On women in Athens, see Keuls, *The Reign of the Phallus* (New York, Harper & Row, 1985). Dover, *Greek Homosexuality* (London, Duckworth, 1978) and Halperin, *One Hundred Years of Homosexuality* (New York, Routledge, 1990) illuminate Greek sexual politics.

Chapter 7

Metaphysics
and epistemology
(Books 5–7)

Metaphysics, very generally considered, asks: what things are real, and in what does their reality consist? Epistemology asks: what can we know, and how do we know it? The two questions may be kept distinct from one another, as they largely have been in philosophy since Descartes, but in the *Republic* Plato interweaves all questions of reality with questions of knowledge, on the grounds that each kind of object in the world corresponds to a different kind of human perception of it. This grand unification of all philosophical inquiries is typical of the middle section of the *Republic*, and is one reason for its philosophical importance.

The problem with particulars (475e–480a)

We have already seen Glaucon object that philosophers resemble dilettantes (475d). Socrates uses this opportunity to distinguish philosophers in terms of the superior objects of their inquiry, and to begin separating those objects from the less perfect ones that the lover of

spectacles pursues. His argument approaches the distinction from both sides, first appealing to the superiority of the Forms (475e–476d), then separately attacking all lower kinds of things (476e–480a).

The Forms (475e–476d)

Socrates begins by speaking of "justice and injustice, good and bad" (476a). Then he speaks more artificially of "the fair itself" (476b), as if that were the same manner of thing. Glaucon expresses no surprise at the new terminology – Socrates seems to be referring to a theory that he has already heard and been convinced of. Indeed, whenever Socrates introduces such language into his argument, it meets with Glaucon's immediate agreement (507b, 596a–b). In Plato's other principal discussion of "(the) X itself" in the *Phaedo*, Socrates again finds his otherwise combative interlocutors prepared to assent without resistance to the existence of entities they somehow already know (100b; cf. 74a).

These passages introduce what we call Plato's Forms. Disinclined to invent a formal technical vocabulary in which each term gets and keeps its own precise definition, Plato uses different words to speak of a Form of X, but most commonly calls it "X itself," to express the perfect way in which a Form holds its property X. Sometimes he calls the Form simply "X," sometimes *eidos*, sometimes *idea* (though the Greek word *idea* does not refer to thoughts in people's minds). "Form" has become the commonest English word for the entity; it captures two important senses of the Greek, both the sense of "species" (a pistol is a form of gun), and that of "shape" or "pattern" (a form letter, a dressmaker's form).

Whatever he calls them, Plato tends to introduce Forms into his dialogues with no argument for their existence. Perhaps his first readers all knew the theory already; perhaps Plato wanted to keep his theory available only to initiates; perhaps he had no argument yet, and posited the existence of Forms in order to get on with the rest of the theory. Perhaps he thought the Forms so obviously existed that they needed no defense. At any rate, in the absence of a proper introduction, we can get to understand the Forms only by determining what Plato expects them to accomplish. In the passage at hand, Socrates defines Forms by contrast with non-Forms. Each of these qualities – justice and injustice, good and bad – is "itself" a single object; "but, by showing themselves everywhere in a community with actions, bodies, and one another, each looks like many" (476a). These "many" are the beautiful sounds and colors through which the beautiful itself shows itself (476b); they "participate" in the beautiful itself but are not identical with it (476d). We have three characterizations of Forms here:

1. *Uniqueness*   The Form of X is the only one of its kind.
2. *Self-predication*   The Form of X is the pure exemplar of the property X.
3. *Non-identity*   Individual X things – actions, bodies, shapes, manufactured objects – have a share in the Form of X, but none of them *is* the unitary Form of X.

Whatever other details about Forms we may argue about (see Chapter 11), their uniqueness, self-predication, and non-identity with individual X things constitute their core properties.

Even this simplest statement about the Forms has its share of vagueness. What does it take to exemplify a property purely? What makes individual things fall short? What can it mean to say that an X thing "participates" in the Form of X? As Books 5–7 progress, Plato will work to clarify his theory, though the answers to these questions always remain open to further elucidation. For example, Plato hints here, by way of explaining participation, that the X thing is "like" the X itself (476c); but what being "like" means will not become clear until later.

This passage does not prove that philosophers stand above the lovers of sensory experience, because those aesthetes may be acknowledged to occupy a lower state of awareness only if we grant that the beautiful things they admire are mere likenesses of beauty itself. To grant this we would have to agree first that Forms exist, and second that X things *owe* their property of being X to the Form of X.

Oddly, Socrates does not fill in these missing steps. But he does concede that this argument will not convince the one who holds opinions without knowledge, for he goes on to add, "[C]onsider what we'll say to him" (476e). The rest of Book 5 sets philosophers apart from their rivals not by proving the existence of Forms, but by developing a critique of non-Forms on independent grounds. When it comes time to defend his metaphysical theory, Plato begins in the realm of ordinary experience. Non-philosophers not only may prove incapable of understanding the abstract theory, but they will be unwilling to do so much as entertain it as long as they remain rooted in their experience. Demonstrating the truth of a theory like Plato's, so opposed to ordinary experience, requires first demonstrating the need for it, by showing that ordinary experience fails on its own terms.

Thus, although Socrates scarcely mentions the Forms in the next argument, he is indirectly arguing for their existence. For the argument against the non-philosopher concludes that ordinary experience cannot lead to knowledge. If there is to be any knowledge at all, then, it must have Forms for its objects.

Knowledge and opinion (476e–480a)

The argument in its entirety says:

1. Knowledge is knowledge of what is, while ignorance is attached to what is not. (476e–477a)
2. Opinion lies between knowledge and ignorance. (478c)
∴ 3. From (1) and (2), opinion depends on whatever lies between what is and what is not. (478d–e)
4. The Form of X is always X. (479a)
5. Beautiful things are also ugly, just things also unjust, holy things also unholy, double things also half, and big things also little. (479a–b)
∴ 6. From (5), a particular X thing is both X and non–X. (479c)
7. From (4) and (6), a particular thing both is and is not, whereas the Form of X is. (479c)
∴ 8. From (1), (3), and (7), the Form of X is the object of knowledge, whereas X things are objects of opinion. (479d–e)

We can narrow our focus to a subsidiary part of this argument, since Plato's principal goal is to demonstrate the failings of the world of ordinary experience. Within this argument for the superiority of Forms there lies the more concise and crucial *argument against knowledge of particulars* (hereafter AKP):

1. Knowledge of an X thing is possible only if that thing is unqualifiedly X (or "always" X, 479a).
2. Individual X things (for at least some properties X) are both X and non-X.
∴ 3. There can be no knowledge of individual X things.

Glaucon accepts (1) without a murmur, when he agrees that knowledge must be knowledge of what is (476e). Along with (1) he accepts a broader unstated assumption, which we shall find hard at work in Plato's epistemology:

⑫ Every level of understanding requires a corresponding level of reality in the object of understanding.

Science would seem to disprove ⑫. Scientific method presupposes that I begin in ignorance about the sun, say, or the human bloodstream, and go on to formulate my first opinions: that the sun revolves around the earth, or that blood ebbs and flows in my veins, out to bodily tissues and back into the heart. After observation and experiment, I abandon many opinions and replace them with knowledge. Now I know that the earth goes around the sun, and that my blood follows a path through arteries and veins. I have gone from ignorance through opinion to knowledge, all concerning the same objects. I could not have reached the knowledge I have without first entertaining opinions, even those that turned out to be false, because opinions lead me to ask more specific questions about the objects I study. On Plato's view, each level of greater understanding ought to find itself attached to a different subject, perhaps non-blood, quasi-blood, and true blood.

That is nonsense, of course, and irrelevant to Plato's concerns, which make better sense if we come to them through a different set of examples, say the respective flavors of coffee and tea, the origins of continents, and the relative lengths of the sides of a right triangle. We have no use for arguments concerning the first. If I prefer coffee and someone else tea, I ascribe the difference between us to taste and leave it at that. In the case of continents there is room to investigate further. But given how long it takes continents to move, any observations that would decide the case are indirect, and work only within a network of fact and conjecture. It is conceivable that new evidence and scientific instruments might lead scientists to discard the theory of plate tectonics. In the third example, I have no such doubts about the future. No evidence will make me give up the Pythagorean theorem, because it does not depend on evidence. Each of these objects admits of a different kind of certainty about it: no certainty at all in the first case, empirical confidence about the second, and unmistakable certainty about the third. These three states stand distinctly apart: no accumulation of evidence about my neighbors' preferences will make me like tea better than coffee, and no amount of evidence will transmute the theory of plate tectonics into a theorem of geometry. Why not call the three kinds of certainty ignorance, opinion, and knowledge? Then Plato is saying only what we too would say, that every manner of thing admits of a different kind of understanding. (For Plato, what we call science is opinion. At 530a–b, Socrates denies the possibility of finding truth through empirical astronomy. The heavens are visible and changeable, he says, two epithets he regularly associates with the objects of opinion. See also *Phaedo* 96a–99c.)

The greatest problem with this defense lies not with the matters of opinion, or matters of taste, about which we agree with Plato that there can be no knowledge; it lies with the objects of knowledge, about which, if ⑫ is true, there can be no opinion. That is, if the Pythagorean theorem *can* be known, then by ⑫ it should not *also* be an object of opinion. But clearly someone ignorant of geometry might discover the Pythagorean theorem without so much as guessing the strategy for a proof. This would not count as geometrical knowledge but as a well-founded hunch; then the same theorem would be both a matter of opinion for one person and a matter of knowledge for another. Can Plato want to deny that? Does he mean that one may not have an opinion about objects of knowledge? Does he suppose that knowledge arrives all at once, instead of emerging through a fog of guesses?

He never asserts such a thing. The slow process by which we come to know the Forms takes us to that knowledge only after long knowledge deprivation (516a–b, 521c, 533c–d). In the passage at hand, Socrates says that the lovers of fair things do not see "the fair itself" (479e), which is to say that they are ignorant of it. So Plato is glad to admit that one may have mere beliefs, or total ignorance, about objects of knowledge; but the close connection that ⑫ insists on between kinds of cognition and kinds of knowledge seems to drive him to deny it.

⑫ will cause more problems later in this part of the *Republic*. We may avoid some of these problems by making sure to take ⑫ in a restricted sense: Plato is asserting not that each level of reality implies *exactly one* level of cognition corresponding to it, but rather that each level admits of *at most* a given level of cognition. Plato does not mind our having opinions concerning the Forms so much as he minds the idea of knowledge concerning non-Forms. I may guess about the Pythagorean theorem, but I will never have a geometrical proof for the superiority of coffee.

Even this much elaboration can lead to more trouble. As our discussion of the Divided Line will show soon enough, there is no easy escape from these questions of detail about levels of cognition. But it is time to return to the second premise of the AKP, which accuses individual X things of being both X and non-X. Here Plato does have an argument at work, but one so compressed as to support a number of interpretations. Socrates says that each of the many beautiful things will also look ugly, each of the just things unjust (479a). The many doubles also appear as halves; so too, *mutatis mutandis*, for big and light things. It follows that every particular thing no more is what one calls it than it is the opposite (479b). Particular things lack genuine properties; they are only half-real. We cannot know them, if knowing them has anything to do with knowing their properties.

The brevity of this argument has given rise to two related questions. First, how does an X thing fail to be X? Secondly, which properties both do and do not hold of a single object? To answer the first question is largely to answer the second, since the properties at stake will be those for which the critique of X things works. When we have answered these questions we will be able to describe the Forms: they will be X in a way that the many X things are not, and there will be a Form of X for every property X to which the argument applies.

Socrates' argument is easier to understand if we set aside beauty, justice, and holiness, and look at the properties that he apparently equates with them. Things we call double, big, or light are so called by comparison with other things. My arms may equally be *double*, if I compare the pair of them with a single arm, or *half*, if I compare them with the group of all my limbs. So doubleness is not an essential property of my arms, but a property that depends on what I compare them with. The question "Is this double?" needs a clear context if it is to make sense. Because any such context-dependent or *relative* term never applies unequivocally to individual things, focusing on the individual things that have that property will not lead to knowledge of the property. I may study a big, thick, heavy mouse for as long as I like, but it will not show me what bigness, thickness, or heaviness consist in. A Form, by comparison, is a pure exemplar of doubleness or heaviness, showing the nature of those properties without appeal to any comparison.

The clarity of this argument, and its echo in Book 7 (see 523a–524a, and pp. 149–50), has led some interpreters to conclude that things fail as exemplars of their properties when, and only when, those properties are relative terms. If that is the case, we should go back and apply Socrates' critique of relative terms to the evaluative terms – beautiful, just, and holy – in the preceding sentence. But the two sorts of properties do not exhibit their ambiguities in the same way. We do not praise a just law only when we have another one to compare it with. Comparison is beside the point. In this sense of "context," evaluative terms are no more context-dependent than color terms. If they are supposed to fail exactly as relative terms do, we must clarify the nature of their dependence on context.

The fault might lie not in the laws or people to which moral terms do and do not apply, but in the bad generalizations we make about those terms. When Cephalus defined justice as returning what was owed, and Socrates refuted him with the example of the madman's weapon, we may interpret Socrates as having shown that returning what is owed is just in one context and unjust in another. This action therefore deserves the predicate "just" in one situation and "unjust" in a second; hence a single act both is and is not just.

Now justice looks more like doubleness in its equivocal application to things. But while this interpretation is insightful, and sensitive to Plato's ethical project, the reader must bear in mind that it is also speculative. Plato never speaks of Forms in any passage that also condemns our naive generalizations about moral terms. In addition, the analogy remains imperfect. This account of evaluative terms extends the notion of "context" from the clear sense of a basis for comparison to the more nebulous idea of a situation. We have lost the point that certain terms only mean something when one object is being compared with another.

If we want to find other explanations of how just or pious persons are also unjust or impious, it may help to look elsewhere in Plato. The *Symposium*, in particular, accuses specific beautiful things of three kinds of shortcomings: their beauty exists in only parts of them; it waxes and wanes; it differs depending on who is looking at the thing (210e–211b). Alongside

1. An X object is not X in every context, but X compared with one thing and non-X compared with another.

we may therefore name three more vivid criticisms of particular things:

2. An X object is not X *in every part*, but contains non-X parts.
3. An X object is not X *at every time*, but increases and decreases in X-ness.
4. An X object is not X *to every observer*, but seems X to one and non-X to another.

Now we have four grounds for calling X things incomplete bearers of their properties.

Of the four, (2) accomplishes the least. It asserts the imperfection of the world's contents, though the purpose of this argument is to prove that imperfection.

(4) works especially well for ethical terms. Nor could anything be more obvious than disagreement about justice. The Sophists had already argued in the time of Plato's youth that this radical disagreement revealed the emptiness of morality. If an action looks brave to one observer and cowardly to another, it cannot have any intrinsic property, whether courage or cowardice. Plato half agrees; he does not take the disagreement to show that nothing is really brave or cowardly but rather to show that no *act* will be either one or the other. This in turn only exposes the inadequacy of the world of opinion by comparison with that of the Forms, about which two informed people would never disagree.

This argument has a disadvantage opposite to that of (1): whereas the argument about context applies neatly to relative terms and obscurely to moral terms, (4) works well in the case of moral terms but makes no sense when applied to others. People do not enter into disputes over whether a thing is light or heavy, is or is not a dog. Only issues of value produce such intractable disagreement. So (4) alone will not account for the entirety of Plato's criticisms of the world.

(3), the most powerful criticism, condemns the physical world to imperfection for its changeability. Since the growth and decay of things prohibits them from holding any properties forever – animals grow from small to large, for instance – no X thing in the world of ordinary beliefs can be held up as a paradigm of X. It will be non-X soon. Perhaps this is why Socrates uses the future tense when he apostrophizes to the lover of sights: "Now, of these many fair things, . . . is there any that won't also look ugly?" (479a). It may be why he says the Forms are *always* what they are (479a, 484b, 485b, 585c). Certainly the changeability of the physical world is at stake when Socrates describes it as a world of generation and destruction (508d, 527b) or decay (485b). Since no one could deny the ubiquity of change, since Plato seems to be concerned to preserve his Forms from change, and since the change of the world indicts every object in it, this argument may work as an elucidation of Socrates' brief comments.

Even this broad critique of the physical world runs into trouble, though. In the first place, the argument in Book 5 restricts itself to evaluative and relative terms. If Plato had an argument in mind that worked against all the furniture of the earth, it is at least curious that he did not name other examples of things' ambiguities. In the second place, the corruptibility of the sensible world does not apply to actions: a courageous act does not decay into a cowardly one, and just laws do not fade into injustice.

It is fair to say that no single interpretation of this passage entirely explains why Socrates criticizes the non-philosopher's absorption in beautiful things. Plato seems to have a bundle of different arguments in mind, each of which shows in a different way, and with respect to different kinds of properties, that an X thing is also non-X. The criticisms have different implications for what kinds of Forms there will be: if (2) or (3) is Plato's core argument, every observable property will have its Form. The changeability of the world implies that even the property of being a dog will hold only partially of any individual thing, since that thing is bound to die and cease being a dog. So there will be a Form of Dog as well as of Beauty and Bigness. If Plato means to rely instead on such arguments as (1) and (4), there will only be Forms of relative and evaluative terms. (See Chapter 11 for more about this issue.)

Whichever argument is at work, a Form of X will be X under all conditions, to all observers, and at all times. This passage has not proved that such entities exist as the objects of knowledge, but that only they *can* be objects of knowledge. Nothing but Forms will serve as objects of knowledge, since individual things lack the necessary relationship to their properties.

One last word about Forms. They threaten to be such perfect objects that human beings cannot possibly come to know them. If the standards of knowledge lie so far away, Plato's theory bars us from reaching them. But the argument of Book 5 is a more sanguine description than that of our ordinary state. While opinion lacks philosophical insight, it also escapes the total absence of knowledge that characterizes ignorance. If opinion, rather than ignorance, is most people's state of mind, then the transition to knowledge becomes dramatically more plausible. For if the unschooled lack all awareness, their acquisition of knowledge must be a spontaneous and unmotivated leap into another state. But if the common state is some jumble of ignorance and knowledge, education has a place to begin. Rather than transform the unphilosophical into new beings, one need only prune away their ignorance.

The Form of the Good (503e–518b)

We skip to the last third of Book 6, when Socrates, mindful of the temptations that philosophers face in the world, returns to the subject of their education. Young guardians must be tested, he says, to see if they are worthy of learning about the Form of the Good (505a). The Form of the Good, as I have said, is intended to unite the pursuits of philosophers, which all too often drift away from human concerns, with the ethical knowledge that makes life worth living (505a–b) and by virtue of which philosophers are qualified to rule in the ideal city.

As things stand, everyone wants what is good; in this respect the good differs from justice, since no one needs to be persuaded to seek it (505d–e). Like the English "good," the Greek word *agathos* can serve both as a narrowly moral concept and as a much broader term of approbation. Even the wicked would rather have good food than bad; they listen to good music without fear of growing saintly. Given this universal desire for what is good, perhaps the ultimate strategy for defending ethics would involve unpacking the meaning of goodness to find a fundamental value on which everyone agrees.

I say "perhaps," because the *Republic* does not go that far toward analyzing the good. Socrates contents himself with a sketch of its function as the supreme principle of metaphysics, and even that is only a sketch. Solid arguments barely enter into this image-laden section of the dialogue; the reader should bear in mind that while some degree of clarification is possible, Plato is trafficking in broad conjectures, of which we should not ask more specific questions than they can answer.

The *Republic* has already provided several examples of Plato's figurative explanations. The noble lie of Book 3 casts the class structure of the city in terms of metals in the soul. The ship of state in Book 6 explains allegorically the hostility that politicians feel toward philosophers. The myth of Er that closes the *Republic* restates its defense of justice in a story about the afterlife. As familiar to Plato's readers as Jesus' parables are to readers of the Gospels, the myths, images, and allegories of the dialogues also resemble those parables in having three distinct purposes. Some *persuade* their audience to do what it already knows it should; others *teach* in concrete language what an unsophisticated audience would otherwise have trouble following; still others *speculate* about matters that no human beings have understood. The noble lie and myth of Er illustrate the propagandistic function of Plato's images, while the ship of state illustrates their pedagogical function. The images we are about to encounter show Plato speculating about the Form of the Good. Like the kingdom of heaven in the Gospels, the Form of the Good needs a metaphor to explain the entire process of the ideal life to those (among whom Plato includes himself) who have not yet completed it.

The image of the sun (507c–509b)

Socrates opens his discussion by assuming the existence of Forms (507b). Here they stand opposed to the objects of human sight (507b–c), and this opposition between the visible and the intelligible suggests an analogy between the sun and some corresponding entity in the realm of the intellect:

Form of the Good	sun
intelligence	eye
knowledge	sight
Forms	visible objects

Just as the eye sees objects only thanks to the sun's supply of light, human reason can know the Forms only thanks to the intercessions of the Form of the Good (508b–e). And as the sun, the source of all energy, also makes possible the existence of every living thing, the Form of the Good not only lets us know about Forms, but causes them to be in the first place (509a–b).

Because Socrates calls the sun a god (508a) and says that the Form of the Good lies "beyond being" (509b), this may sound like the beginnings of mystical theology; Plotinus would later use this passage to elevate the Form of the Good into a divine principle. But while there is a mystical element to Plato's thought, this is not the place to look for it. The traits of the Form of the Good make it not a divinity but a Form of Form-ness, a next level up from the Forms in abstraction and reality and therefore a capstone to Platonic metaphysics.

To reach this further level of abstraction about the Forms, we need to ignore their particular contents and identify their common traits. Recall that each Form is the exemplar of whatever property it is the Form of. The Form of X captures what it is to be X, or to be a *real* X; but this is the same as what it is to be a *good* X. "That's really a motorcycle" is a way of praising the motorcycle, calling it good, while "This isn't much of a dog" describes a bad dog. Every use of "good" in the world of opinion points toward the Form of the property for which the particular thing is being praised.

In the case of Forms of X, we determine their content by surveying X things and looking for their common or essential features. If we wanted to define the Form of Form-ness, we would similarly take the Forms together and find *their* essential features. But we have just seen that each Form of X is the best X there can be. So the Form of Form-ness must be the Form of the property of being best – which is to say, it must be the Form of the Good. Since a Form is that which "is," in the vocabulary of Book 5, the Form of the Good lies "beyond being" in the sense of surpassing the Forms in much the way that they surpass particular things.

The Form of the Good makes knowledge of other Forms possible through this same ideality of Forms. In order to ascertain the content of the Form of Justice, one must first get into the practice of looking for ideal justice. Looking for ideals means looking for the best version of a property; so the Form of the Good, as a hazily glimpsed goal of all inquiry, makes Forms available to the mind, in the same way that the sun makes things available to the eye.

The Form of the Good is the supreme principle of metaphysics, by virtue of its superiority to other Forms, as well as the supreme principle of epistemology, the entity that must be understood if one wants to know the complete nature of the Forms. So the two functions of the Form of the Good, corresponding to the sun's causation both of visible things and of our sight of them, unite metaphysics with epistemology. At the same time, just because it is the Form of the *Good*, it represents the goal of life, a principle to make sense of and justify all human behavior that is governed by the pursuit of value.

On these last grounds the theory has already begun to falter; despite Socrates' introduction of the Good in ethical terms, he has stopped referring to any role it might play in human ethics. I suspect that Plato did not know how to make his vision of a highest principle of philosophy do useful work in ethics, unless that work is very indirect, a product of the role that the Form of the Good plays in the operation of reason.

The Divided Line (509d–511e)

The argument from analogy

Socrates still has plenty to say about the place of the Form of the Good in his metaphysical system, and how a philosopher might hope to reach it. In the remainder of Book 6 he returns to his distinction between objects of opinion and objects of knowledge, complicates that distinction, and arranges the entire structure into a path toward the Form of the Good. He describes an unequally divided line, with each part redivided into the same unequal proportions. The two segments resulting from the first cut correspond to the objects of knowledge and opinion. The objects of opinion, or visible things, are then separated into ordinary physical objects and their shadows and reflections (509d–510a). The higher class of objects in turn admits of division (510b) into Forms and mathematical objects ("the odd and the even, the figures, three forms of angles," 510c). Assuming that greater length corresponds to greater intelligibility, the Divided Line looks like Figure 2.

What began as a simple comparison between the sun and the Form of the Good has become a bewilderment of analogies. The complexity results from Plato's desire to use the Divided Line to make two points at once. First, it explains to an unphilosophical audience how the objects of opinion are related to objects of knowledge, by inviting that audience to see the visible world as a mirror image of another, more solid place. The reflection relationship uses our ordinary conception of greater and lesser reality to point beyond ordinary experience toward a greatest kind of reality. At the same time, the Line lets Plato find a special place for mathematics, the inquiry that he has set above all other skills as a propaedeutic to philosophy. This double function of the Divided Line gives rise to architectonic rococo, but it finally issues in a unified account of all objects.

Kinds of cognition and their kinds of objects

As mentioned on p. 135, Plato wants to retain some bridge connecting objects of opinion with objects of knowledge. He also insists on the

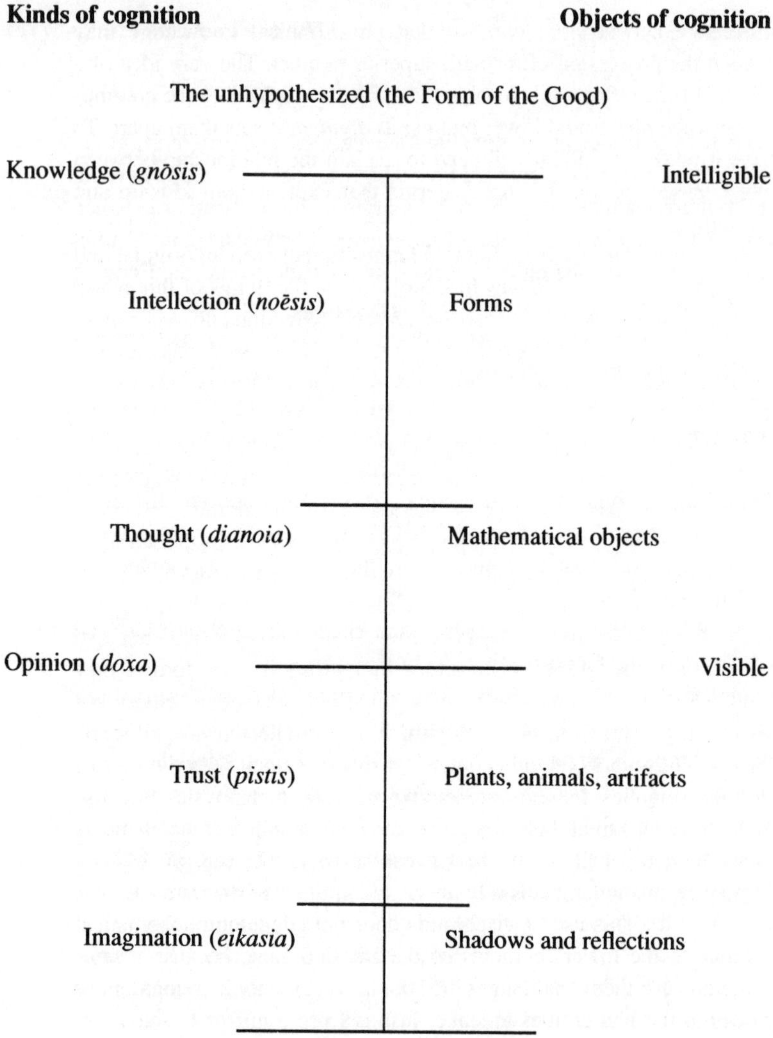

Kinds of cognition   **Objects of cognition**

The unhypothesized (the Form of the Good)

Knowledge (*gnōsis*) ——————————————— Intelligible

Intellection (*noēsis*)   Forms

Thought (*dianoia*)   Mathematical objects

Opinion (*doxa*) ——————————————— Visible

Trust (*pistis*)   Plants, animals, artifacts

Imagination (*eikasia*)   Shadows and reflections

FIGURE 2   The Divided Line

difference between the two, so that philosophical knowledge may remain the possession of a small, superior number. The very idea of a Divided Line reflects this tension: as a *line*, it emphasizes the continuity between higher and lower realms; as *divided*, it sets them apart. To have it both ways, Plato will need to explain the relationship between any two sections of the line in terms that express both kinship and difference.

Hence Plato's appeal to the relationship between an original and its likeness or image (*eikōn*). In Plato's terms, the things of this world possess a more substantial reality than their reflections do. My reflection depends on me for its existence, but not vice versa. I make a more reliable object of knowledge than my reflection. Mirrors may distort my appearance and cannot inform me about things like my weight. Yet there is no denying the similarity between us – no house would have mirrors in it if reflections did not bear their special relationship to the thing reflected. The metaphor of likeness and original, then, tells non-philosophers what they are missing when they wallow in the world of the senses, and also hints at how they might come to attain it.

Mathematics belongs to the realm of knowledge because the truths it discovers do not concern objects of sensory experience. To know that seven chairs, when added to a group of five, form a new group of twelve chairs, is to know something not about chairs but about the properties of numbers, which are "intellected but not seen" (507b). Thus numbers and geometrical shapes belong with the Forms. But mathematics remains something beneath metaphysics because mathematicians treat their objects as known, when in fact the elements of mathematics call for further investigation (510c; see pp. 142–6). Moreover, mathematicians rely on visible things like diagrams in their work (510d). This use of visual aids does not condemn mathematical practice to the lower segments of the Divided Line, because mathematicians use them "as images" (510b, e; 511a), only as reminders or guides to the real entities at stake, just as I use a mirror to shave my flesh-and-blood face, not the reflected one.

Plato bases his evaluation of mathematics on its practitioners' methods. In Book 5 the X things of this world were themselves at fault; here the fault lies not with triangles, but with what Plato considers the complacency with which mathematicians think about them. Likewise, those visible things that had seemed capable of consigning anyone who looked at them to the level of mere opinion, seem not to have that effect on mathematicians, because mathematicians use them as images. What becomes of ⑫? Do objects determine the levels of cognition about them or not? Plato cannot say simply that they do, because everyone would be stuck at the level of opinion, since everyone begins life with only visible objects of experience available. There would be no hope for philosophy; mathematics could not exist. So Plato grants that there are different ways of treating one and the same object, and therefore that a single object can lead to different states of the soul in different observers. In that case, though, why speak of different classes of things, instead of four different views of a single class? Plato does not want that alternative either, for he wants philosophy to concern itself with something more real than the objects of unphilosophical scrutiny. Packing mathematics into the Divided Line, and trying to make each division the image of the one above it, leads him, at the very least, into puzzles that call for much more complex solutions.

Destroying hypotheses

The most debated issue concerning the Divided Line has to do with these faults of mathematics. Dialectic, by contrast with mathematics, neither rests content with hypotheses nor uses sensory images (510b, 511b–d), but investigates its own basic principles until it has arrived at an unhypothetical starting-point (510b, 511b). (In Book 7 Socrates calls this investigation the work of "destroying hypotheses": 533c.) Once in possession of that first principle, philosophical argument "goes back down again to an end" (511b).

What are these hypotheses, and what do they have to do with visual images? Socrates ties the hypothesis-mongering of mathematicians to their unwillingness to give accounts of mathematical objects, "as though they were clear to all" (510c–d). This tells us something: numbers, figures, and other mathematical objects need to be given more complete accounts. But this context permits the further account to be either a *proof* of basic postulates about those objects, or a *definition* of the objects themselves.

The geometry of Plato's day could legitimately have been accused of lacking both proofs and definitions, for even Euclid's *Elements*, some fifty years after the death of Plato, treated certain statements and terms as given. The best-known statement of this sort is the Parallel Postulate, the claim that through a point not on a line exactly one line passes that is parallel to the line. The Parallel Postulate is a complex assertion about geometry, but in the system that spells out demonstrations for every statement about lines and figures, it goes unproved. If we draw lines and points on flat surfaces, we probably will never notice that the postulate even needs proving. Only with the flowering of non-Euclidean geometry in the last hundred years did mathematicians appreciate its arbitrariness. It needs a better account, though geometers' reliance on visual images blinded them to this need. So unproved assertions about mathematical entities might be what Plato means by hypotheses.

However, Euclidean geometry contains undefined terms as obviously as it does unproved assertions. Euclid calls a point "that which has no parts"; this is not a genuine definition, but anyone engaged in reasoning about points and lines would consider their meanings clear enough. Again, non-Euclidean geometry gave the lie to this traditional confidence, by showing that points, lines, and planes admit of radically divergent interpretations. We may understand a plane as the surface of a sphere and lines as the sphere's great circles, instead of the flat surface and taut segments we are used to. This openness of the terms of geometry to rival interpretations means that no clear definitions have yet been provided for them: if "line" had a precise definition, it could not have been interpreted in a new way. Therefore, undefined terms exist in geometry, and produce an obscurity about the discipline that Plato may have had in mind when he complained about mathematicians' hypotheses.

Once we know which complaint Plato means to make, we can say what he expects from the highest philosophy and the Form of the Good. If the problem with hypotheses is the absence of proofs for fundamental assertions, then Plato is calling for dialectic to discover a philosophical foundation for mathematics. Ascending from the hypotheses amounts to finding more fundamental principles from which they can be derived. The unhypothetical beginning will be a super-axiom requiring no proof, from which every truth about the Forms and about mathematics can be derived. Philosophers work by finding increasingly powerful principles until they reach this axiom, then "go back down again" to prove the truth of those lower principles that mathematicians had accepted as postulates.

This picture of the ascent up the Divided Line, the axiomatization theory, has captured many imaginations, especially given the quest for logical axiom systems in the late nineteenth and early twentieth centuries. Just as Frege and Russell searched for axioms from which they could prove the elementary truths of arithmetic, Plato wants to find a foundation for all mathematics, and somehow for metaphysics at the same time. One must not press this historical analogy too far, but surely we may ascribe to Plato a desire for unwavering truth, what we now call logical certainty (477e). He does not explicitly talk about proofs in this passage, but that does not threaten the axiomatization interpretation, since the passage contains so little explicit, unmetaphorical talk of anything.

The greatest problem for this interpretation arrives when we try to describe the unhypothetical beginning, which seems to be the Form of the Good. Nothing in any of Socrates' remarks, here or elsewhere, about the Form of the Good or about Forms in general, will let us think of the highest entity of metaphysics as a super-axiom. Still less does it seem capable of generating the basic truths of mathematics.

A competing picture, which begins by seeing hypotheses as undefined terms, takes the ascent up the Divided Line to be a quest for definitional *clarity* rather than for axiomatic *certainty*. If mathematical objects lack further accounts in the sense of remaining undefined, then dialectic will define each one on the basis of simpler, broader, more abstract terms. Plato's *Phaedrus*, *Statesman*, and *Philebus* all describe dialectic as a method of reaching definitions, and though the process of finding definitions at work in the *Republic* might differ from the one those dialogues lay out, it would probably be, like them, a search for ever more general terms, under which we subsume more and more specific terms until we can define everything on the basis of one unhypothetical concept.

This reading has its difficulties as well, particularly if we import the definitional method of the three other dialogues, all written later than the *Republic*, back into a context they might not fit. But it has two advantages over the axiomatization reading. First, we can find some continuity between a project that aims at definitions and the enterprise of the historical Socrates. When Socrates elicits definitions from his interlocutors in the early dialogues, he often criticizes them for defining a virtue too narrowly: he wants to elucidate moral terms in the broadest possible language (*Meno* 72a–c; *Euthyphro* 6d–e; *Laches* 191c–e). At one point he even suggests that all specific definitions must be guided by knowledge of the good (*Charmides* 174b; compare Socrates' comments about "the good" at *Laches* 199d–e); though this "good" cannot bear a very close relation to the *Republic*'s Form of the Good, the similarity of terms might mean that Plato saw affinities between his own enterprise and his mentor's more primitive one. Plato often departs from Socrates' views, but where he can he tries to link their projects, and the definitional reading of dialectic would make such a link possible.

The second advantage of this reading follows from its more natural interpretation of the Form of the Good. Hopeless as an axiom from which to derive the truths of mathematics, the Form of the Good has a chance of working as the broadest concept found in the realm of knowledge. If mathematical objects bear any resemblance to the Forms, it is their quality of being ideal. A triangle understood in strict geometrical terms is something superior to any drawing of a triangle. The proof that every triangle's internal angles add up to 180 degrees will apply only ambiguously to drawings, but to the triangle as it is strictly defined the proof applies perfectly. Again, a line, as defined, has no width; but the nature of physical marks guarantees that any line I draw will have some width. Hence the triangle and line conceived as abstract entities are better than the ones drawn on paper, precisely as the Form of Justice describes a better justice than that found in any person, act, or institution. If the Form of the Good is a Form of Form-ness by virtue of capturing the ideality of Forms, then it will also capture the ideality that characterizes mathematical entities. The Form of the Good will therefore play an indispensable role in every definition of objects of knowledge; we may call it the ultimate term in all theoretical definitions.

Destroying hypotheses means destroying the "everyone knows what it is" attitude that mathematicians take toward the primitive terms of their enterprise. To a modern audience this interpretation may seem too modest, if dialectic leaves mathematical postulates clarified but not proved true. And as I have said, we need to exercise caution about insisting on any reading of this passage. But we have a clearer sense than before of what Plato expected from philosophy, and how he thought it might grow into a unified discipline on which all his philosophers could work together.

The Allegory of the Cave (514a–517c)

After puzzling over Plato's critique of mathematics, every reader will arrive relieved at the Allegory of the Cave. Here again is the *Republic*'s rhythm of an abstract point for specialists succeeded by a popularization for others: the Allegory of the Cave translates the Divided Line's distinctions among kinds of knowledge back into the imagery of sun and light that first illustrated the Form of the Good. The four stages of things that the liberated prisoners see – the shadows (cast by firelight) of the statues of things; the statues themselves; shadows (cast by sunlight) of those things of which the statues are images; then the things themselves – correspond to the four stages of objects of cognition along the Divided Line.

For a better understanding of how the allegory works, though, we need to ask more precise questions about its illustration of the Line:

1. Is the allegory an image of all human life, or only of life outside the good city?
2. How well does it match the Divided Line?

The Allegory of the Cave returns the conversation to political questions by illustrating the political consequences of the hierarchy of knowledge. Since the allegory depicts a prisoner being led out of the cave and returning to help the other prisoners, it may be said to translate the static imagery of the Divided Line into images of education and governance. Described in this way, it sounds like an image of life in the ideal city. Socrates' language at 519b–520d and 540a–c shows that he imagines the cave's escapees as the guardians of his city. But we can hardly square this interpretation with the bitterness of 516e–517a, which pictures the enlightened thinker stumbling back into the cave, forced to compete with his unfreed companions, and ridiculed by them for his ineptitude in worldly affairs. If these remarks allude to Socrates, as they certainly seem to, then the cave's perpetual prisoners must represent Athenians, not citizens of the unfounded city. (Hence Socrates' discouraging words at 515a: "They're like us.") Perhaps Plato means the cave as an image of all human life, whether ideal or actual.

In that case, the great majority of all human beings will always find itself bound to the lowest sort of experience. According to the Divided Line, the lowest level is "imagination" or "image-thinking" (*eikasia*), restricted to the sight of reflections and shadows and presumably the sound of echoes, which even the flabby standards of this world of opinion must judge as only virtual reality. Surely Plato has erred in claiming that most human beings remain beneath even the level of empirical knowledge. Has he overstated his case so egregiously in a furious wish to insult ordinary experience? Or has he invented an image of the Divided Line that works only in its broadest outlines, and fails when we try to work out its details?

Either guess may be right. But we may also read *eikasia* more metaphorically, and accuse the general run of humanity not of gazing like Narcissus at reflections, but of occupying itself in some other way with the images of visible things. When Socrates is not speaking technically, he uses the word "image" (*eikōn*) in the *Republic* to refer to his own metaphors and stories (375d, 487e–488a, 489a, 514a, 531b, 588b–d); the word seems capable of describing any non-literal use of language, often with no pejorative connotation. But "image" also covers non-literal language to which it *does* ascribe inferiority. In Book 3 Socrates calls the imitative poet's creations "images" (401b, 402c), and even though he will not use the word in Book 10's condemnation of poetry, that condemnation would easily let imitative poetry take its place alongside the images of Books 6–7.

Now, in the allegory, Socrates equates the cave's shadows with issues disputed in court (517d–e). Since Athenian legal disputes were famous for their rhetoric (see *Phaedrus* 272d–e), it is safe to identify figurative language, and especially the uninformed variety, as the imagery that most commonly captures the public's attention. All their lives people take in mere allegations about important issues, colorful poetry grounded in ignorance, and every artistic or political performance that, by drawing more attention to the flash of its form than to the solid matter of its content, leaves its audience more ignorant than ever. The prisoners who squint at and squabble over shadows represent all those citizens who believe what politicians and artists tell them.

If the allegory describes the state of all human beings, in the ideal city or out, it implies that, even given the best political institutions, most of a city's members will mill around poets and demagogues. The Platonic city will be as full of the ignorant rabble that Plato wants to escape as Athens ever was. Either the Platonic city remains far from utopian, kept by inevitable human weakness from becoming a perfect community, or else Plato has not thought through the implications of his elaborate analogy.

A greater problem with accommodating the allegory to the Line arises over the existence of mathematical objects. As we have seen, Socrates distinguishes mathematics from dialectic on the basis of its practitioners' methods instead of its objects' reality. But the Allegory of the Cave identifies a specific kind of thing for every step on the Line. Whereas the Line loosens the hierarchy of knowledge and being to permit emphasis on humans' approaches to what they know, the allegory adheres to the strict assumption (⑫) that for every kind of knowing there exists a separate thing that is known. The allegory does not exactly match the Divided Line, then, but papers over its complications regarding the objects of cognition.

An education in metaphysics (521c–539d)

Once Socrates has shown his best guardians progressing toward dialectic, he will have completed his argument for the philosophical city, and can return to the species of injustice he had promised to catalogue. Amid the curricular proposals in these pages, a few arguments refer back to the Divided Line and deserve a look before we go on to Book 8.

The problem with particulars, again (523a–525c)

In search of studies that lead the soul to higher thinking, Socrates distinguishes between objects that "summon the intellect to the activity of investigation" and those that do not (523b). The former involve what we have called relative terms (pp. 132–4). On this occasion, Socrates takes the inferiority of particular things to prove the merits of arithmetic:

1. Because a finger does not also appear not to be a finger, sense-perception suffices to form the true judgment, "This is a finger." (523c–d)
2. Because a large, thick, or soft finger also appears small, thin, or hard, sense-perception cannot make clear judgments about those properties. (523e–524a)

∴ 3. In the case of the latter properties, the intellect needs to examine the properties apart from perceptions of them. (524c)

4. Every number appears not to be true of a particular thing at the same time that it appears to be true of it. (525a)

∴ 5. Arithmetic, which is concerned with numbers, leads to the truth. (525a–b)

This argument resembles Book 5's argument about knowledge and opinion closely enough to count as a further implication of that argument. As such, it supports the view that only relative terms will have Forms. Since the inferiority of individual things in Book 5 rested on the ambiguity of their properties, this passage would deny the existence of a Form of Finger.

Why does mathematics suddenly enter the present argument? Because numbers form a special case of opposable properties. They appear in particular things in the same confusing way that other relative terms do: 525a may mean, for instance, that my hand is simultaneously one (hand) and five (fingers). But numbers belong to existing disciplines. Philosophers might hope for an education that leads to the systematic study of justice and beauty, but they can take heart in the existence of some disciplines that have already studied some confusing terms without reference to their empirical manifestations.

The tone of this passage, a dramatic change from the belittling language of Book 5, suggests an inconsistency in Plato's view of the physical world. How can the bigness of a finger both condemn the student of the sensory world to a life of mere opinion (479d–e), and be the stimulus that leads that student up to being (523a)? It all seems to depend on the observer's attitude toward the phenomena. If I take the physical world to be the sum of existence, then the incomplete way in which certain predicates apply to that world will leave me possessed of mere opinion. But if I look for a theoretical understanding of those predicates in a realm beyond the physical, I have a chance of reaching knowledge. Images have their epistemic merits, as long as we value them not for their own sake but for their capacity to point beyond themselves to greater knowledge. The world of the senses is like a puppet show, a source of deception only to those who do not think to look for the puppeteers outside the marionette world.

We are back at the problem of objects of cognition. The critique of particulars in Book 5 presupposed that attention to a kind of object commits a person to the corresponding kind of cognition. The present passage allows the kind of knowledge available from a given object to vary with the investigator's method of studying it: the same finger can leave me swamped in my confusion or guide me out of it. But if my level of awareness determines which thing I am thinking about – Form of Thickness or one thick finger – then ⑫ cannot be true in any form that permits the argument of Book 5 to work. This concession to the investigator's antecedent frame of mind means, as the discussion of mathematical objects in the Divided Line also did, that Plato's distinction among kinds of objects muddies the waters more than it clarifies them.

Dialectic again (531d–537d)

After defining his mathematical curriculum, Plato returns to dialectic, here the final phase of a philosopher's education. We see, first, that although Socrates' praise of mathematics had seemed to forget the earlier criticism of mathematical method (529c–e, 530e–531c), that criticism returns when he comes to speak of dialectic. Given their adherence to unexamined hypotheses, mathematicians only dream about reality (533b–c). Dialecticians destroy those hypotheses in order to lead the soul to superior knowledge (533c–e). So the inclusion of mathematics in the curriculum does not imply any change of heart about its truth.

Secondly, the Form of the Good is named as the goal of dialectic (534b–c; cf. 532a). The unhypothetical beginning at the top of the Divided Line must indeed be, as we had thought, the Form of the Good. And here Socrates links dialectic to the ability to form an "overview" of every other subject (537c). Since an overview, or a most general possible statement of the nature of each thing, is closer to a broadest term of definition than to a first axiom from which all others follow, this passage favors the definitional interpretation of ascent up the Divided Line (pp. 142–6).

Review of Books 5–7

Plato's motion back and forth between political and metaphysical discussions leaves these books of the *Republic* resistant to summary. As Aristotle complained (*Politics* 1264b39), much in them lies outside the main argument of the *Republic*. To some extent these books even actively threaten the rest of the dialogue, for they relegate the question of justice to a position of secondary importance (504b–505a, 506a). If Plato really believes this, he must consider the *Republic*'s main argument little better than a philosophical primer, suitable for those who cannot understand the Form of the Good, but a crude approximation for those who can. If unwilling to disparage the *Republic* so completely, he must see it as raising further, more fundamental questions that he is not yet prepared to answer.

Still, much in these three books is essential to the political and ethical arguments of the dialogue. As a document of political philosophy, the *Republic* needs to lay out the plan for a good state, in order to specify which structural features of existing states engender the injustices that human beings have experienced. Without the details of Books 5–7, the *Republic*'s good city would be too vague to work as a model for political change. The equality of women and the abolition of property and family for the city's rulers clarify the degree to which a city must subsume other interests to the pursuit of justice. Even if these changes seem repellent, the reader must acknowledge them to make the point that tinkering with details will never produce a just society. In this sense all revolutionary political thinkers owe a debt to Plato, for imagining radical change instead of reform.

Plato's boldest proposal, that philosophers rule the city, becomes indispensable as soon as he decides to consider the practicability of his political dream. The city will not work without philosophers at its helm. But to say that is to grant the importance of the Form of the Good to the *Republic*, for in the Form of the Good Plato is able, however schematically, to unify the theoretical pursuits of philosophers with the moral expertise required of rulers. We might say that the Form of the Good, in a burst of rationalistic optimism, denies any distinction between "knowing how" and "knowing that" in ethics, between the insight we find in morally wise individuals and the learning we attribute to scientists and scholars.

Thus the middle books give the *Republic* a good measure of its power as a political text. But the *Republic* is also an ethical text, an argument that the life lived according to moral principles is the life most worth choosing; to this argument the digression is also essential. Reason, in Book 4 a coordinator of the soul, acquires content in these books. In Book 5 it is the passion of philosophers, with motivational force of its own (⑪), therefore a force that in critical situations may overpower the soul's other parts. In Books 6 and 7 we find out specifically what work reason accomplishes, always drawing the soul away from the seductions of the physical world and toward an abstract principle of goodness. The argument for the pleasantness of a just life will turn out to depend on the conception of reason that these books make possible. So we return from the digression to the main argument with a better understanding of its elementary terms.

Where does the theory of Forms belong in this story? What is it a theory about? What work is it supposed to do: explain? predict? This is not just the complaint that we never see Forms. Every scientific theory contains some entities, whether atoms or black holes, that do not turn up in ordinary experience and to some degree have been hypothesized on the basis of more direct observations. But in the case of science we have a clearer understanding of what the theory and the theoretical entity might do: unite disparate phenomena under general principles; explain the properties of plant cells; predict where Mars will appear in the evening sky, and when. We swallow talk of atoms and black holes because those things form part of a broad and instructive account of the world.

Can we accept talk of the Forms in the same way? In one sense they violate the most fundamental requirement of scientific theories, namely to explain or account for the world as it is. The theory of Forms principally sets itself to describing theoretical entities that stand *apart from* the world of ordinary experience and judge its shortcomings. The Forms bear their properties in a manner that individual things cannot: the Form of X is unequivocally, purely, and completely X, whereas X things are only partly X. Specific properties aside, the Forms enjoy a kind of eternal existence that no individual thing can match. It can seem as if the theory of Forms works only as a condemnation of the ordinary world, and hence accomplishes no more in the way of explanation than a geography of heaven would accomplish for earth-bound cartographers. But this is not all there is to Forms; for if it is undeniably true that an individual X thing is not entirely X, it is just as true that the thing is not *not*-X either. It falls short of perfectly exemplifying what it is, but to some degree at least it does exemplify the property in question. So while the Form makes clear what the X thing is not, it also shows what that thing can be.

In this sense, the Forms are vital to much more than the *Republic*. In Plato's conception of philosophy, every inquiry into abstract terms, which ultimately is to inform our vision of the non-abstract world, needs some object to study; the Forms offer something lucid and real to look at when the physical world, because of its ambiguity, incompleteness, or corruptibility, seems incapable of being studied. That is, understanding the justice of laws in our world, or the beauty of people, presupposes clear theoretical knowledge of justice and beauty "in themselves." The point is still to understand this world. But what *is* the justice of a law or a person? What do we study when studying a just law? Plato appeals to the Forms: the "participation" of the Form of Justice in a person or law makes for whatever in that person or law is just. To put it another way, whatever is just in a person or law reflects the properties of the Form of Justice, much as the mass of a table, and the properties of that mass, are really the mass of its constituent atoms.

Then there is some similarity between the theory of Forms and a scientific theory. Our knowledge that there are fundamental physical entities assures us that all physical objects will obey the same general laws of physics, that tables and cows alike will be held to the earth's surface by gravity and cast shadows. Plato's belief that Forms of disputable terms exist assures him that all examples of those terms will manifest similar properties, which is to say that there is a point to discussing the justice of laws or the beauty of colors, that such discussions amount to more than subjective taste (see *Parmenides* 135b–c).

Suggestions for further reading

This is the chapter that the reader will want to respond to the most cautiously, as a springboard to the questions of Plato's metaphysics. White, *A Companion to Plato's Republic* (Oxford, Blackwell, 1979) and Cross and Woozley, *Plato's Republic* (New York: St Martin's Press, 1964) offer valuable general discussions of Plato's metaphysics, and might be the best readings to begin with. My discussion in this chapter is especially indebted to Annas, *An Introduction to Plato's Republic* (Oxford, Oxford University Press, 1981).

The argument in Book 5 about the failings of particulars has proved one of the most difficult to understand. For comments on Plato's phrase that some things are and are not, see Kahn, "The Greek verb 'be' and the concept of being," *Foundations of Language* 2 (1966): 245–65, and Fine, "Knowledge and belief in *Republic* V," *Archiv für Geschichte der Philosophie* 60 (1978): 121–39. For more on Plato's epistemological concerns, see Cherniss, "The philosophical economy of the theory of ideas," *American Journal of Philology* 57 (1936): 445–56, and Moravcsik, "Understanding and knowledge in Plato's philosophy," *Neue Hefte für Philosophie* 60 (1978): 1–26. On the problem with particular things, Allen, "The argument from opposites in *Republic* V," in J. P. Anton and G. L. Kustas, eds., *Essays in Ancient Greek Philosophy*, vol. I (Albany, SUNY Press, 1972), pp. 165–75, Brentlinger, "Particulars in Plato's middle dialogues," *Archiv für Geschichte der Philosophie* 54 (1972): 116–52, Nehamas, "Plato on the imperfection of the sensible world," *American Philosophical*

Quarterly 12 (1975): 105–17, and Vlastos, "Degrees of reality in Plato," in R. Bambrough, ed., *New Essays on Plato and Aristotle* (London, Routledge & Kegan Paul, 1965), pp. 1–19, all help with Plato's arguments.

On the Form of the Good and its ethical implications, see especially Cooper, "The psychology of justice in Plato," *American Philosophical Quarterly* 14 (1977): 151–7; also Joseph, *Knowledge and the Good in Plato's Republic* (Oxford, Clarendon Press, 1948) and Santas, "The Form of the Good in Plato's *Republic*," in J. P. Anton and A. Preuss, eds., *Essays in Ancient Greek Philosophy*, vol. II (Albany, SUNY Press, 1983), pp. 232–63. The Divided Line has inspired a quantity of interpretive effort; see Elias, " 'Socratic' vs. 'Platonic' dialectic," *Journal of the History of Philosophy* 6 (1969): 205–16, Gulley, *Plato's Theory of Knowledge* (London, Methuen, 1962), Hamlyn, "*Eikasia* in Plato's *Republic*," *Philosophical Quarterly* 8 (1958): 14–23, Patterson, *Image and Reality in Plato's Metaphysics* (Indianapolis, Hackett Publishing Co., 1985), Robinson, "Analysis in Greek geometry," in *Essays in Greek Philosophy* (Oxford, Clarendon Press, 1969), pp. 1–15, and *Plato's Earlier Dialectic* (2nd ed., Oxford, Clarendon Press, 1953), as well as Vlastos, "Elenchus and mathematics," *American Journal of Philology* 109 (1988): 362–96; see also Burnyeat, "Platonism and mathematics," in A. Graeser, ed., *Metaphysik und Mathematik* (Berne, P. Haupt, 1987).

On the Allegory of the Cave, see Morrison, "Two unresolved difficulties in the Line and the Cave," *Phroneses* 22 (1977): 212–31, and Raven, "Sun, Divided Line, and Cave," *Classical Quarterly* 3 (1953): 22–32.

Chapter 8

Injustice
in the soul
and in the city
(Books 8–9)

Books 8 and 9 round out the argument that began in Book 2 with the two purposes of defining justice and showing its profitability. It might appear that by the end of Book 4, in which he described justice in the soul as a harmony akin to health (444d–e), Socrates had already achieved both aims. However, the challenge from Glaucon was not merely to pay justice a compliment, but to demonstrate on universally acceptable grounds that the just soul is the happiest of all possible souls (⑧). Book 8 therefore begins with the announced aim of contrasting justice with every form of injustice, in order to show that each of these will generate less happiness than justice does, both in the private person and in the city.

Given the limitations of space in this book, some parts of the *Republic* have had to be done an injustice. Books 8 and 9, which are full of textured, perceptive accounts of both political and psychological decay, suffer the most. To some extent my brevity, especially as regards Book 8, may be excused on the grounds that

there is much less rigorous argument here than in the preceding sections of the *Republic*, and the reader who has reached this point will be able to digest the material alone; but this in no way means that Books 8 and 9 do not deserve close study.

Much in Book 8 and the first pages of Book 9 relies on anecdotes and examples. Plato's sociological and psychological profiles of vice sometimes even take precedence over his theoretical diagnoses. The theoretical structure returns in force in Book 9, when Plato finishes his catalogue of bad cities and people and looks only at the most just and most unjust individuals; at that point he introduces lines of argument conceptually unrelated to the preceding parade of vices, lines of argument which moreover take his conclusions in a direction we could not have foreseen at the end of Book 4.

Degenerate forms of the city and the soul (544a–576a)

The four kinds of injustice

Socrates identifies the four species of injustice (see 445c) with governments already existing in the world: timocracy, oligarchy, democracy, and tyranny. There is a psychological constitution corresponding to each, so that we may speak of the oligarchic soul as naturally as of the oligarchic city (544a, d–e). After its disappearance in Book 5, the analogy between city and soul returns in full force.

It is not evident why Plato should have settled on *five* kinds of constitution: one just and four types of unjust city. He probably bases this claim on his empirical observation of existing governments, as sound a reason as we could ask for, and a sign of his attention to the ways of the world. But we can already guess that the five types of government will fit uneasily into his prior political analysis that all citizens fall into one of *three* classes. Five human characters should prove just as hard to describe theoretically, given only three parts of the soul. Many of the complications in the coming argument grow out of this bad fit between theories.

The account of timocracy works best, both for cities and for souls. Both timocracies arise when the rational part has lost its hegemony over the whole (547b; 550a–b). The productive class in the city, and the appetites in the soul, insist on their claims to satisfaction. In a compromise between lowest and highest, the spirited part between them comes to rule. As he often does elsewhere, Plato shows his respect for Sparta, the second-best type of government (544c), which lacks only the intellectuality exemplified by Athens. (Despite his undeniable fondness for Sparta, Plato understood its limitations. Though his city would differ from Athens in many respects, it would share the "love of learning" that Plato recognized in his home city: see 435e–436a.) We might think of Napoleonic France or the early Roman Empire – for that matter, Napoleon and Caesar come to mind as timocratic people, as Glaucon comes to mind for Adeimantus (548d). Although this form of life enjoys considerable stability, the fact that the spirited part achieves rule in the midst of conflict shows that the timocracy will contain less unity than we found in the best soul and city.

With the transition to oligarchy, the third class or part of the soul takes the place of the second. Once the productive class takes charge, money becomes the dominant force in a society; thus it will not be the whole of that class, but its richest members who rule the oligarchy (551b). In the soul the desire for money likewise takes charge, for of all the bodily desires it most resembles an organizational force. Unlike lust and hunger, greed at least knows the value of discipline (however anxious: 554d) and long-term planning (however ignobly aimed: 554e–555a).

From these first stages of degeneration we can generalize to three characteristics of vice. First, Plato fits his account of social decay into his definition of justice as the performance of natural functions (⑥). Trouble begins when the wrong children enter the ruling class (546b–547a). Species of political vice are identified by the class that inappropriately rules the city. The greatest social disease, people who live off liquidated assets (552a, 564b), most flamboyantly breaks the rule of distributed labor.

Secondly, bad constitutions possess only spurious signs of unity. The oligarchic soul controls itself as if virtuous, but it lacks the harmony of virtue. (Think of Cephalus.) A single appetite *dominates* the oligarchic soul, but that appetite cannot *unify* it. For unlike reason, which inspects every motivation, then chooses which ones to permit, avarice rules simply by insisting on its own goals. Avarice knows no way of reining itself in: not having been born to rule, it lacks the capacity for self-examination. Plato would cite billionaires, who crave money beyond anything they could spend, as proof of the unfitness of greed to rule the soul.

We see, finally, that any ideal other than justice, once permitted to dominate, will bring the soul and city into worse injustice, through an inner logic of the degenerative process. Every ideal but justice engenders an instability or tension that then resolves itself in a worse political system. The competitive spirit of the timocracy's citizens prompts them to accumulate ever more private wealth (550e), and finally turns them into oligarchs (551a). When the oligarchy carries its avaricious ideal too far, it impoverishes its formerly solid citizens (555d–e) and encourages licentiousness (555c, 556c–e). This observation reinforces the last. If every configuration of the city, apart from the ideal configuration, grants pride of place to the very value that will degrade the city further, there is something wrong with those values as guides for the city or the soul.

Democracy carries disunity and built-in decay to their logical conclusion. Democracy presupposes disagreement, not as a temporary evil to be overcome in some unanimous final state, but as an inherent condition of society. No value predominates in the democratic city, unless it is the tepid value of toleration (557b, 558a). Because the citizens can agree only to disagree, they appeal to no common value and encourage no public virtue. The idea of unity, or of a ruler superior to the citizens, has become repulsive to them. Equally egalitarian, the democratic soul prefers not to choose among its desires – certainly not to condemn any objects that its desires hanker after (561b) – but indulges each as it arises. Desires may be necessary or unnecessary (558d–559c); and whereas the oligarchic soul also denied itself every higher impulse in the service of desire, at least that desire originated in natural need. Having lost the power to tell necessary from unnecessary, the democratic soul has no principle to guide its steps, not even the drab and crass principle of avarice.

It might seem from this description that democracy's confusion leaves it at the other end of the spectrum from the Platonic city. But Socrates still has tyranny to speak of. The greatest dictatorship arises out of the greatest anarchy (564a). In the soul, the democratic person's refusal to judge among desires brings one of those desires, lust (*erōs*), to outgrow all the rest (572e–573a). (Here Socrates seems to despise *erōs*. But we must not jump to conclusions. Elsewhere he recognizes its importance: 458d, 474d–475b. In the *Symposium* and *Phaedrus* Plato finds metaphysical significance in sexual love; the *Timaeus* lists the bad effects of celibacy at 91b–c; cf. *Laws* 930c.)

In one sense this development returns us to the oligarchic soul, for like it the tyrannic soul follows the command of a single desire. We can see Plato struggling to make his psychological theory account elegantly for the phenomena: he draws yet another distinction among desires, this time separating the unnecessary ones further into the law-abiding and the lawless (571b). The worst of the latter is lust, especially monstrous lust for the most forbidden persons, foods, and deeds (574e–575a). Unlike the oligarch's greed, this transgressive lewdness has nothing to do with self-control, perverted or otherwise. A lawless drive, it rules lawlessly in the soul.

Of all the psychological portraits, this one (reminiscent of the elderly Baron de Charlus in Proust) sounds the most modern. Unfortunately, the portrait of a depraved soul, for all its realism, strains Plato's psychological theory. On top of the ad hoc subdivision of desires, we get the claim that someone compelled by a single desire nevertheless experiences less psychological unity than the person whose soul follows the promptings of any number of desires. Both the structure of the soul and its disunity when unjust have become confused by Plato's efforts to make every soul fit his theory. In reality, the political and psychological transitions from democracy to tyranny are not obviously symptoms of growing chaos. If anything, they may show that chaos engenders a new repressive order. In the case of the soul, Socrates' repeated distinctions among the various desires brings to mind a question we raised about Book 4, whether this baggy category of "desire" had any informative function, or merely gathered under a single meaninglessly broad heading motivations that had nothing to do with each other (see pp. 87–91). If rule by the appetites can equally produce oligarchy, democracy, or tyranny in the soul, the appetites must have even less to do with one another than we had thought.

Limitations of the comparative method

Book 8 and its conclusion in Book 9 stand out in many readers' minds, thanks to their psychological insight and their applicability to states and people beyond any that Plato could have known. By the time the tyrannical soul has been described (576c) there seems little left to do but agree that Plato has indeed laid out these cities and souls in order from best to worst, and that the good city surpasses its political competitors, the corresponding soul all its psychological competitors.

But what has this catalogue of injustices accomplished? Grant that each city and soul is more prone than its predecessor to engage in unjust acts. We knew that before looking at the cases, since *ex hypothesi* each was to be more unjust than its predecessor. If Plato is to answer Thrasymachus, he also needs to show that what makes a soul *worse* makes it *unhappier*. In timocracy and oligarchy power passed ever further from the rational part or class, which is most equipped to rule, to the appetitive, whose selfishness assures that its rule will never bring about the willing cooperation of the parts being ruled (552e). If every step into greater injustice could likewise be shown to follow from a further loss of unity, we might have the basis for an argument: harmony in the soul being pleasant, and inner conflict a source of unhappiness, the arrangement that produces good works will simultaneously lead to happiness (⑧).

I have pointed out that this progress into disintegrity applies to the types of city and soul only until we reach the tyrant. The parts of the soul then cease to illuminate, since Plato complicates the desiring part beyond recognition. And although we know what Socrates means when he finds "anarchy and lawlessness" in the tyrannical soul (575a), he has not shown that this lawlessness follows from the disunity warned of in Book 4. Since Socrates' explicit comparisons of justice with injustice (576b–588a) use tyranny to represent all injustice, this deviation from the theme of unity is no small matter: unity of a sort we clearly recognize disappears just when we are about to put the picture of disunity to work.

Other details of this section also fail to work out. Each city is shown to lead by inevitable historical laws to the next; each soul is put into a man whose son degenerates into the worse type. To what extent does Plato himself believe to be telling a causal story? The tale of generational decline is too simplistic to believe; and since Plato gives no hint of how upward progress might work, we have to assume this devolution to be terminable and irreversible, so that within five generations of its establishment every human community would consist only of sex-crazed burglars. As a factual claim this is neither true nor fresh, but the oldest complaint ever made about younger generations.

Concerning the city, Plato would surely have known that the transitions he speaks of are not the only ones possible. During his adulthood Athens recovered from the Thirty Tyrants and returned to democracy. So ordinary governments may grow naturally out of a worse form into a better one. Moreover, if every city declines from a better one, then the best city, which would improve on every other, can never be born in this world whose history always goes from bad to worse. Plato's "history" makes better sense as a lively vehicle for presenting a hierarchically ordered series of governments. The fiction that each type slides down further from its predecessor permits Plato to look for the single characteristic that sets democracy apart from oligarchy, and oligarchy from timocracy. His argument would work equally well if cities changed haphazardly; to prove that justice benefits a city Plato needs only to show that each type *is better than* the one below it, even if it does not *transform itself into* that type.

Unfortunately, translating the narrative of cultural decline into a taxonomy of governments turns a strong (though false) claim about the world of politics into a truer but much blander one. We lose any sense that Plato locates the characteristics of various cities in specific material conditions. If this is not really history, we need not take its accounts of political change seriously.

As for the analogy between the city and the soul, that seems at the beginning of Book 8 to have an important role to play in Plato's argument. Glaucon's introduction expects the worse regimes to shed some light on the four worse kinds of people (544a–b). Socrates adds that each regime will be populated primarily by the people whose souls correspond to the form of government (544d–e; see 435a–c). If this is true, the timocratic soul will both share its general structure with the timocratic city, *and* turn up more frequently than any other personality type in the citizens of that city. Then individual psychology explains a great deal about politics, for a city will reflect the character of its citizens. Such a tight relationship between the city and the private person would retrospectively justify the *Republic*'s argumentative strategy by unifying its treatments of souls and cities.

But the analogy breaks down. When Socrates imagines the development of timocratic and oligarchic men, he pictures their private lives in cities unlike either their own souls or their fathers'. The timocrat's father, the best sort of man, lives in a city that is not well run (549c), therefore not the best city that would correspond to his soul. The young oligarch grows up in a city swarming with informers and lawsuits (553b), which is to say in a city more like democracy than oligarchy. The tyrant offers the clearest disanalogy, for in drawing attention to the special misery of a tyrannical person who gains a tyrant's power, Socrates is suggesting that this conjunction of pathology and power will be the exception rather than the rule (576b–c). So psychological tyranny need not have anything to do with dictatorship. Socrates expects tyrannical men to band together within a city (575a–c); but if they form a small group in *any* given city, they cannot be that city's representative types.

Plato must be saying only that certain sorts of people are reminiscent of certain states. There is something metaphorically democratic about a democratic person's soul, and metaphorically oligarchic about the oligarchic soul. In practice this connection has only one definite consequence: "With respect to virtue and happiness . . . the relation between man and man [will] be that between city and city" (576d). The oligarchically souled will be better, more self-controlled people than those with democratic souls, as oligarchies in cities are more self-controlled, hence more virtuous, than democracies. We will rank souls exactly as we rank the cities. This does help the argument; but Plato could have shown one kind of soul to be worse than another much more directly than by constructing such a complex analogy. The analogy between city and soul, like the account of each city's degradation, fails as a literal statement, and as a metaphorical version of the truth becomes much less significant than it had first appeared. The general effect of this discussion is one of a vast machinery being assembled and then sitting idle.

Three comparisons between just and unjust lives (576b–587b)

This needless complexity is especially striking when we bear in mind that Socrates has narrowed down his immediate goal: not to show each form of unjust soul worse and unhappier than the just soul, but to contrast the soul of the most just person with that of the most unjust (545a). The narrower agenda reflects Glaucon's original comparison of perfectly just and perfectly unjust people (360e–362c). So after elaborating on each kind of person and regime, Socrates drops the intermediate types and compares the lives lived at the two extremes.

The psychological profile (576b–580c)

The first comparison follows the language and the descriptions we have just gone through. Look at the tyrannical soul, Socrates says: for all its delusions of wielding power, it represents the most enslaved state of all (577d). Like a city in a despot's hands, this soul lives wretchedly in confusion, regret, and fear (577e–578b). A man with a tyrannical soul who has the bad luck to rule an actual city comes off the worst of all (578b–580a). This is not really an argument, only a summation of the catalogue of injustice. Justice has revealed itself by now as more appealing than injustice, as health is more appealing to see than disease. And thanks to guarding the just from the anxieties and obsessive desires that injustice brings to the soul, justice also surpasses injustice in its consequences.

As in Book 4, justice is conceived as a harmonious relationship among the soul's parts, on the basis of which the soul escapes inner conflict. By ruling the other parts, reason brings happiness to the person. To the extent that Socrates spells out any argument in this passage, it comes at 577d–e:

> If, then . . . a man is like his city, isn't it also necessary that the same arrangement be in him and that his soul be filled with much slavery and illiberality, and that, further, those parts of it that are most decent be slaves while a small part, the most depraved and maddest, be master? . . . Therefore, the soul that is under a tyranny will least do what it wants – speaking of the soul as a whole.

The soul whose reason does not rule is the soul that does least whatever benefits it "as a whole"; therefore, the work of reason in this
passage, as it has been implicitly since the beginning of Book 8, is the
supervision of the whole soul that we saw at work in Book 4. I note
this apparently obvious fact, because Socrates is about to complicate
our conception of reasoning.

The philosopher as best judge of pleasure (580c–583a)

Here is another proof, says Socrates (580c). Each part of the soul has
its own desires, and the pleasures that derive from their fulfillment.
The appetitive part loves gain, the spirited part honor, and the rational
part wisdom and learning (581a–c). Everyone ruled by one part of the
soul will find the fulfillment of that part's desires the most pleasant
experience (581c–d). (Although Plato offers no argument for this last
claim, it is a consequence of his psychological theory: to be ruled by
a part of the soul is to make that part's values one's own, hence to find
the objects of its desires the most pleasant objects to acquire.) Disputes
over rival pleasures need judges. But the best judge of any matter is
the one with the widest experience; since the lover of wisdom
(*philosophos*) knows the pleasures of bodily appetite and honor as well
as those of learning, that will be the best judge (582a–d). Since judgments rely on arguments, and philosophers use arguments better than
anyone else does, they emerge again as the best judges (582d–583a).
Having accepted philosophers' judgment as best, we must say that
their own life, the life of the just, defeats the life of the unjust a second
time (583b).

Socrates has turned his attention from the best life to the most
pleasant. He had never planned to speak of pleasure. But we should
understand the pleasure under discussion as broadly as possible: it is
not some feeling common to all three lives, but an ingredient of each
life's experiences that makes that life worth choosing. Besides,
Glaucon had asked Socrates to show the superiority of justice over
injustice with respect to its natural effects on the soul. He cannot
legislate in advance which consequences Socrates may appeal to. If
Socrates chooses to identify pleasure as one, he has not strayed from
his mandate.

The boldest assumption in this argument arrives when Socrates assigns a characteristic desire (*epithumia*) to each part of the soul. When Socrates first named the parts of the soul, he assigned all desires to the third and irrational part (437d, 439d): the function of that part had been specifically to yearn for and pursue objects, while the other two found their expression in behavior *not* aimed at objects. Now Socrates makes official his implicit premise of Book 6, that the rational part has desires of its own (⑪). This change significantly modifies the *Republic*'s psychological theory, by adding a second feature to reason much different from its original characteristic of serving as an overseer to the whole soul. Now that reason rules (to all appearances, only) in the philosopher, its desire for learning becomes specifically love for philosophy. From just and unjust men we have moved to the philosopher and the tyrant.

Real and unreal pleasures (583b–587b)

In this last and most difficult argument, Socrates continues to think of the just life as the intellectual life, its pleasures therefore the joys of abstract thought. This argument ambitiously tries to prove that the pleasures available to a philosopher exceed everyone else's pleasures in both truth and purity (583b).

First (583c–585a) Socrates distinguishes among the three states of pain, pleasure, and the intermediate repose that contains neither (583c). This middle state sometimes feels like pleasure and sometimes like pain, depending on what precedes it. Then the argument moves in two different directions, so tersely as to resist clear summary. Plato first takes up a point from the previous argument, to the effect that a philosopher makes a better judge of pleasures than anyone else. The state of repose, because we experience it sometimes as pleasure and sometimes as pain, cannot genuinely be either (584a); therefore, those pleasures brought about by relief from pain only *seem* pleasant. But if pleasures can be false, "pleasant" only from an unenlightened point of view, we must acknowledge the possibility of expertise with respect to pleasure (584e–585a). That expertise will tell the true from the spurious, a task that reminds us of Book 5's portrait of the philosopher. Plato wants to remove the subjectivity from our discussions of pleasure. We may think that a pleasure is exactly as good as it feels, but the condition that now brings the happiness of pleasure may as easily bring pain on another occasion, or nothing at all. Even in ranking our brute sensations, we have to defer to the expert; we will not accept the word of the unjust that their lives are more enjoyable than the lives of the just. The argument may sound undemocratic, but it is rooted in the everyday observation that some people are wrong about what they expect to satisfy them. The insane, and those addicted to debilitating drugs, provide the most dramatic examples; but "That's not really going to make you happy" is said to plenty of others as well.

Socrates next moves to draw out what he calls an illumination of this point (585a–587b), which, however, departs from the previous argument. Most pleasures of the body and soul relieve a person not simply of pain, but specifically of the pain of emptiness (585a–b). If pleasure is fullness, it will be a greater fullness if that which replenishes the person possesses greater reality. Since the objects that the philosopher studies are more real than those a hungry person eats, the pleasures of the philosophical soul surpass those of the less philosophical body (585b–e). Pursuing intellectual pleasures offers permanent relief from the doomed cycle of desire and fulfillment. Thanks to their greater reality, the objects of philosophical knowledge will not disappear again as food does in the stomach, but keep the philosopher at a steady state of fullness. Plato is appealing again to ⑫, the claim that kinds of understanding correspond to different levels of reality in their objects; despite the trouble that ⑫ causes for an account of knowledge, it is essential to this defense of the philosophical life.

The halves of this argument sit uneasily together. The first calls for an expertise that we can imagine judging among *all* the pleasures available to a person. Such expertise fits our image of reason as a coordinator of the demands that come from the rest of the soul. The second half of the argument, though, identifies all true pleasures with the joys of the intellect, as if the appetitive part of the soul should *never* have its way.

There is a more profound contradiction. For, whereas the first half of the argument shrank from praising any pleasure that follows from the relief of pain, the second half endorses the relief from ignorance as though it could raise a person higher than the middle state of calm (586a). Nothing in the argument prepares for this claim, which feels like a gratuitous insistence on the pleasures of philosophy. It seems as if Plato wants so badly to demonstrate the superiority of the contemplative life that he will even downplay an essential characteristic of P-justice, namely that it gives each part of the soul its fair share of satisfaction.

Two conceptions of reason

The comparisons of justice and injustice force an issue we can no longer avoid. Does justice require philosophy, or may we continue to think of it as the harmonious interrelation among the soul's parts? Socrates seems not to distinguish the two conceptions, but takes every defense of philosophers as a defense of "the just" (e.g. 582e–583b). At the end of the preceding argument he overtly identifies the two:

> [W]hen all the soul follows the philosophic and is not factious, the result is that each part may, so far as other things are concerned, mind its own business and be just and, in particular, enjoy its own pleasures, the best pleasures, and, to the greatest possible extent, the truest pleasures. (586e)

Plato assumes that intellectual pleasures belong always and only to the person whose intellect controls the soul's other parts. He assumes that the rational faculty that is capable of grasping abstract truths will be the same rational faculty that effectively directs traffic among the parts of the soul. The highest knowledge and the sanest personality go together.

However difficult to accept, this assumption follows directly from Plato's defense of philosopher-rulers in Chapter 6: see ⑨ and ⑩. To justify government by philosophers, Plato expanded his conception of reason; he cannot give up the expanded function of reason now without giving up philosophocracy. So Books 8 and 9 have to defend the ethical life both from within the psychological theory of Book 4 (so that the Republic's overall argument remains coherent) and from within the rationalistic conception of ethics developed in 5–7. In the argument we just looked at, Socrates conflates the two views of virtue. The discord in that argument is perhaps all the evidence we need that theoretical and practical wisdom will not mesh together easily.

Conclusion (587c–592b)

Plato closes with familiar rhetorical gestures. In his way of playing with mathematics, he has Socrates calculate the exact proportion between the lives of the just and of the unjust (587e). Inclined as ever to give his theory an image, he pictures the soul as the biological union of a human being, a lion, and a many-headed mythological beast (588b–589a). The fate of reason, represented as the only human part of our souls, is to find itself trapped with a dangerous if educable creature, and another, far more lethal and loathsome, which the little human can master only with the help of the intermediate beast. After this image, and most familiar of all, comes the disclaimer that although the good city might never exist, it is still valuable as the pattern for justice that private citizens can use as a guide for life (592a–b).

Amid these perorations, a couple of important points are made. Notice first that Socrates calls the ideal relationship among the parts of the soul a friendship (589a, b). However puritanical a modern reader might think Plato's ethical theory, Plato does not conceive of justice as a state of constant repression, but as a discipline that the just person finds gratifying. Natural desires exist to be expressed, not denied. Secondly, Socrates reiterates the importance of acts commonly called just for the maintenance of justice in the soul (589c–d, 590a–c). He had claimed as much in Book 4 (444d–e), in the course of arguing for ⑦: the precepts of conventional morality, though they need justifications that only philosophers can provide, suffice to produce in the soul even the elevated justice that a philosopher praises. In the present section Socrates takes his respect for popular opinion even further: not only do the rules of ordinary justice *happen* to conduce to Platonic justice, they were *made* to serve that purpose. Plato has never lost sight of ordinary morality, but returns at the end of his praise for philosophical virtue to recognize the worth of virtue at its most unphilosophical.

Suggestions for further reading

On the types of government and types of souls, see Guthrie, *A History of Greek Philosophy*, vol. IV: *Plato* (Cambridge, Cambridge University Press, 1975) for exegeses of the faults Plato finds in each stage. On the tension between two conceptions of justice at play in Book 9, see Nussbaum, "The *Republic*: true value and the standpoint of perfection," in *The Fragility of Goodness* (Cambridge, Cambridge University Press, 1986), pp. 136–64, for both a sharp analysis of how Plato expects us to live, and a sympathetic appraisal of the merit he finds in that kind of life. See also Irwin, *Plato's Moral Theory* (Oxford, Clarendon Press, 1977), Murphy, *The Interpretation of Plato's Republic* (Oxford, Oxford University Press, 1951), and Shorey, "Plato's ethics," in *The Unity of Plato's Thought* (Chicago, University of Chicago Press, 1903), reprinted in Vlastos, ed., *Plato* (Garden City, Doubleday, 1971) vol. II, pp. 7–34.

Chapter 9

Art and immortality (Book 10)

The shift from Book 9 to the start of 10 is so abrupt that even the reader whose mind has wandered during the long saga of the city's decline will realize immediately that something has happened. From the comparison between justice and injustice that took two books to prepare, and that harked back to an intricately structured argument spanning the length of the *Republic*, we move to what seems a slapdash collection of arguments about the arts, only tangentially related to the dialogue as a whole. Even more suddenly, this discussion lurches into an argument for the immortality of the soul; this is followed by a myth, warning of the price for an unjust life, and apparently therefore taking back the *Republic*'s long and patient defense of justice in the terms of this world. Then the dialogue ends.

It is almost as if someone had tacked on marginally relevant arguments to the preceding sections of the *Republic*, in the belief that more deep thoughts may as well go there as elsewhere. But to complain seriously that Book 10 has in any sense been tacked on is to

173

misrepresent the Republic, whose central ordering principle admits of ample asides. Moreover, Book 10 amplifies a dominant theme of the dialogue, that a good life requires the rule of reason. Socrates opens his critique of poetry, for instance, with the comment that the earlier censorship (398a–b) has found further justification "now that the soul's forms have each been separated out" (595b). Indeed, every issue in Book 10 reflects back on the psychological theory (Book 4), and on the vindication of a life in which reason rules the roost (Books 8–9). Given that Socrates has just finished defending the life of reason, it becomes less strange than it had first appeared to see Book 10 going on about the nature of that life.

The argument against all poetry (595a–608b)

However difficult the details of the first half of Book 10, the general argument is clear enough:

1. ⑬ Poetry imitates appearance. (595b–602c)
∴ 2. ⑭ Poetry appeals to the worst parts of the soul. (602c–606d)
∴ 3. Poetry should be banned from the good city. (606e–608b)

Because the argument concludes with (3), agreeing or disagreeing with Plato may appear an issue of personal liberty. But Plato's interest lies in the new discoveries he has made about imitation in poetry. He gives no argument for the move from ⑭ to (3), considering it obvious that if he can show poetry to yield deleterious effects, he will have made the case for its abolition. The work consists in showing where those effects come from. So he will first argue that poetry is a phantom (⑬), then use ⑬ to expose its psychological effects (⑭).

Imitation (595a–602c)

We learned in Book 3 that poetry presents its characters by means of *mimēsis*, i.e. imitation or representation (392d). Book 10 will add that artistic imitation is an imitation of appearance. The things imitated, and the bad species of imitation, remain the same in both discussions: poetry as it now exists imitates human beings (393b, c; 395c–396d; 605a, c), but in the ideal city will imitate only the best of them

(396c–397b, 604e, 607a). If Plato has changed his view about poetry from the earlier discussion to this one, the change concerns the nature of imitation. In Book 3 the process was left unexplained, but since that point Plato has introduced a theory of knowledge and reality that lets him analyze it more closely.

Painting (596a–598d)

Socrates begins with an analogy between poetry and painting, which both "imitate" their subjects. Both genres are or can be representational. This point of comparison suggests that looking at painting may clarify an elusive characteristic of poetry, perhaps as looking at birds' mating behavior clarifies the otherwise too complex mating behavior of humans.

In the description of painting, the Forms unexpectedly arrive to complicate the argument (596a–b). Moreover, they arrive in an unexpected style, since these are not Forms of relative terms, but of every kind of thing belonging to a general category. Craftspeople use these Forms as models: the carpenter who builds a couch or table does so by "looking to" the Forms of Couch and Table (596b). The painter of a couch or a table, by comparison, looks only at the individual things and copies their appearance (597e–598b).

This elaboration tends to confuse more than it helps. Plato does not need the Forms to make his point in this passage, that the skill of imitation is inferior to other skills. To establish that point he needs only to argue, as he will at 598b, that the painter is ignorant of a thing's nature. The Forms serve to diagnose the failing of the imitator. We cannot say that the painter fails on the grounds of copying a particular table, for a carpenter may also use one table as the model for another. The difference consists in *how* each uses the object. A carpenter sees the table, as a geometer sees the drawing of a triangle, as the image of some greater reality; thus one may "look to" the Forms even by looking at an individual table. Because carpenters examine the construction of each joint, the cut of the legs, and the proportions of each piece, they rise above the particularity of the model table in a way that painters do not. What makes a painting the imitation of appearance is the painter's ignorance of the relevant Form. Though a table belongs to a lower order of being than its Form does, it still bears some relation to that Form, as X things generally "participate" in the Form of X (476d). But an imitation of the *appearance* of an X thing leaves out any reference to the Form of X. Artistic imitation only partly duplicates the imitated object (598b), because the imitators' ignorance lets them present only its look to the audience of other ignoramuses.

Poetry (598d–601a)

Assuming that we agree about the similarity between painting and poetry, we have arrived at

⑬ Poetry imitates appearance.

The problem with moving so precipitously is the vagueness of *mimēsis*. We may legitimately ask how artistic imitation can be relevantly the same in both genres. This leads us to live issues in aesthetic theory: how might music also be representational? What is the difference between the representation of a person in drama and the "same" representation in fiction? How do we compare a painting with a sculpture?

For the purposes of understanding Book 10, however, we may leave such questions aside. The emphasis in Book 10 is not on imitation itself, but on what we may call the most general description of its object, the appearance of a thing instead of the thing's true nature. Even if the imitative relationships present in the different arts have nothing to do with one another, this claim about appearance can still hold true. All we need to say about poetry, then, to preserve what matters of the analogy, is that poets are as ignorant as painters about the truth concerning their subjects.

That is the point Socrates turns to in his exposure of Homer's ignorance (599c–601a). Homer's ignorance underscores the merely apparent nature of a poet's understanding of human beings: Homer's skill lay entirely in his ability to create convincing portraits of heroes in action, not in any deeper comprehension of morality. Poets are therefore ignorant in the same way that painters are; hence they too imitate appearance alone.

The champions of art sometimes respond that ignorance is

irrelevant, that one may be ignorant and still a splendid poet, Plato certainly acknowledges that point; it is his own point. From Plato's perspective the problem is precisely that whether the poet is knowledgeable or ignorant makes no difference to the merit of the poetry. One cannot be ignorant of medicine and still a splendid doctor; but Homer's ignorance shows that one can be a poet without being knowledgeable, therefore that it is not part of poets' imitative job to learn the facts about the things they write about. Since poetic imitation can be accomplished without appeal to the facts of the matter, it cannot be an imitation of a thing's true nature.

User, maker, imitator (601c–602a)

In a coda to this argument, Socrates ranks the levels of understanding available to the user of a thing, its maker, and its imitator. The first possesses knowledge (601e) and the second "right trust [*pistis*]" or "right opinion [*doxa*]" (601e, 602a), while the imitator, lacking both knowledge and justified belief, remains ignorant (602a).

It is hard to see why Plato should want this complication of his view. He does not normally assume the user of an artifact to enjoy such unimpeded access to the Forms. But at least this passage shows us how to tie the discussion of art to the Divided Line: the words for "trust" and "opinion" in this passage are the same words Socrates used there to name our perception of physical objects (511e; cf. 534a). Since the imitator possesses something worse than this trust, artistic imitations must belong in the lowest part of the Divided Line, together with shadows, reflections, and all other "images" (509e–510a). As such, works of art are objects of "imagination" or image-perception (*eikasia*), the cognitive awareness furthest from knowledge.

This passage is also useful for moving from artistic imitations *simpliciter* to their effects on their spectators. In what follows, Plato will argue explicitly that distinct states of the soul mark the audience of art, and that these states corrupt the soul. The present excoriation of poetry's *epistemic* status will serve as a preliminary to a *psychological* criticism.

The arousal of unreason (602c–607a)

Painting and the irrational (602c–603b)

Socrates asks what it is in the human being on which imitation has its effect (602c). He contrasts the sense of sight, easily duped by artistic shams, with the calculating faculty that combats illusion by means of sober measurement (602d–e). Since sight and reason disagree about whether a stick in water is bent, and since a single part of the soul cannot disagree with itself (602e), the part of the soul taken in by visual images must be distinct from the calculating part (603a). This argument duplicates the passage in Book 4 that first separated the parts of the soul, also on the basis of internal disagreement (436b). If the present separation of parts matches up with the earlier one, artistic imitation may be said to appeal to the lower impulses we have already encountered. Then Socrates has outlined a succinct argument for the depravity of artistic imitation:

1. ⑬ Art imitates appearance and not reality.
2. Reality is the object of knowledge, perceived by the rational part of the soul.
∴ 3. From (2), appearance *without* reality appeals to a non-rational part of the soul.
∴ 4. From (1) and (3), art appeals to the irrational in human beings.

⑭ is only (4) as applied to the case of poetry; so if the argument applies to poetry, ⑭ is true.

As the argument stands, however, it plays off an ambiguity that threatens to keep its focus too narrow. For the "non-rational," when we speak of painting, means only the bodily organs susceptible to making mistakes about experience. This is rather a neutral sense of non-rationality, far from what we mean when we speak of irrational anger, fear, or dislike. But the argument against poetry requires the irrationality encouraged by art to include all the passions that a person falls prey to. The problem is that, while Book 4 had separated the part of the soul that exercises self-control from the angry part and the lusty, thirsty part, the present argument addresses itself to the part taken in by optical illusions and the more sober part that remains unfooled. One's sense of sight, however fallible, has nothing to do with human desire. To keep his argument from applying only to optical illusions, Plato will have to equate the propensity to error with the propensity to passion.

Poetry and the irrational (603c–607a)

So Socrates turns directly to poetry (603b–c), to show how its imitative practice allies it with the soul's lower parts. (In these critiques of poetry we find Plato concentrating on drama, with Homer a tragedian *avant la lettre*: 595b, 598d. Since Homer and the playwrights occupied pride of place among all poets in classical Athens, Plato has to attack them to show how far-reaching he means his criticism to be.) The argument makes two distinct points: first, that poets tend to imitate the soul's worse impulses instead of its better ones (603c–605c), and secondly, that poetry leads its audience to privilege those parts of the soul that ought to be kept in a subservient position (605c–607a).

The first argument sets the soul's deliberative faculty against its other impulses. In every crisis that leaves people torn between the desire to react passionately and the desire to control their reactions, the latter desire – which we recognize from Book 4 as the work of reason (439c–d) – is the impulse to decide what really has happened. Suppose a man's son dies: his reason will be the part of him that asks what human life amounts to (604b–c), while his grief flows from the part that "believes the same things are at one time big and at another little" (605c), i.e. the part that finds a young man's death monumental when the young man is a son, trivial when he is a stranger.

This last step reveals the radical move in Plato's argument. Self-control, the work of reason, is not only a psychological impulse, but also on every occasion the result of philosophical inquiry. The desires lack awareness of their own importance or insignificance; therefore, the impulses that do not come from reason will always make mistakes. So the expression of any passionate or desiring impulse rests on an error about the importance of that impulse's objects. The soul's irrational parts do resemble the sense of sight, because in the domain of human action they are the source of all misjudgment.

Plato apparently expects people never to give extra weight to their own desires and emotions. Deliberating about his son's death requires a man to deny the special, very particular relationship between himself and his son, to treat himself impersonally as one more human being among many. Reason takes on the appearance of an inner command that denies the importance of personal ties and desires to a healthy human life.

Whether or not Plato wants us to become quite so detached from our desires, he certainly expects us to subject them to scrutiny, to weigh each non-rational motivation against a philosophical evaluation of its worth and meaning. This picture of behavior illustrates ⑪, which first appeared in Book 5 and then grew in significance in Book 9. The rational part of the soul has its own desires, not only governing all the other impulses, but also aiming at philosophical understanding. Because the ruling part of the soul is also the part that looks philosophically at every issue, a well-run soul must force its irrational impulses to meet philosophical standards of appropriateness.

Plato supports his position by arguing, independently of the painting analogy, that poetic imitation appeals to and encourages the emphatically irrational impulses in the soul. He finds dramatic poets always depicting human passions, instead of the sober calculating faculty that reins them in (604e–605a). Whatever his agenda, Plato has a legitimate point. An actor once complained to me about having to portray a perfect salesman in a training film for hospital-supplies distributors, while another actor displayed the techniques that distributors should avoid. "Mr. Bad Catheter had the fun," he said. "I had to play it straight." Most actors and most playwrights would feel the same way. To play an idealized character is to leave out the bumbling and the vice, all the flaws with which actors show their skill. Plato knows how much the dramatic arts thrive on the portrayal of imperfection; since imperfection belongs in the domain of the irrational, he can hardly help seeing the dramatist's fondness for deviance as an unseemly preference for error over truth. (Given the nature of the antipathy that Plato developed toward the theater, we can understand better why Socrates should have become such a stiff, saintly figure in Plato's own works of this period: Socrates' is the good and intellectual soul that no actor would want to portray.)

In his final argument, Socrates convicts the audience of poetry of the same perverse preference (605c–607a). For whatever reason, we let ourselves enjoy actions, passions, jokes, and drives in a dramatic or fictional work that we would never tolerate in our private lives. (Think of the sympathy that Satan elicits from readers of *Paradise Lost*.) Our enjoyment amounts to privileging non-reason over reason, because every appeal to the emotions is a seduction away from the use of reason. Emotions by themselves are not bad; nor can something like grief be suppressed entirely. But preferring an emotional response to a rational one is like asking the army what its leaders ought to order it to do. And just as too many calls for votes in an army would weaken its officers' power, so too every indulgence of an irrational impulse leaves it stronger (606b–d; cf. 444c, 589c–d). The enjoyment of poetry leads to injustice in the soul.

Appearance vs. the imitation of appearance

If the imitative arts produce objects of low metaphysical status, that is not reason enough to outlaw them. We ranked poems with reflections and other images; but surely mirrors and shadows should not be expelled from the city. To put the problem another way, Plato finds poetry dangerous. But his analysis of artistic imitation puts poetry on a par with the most insignificant objects imaginable. Why get exercised over such trivial entities? How can works of art affect the soul when they are no more than shadows?

Plato must think that imitations possess some additional quality that gives them a power unmatched by other images. Consider the painting of a table, in which the front legs are made shorter than the rear. In one sense this misstatement about the world resembles a stick that looks bent in water. But while I may pull out the stick and hold it against a straightedge, it never occurs to me – it is irrelevant – to measure the legs of the painted table. The painting pleases me as it stands; to enjoy a painting is to give up such pedestrian considerations as the object's actual proportions. In this way the painting seduces me away from using my powers of calculation, as an apparently bent stick does not. Something about the artistic image holds my attention, keeps me from asking rational questions about it.

That "something" is the added element that inspires Plato's mistrust of the artistic image. On his account, the special character of poetry includes the sweetness (607a) and beauty (598e, 602b) of representations, and the audience's pleasure (605d, 607d), but it goes beyond them. Poetry exercises what Socrates calls "charm" (*kēlēsis*; 601b, 607c), an appeal tantamount to enchantment. A pleasant image – the sharp shadow cast by a denuded tree – however inappropriate as an object of knowledge, does not warrant the condemnation that Socrates heaps on imitations, because no naturally occurring image would seduce its spectator in the fascinating way that an artistic image does.

Now we have a better argument. The products of artistic imitation lure the spectator into preferring them over objects that might lead to knowledge. Their charm is the origin of their seductiveness. Plato seems to have acknowledged this charm earlier in the *Republic*, when he arranged his young guardians' education to take advantage of it. For in Book 3 he shows the guardians learning to develop aesthetic reactions to good and bad deeds, with the help of moral lessons dressed in the attractive speech of poems (401b–d). There, poetic charm seemed a force capable of good; but this difference between the two passages only underscores the general difference between Books 3 and 10, namely the difference between Plato's attempt at first to find some poetry that is good and his later suspicion that there is no such thing (see pp. 209–14).

Assuming some explanation of charm, this argument might work. Socrates attributes the charm of poetry to its rhythm, meter, and harmony (601a), but that only calls for further explanation. Where do those poetic devices get their appeal? Here the *Republic* is silent. In the *Ion* and the *Phaedrus* Plato tries to say more, accounting for the power of poetry with a divine madness (akin to what we call inspiration) that possesses the poet and gives every good poem its inexplicable attractiveness to its audience (*Ion* 533d–534e; *Phaedrus* 245a). Plato says nothing about divine madness in the *Republic*, probably because it threatens to elevate poetry to a more exalted level than the *Republic*'s ungenerous criticism will permit. But without some such explanation of their charm, the danger inherent in works of art must also go unexplained. Given their epistemic worthlessness, they can seduce their audience only by virtue of their charm. Either Plato must explain the bewitchment of art in terms that do not praise it, or he must concede that such error-riddled productions could never corrupt the soul.

More consequences of justice and injustice (608c–621d)

The second half of Book 10 takes pains to close Socrates' discussion with Glaucon and Adeimantus in tidy references back to the issues they had raised in Book 2. In justifying their original challenge, Glaucon and Adeimantus had made peripheral points – Glaucon about the unfair wages that accrue to the just and the unjust, Adeimantus about the disrespect for virtue evident even in his culture's praise of it – that Socrates will address in finishing his argument.

The *Republic* has defended justice on the grounds (1) that the just enjoy greater psychological peace than the unjust, and (2) that the intellectual pursuits to which the just find themselves drawn yield pleasures unknown to anyone else. Whatever the merits of these claims, we must recognize that to a certain sort of listener they will sound empty. Someone whose life is concerned with fame and physical joy will find it easy to shrug off the promise of psychic harmony, to say nothing of the vaguer promise of intellectual pleasures. Plato knows he cannot win over a reader who has not already begun to think philosophically: Book 5's lover of opinion cannot simply be told about the Forms, but first has to stop focusing on the things in the visible world. Throughout the *Republic* we have seen Plato respond to this gulf between his philosophical and unphilosophical audiences by offering two different kinds of arguments for a single point. The dozen remaining pages serve the same purpose: after arguing for the deep, important benefits of justice, Socrates says a few words about its superficial benefits, to satisfy the reader on whom those better arguments were wasted.

Immortality (608d–612a)

As a preliminary step toward the final propaganda for justice, Socrates argues that the soul is immortal. Especially during the period of the *Republic*, Plato kept returning to this subject. The *Phaedo* devotes itself to seeking a proof of immortality; other dialogues include arguments in passing (*Meno* 81b–86d, *Phaedrus* 245c–d); still others assert immortality without argument (*Laws* 959b, 967d; *Timaeus* 41c–42e). Here immortality gets a minor argument:

1. The evil connected with every thing is that which can destroy it. (608d–609a)
2. Injustice, licentiousness, cowardice, and ignorance make a soul bad. (609b)
∴ 3. Vice is the specific evil of the soul.
4. The presence of vice never results in death. (609c–d)
∴ 5. The soul is immortal. (610e–611a)

The heart of this argument comes in (4), an important observation. A knife, when blunt enough, stops being a knife at all; but a bad soul does not find its being threatened by its badness. Though for Plato being morally bad also means being *bad at* the work of the soul, this failure to live up to the soul's duties does not make the soul expire. The disease of the soul is not a sickness unto death. Plato concludes that the soul possesses remarkable resilience.

Here his argument falters, for immortality is far from the only explanation we can give of (4). We might equally use the undeniable truth of (4) to turn Plato's own argument around: since vice does not bring death, vice cannot be the soul's specific evil. Vice works against the harmony of the soul by attacking its natural system of governance. But that governance is no more identical with the soul than a nation is identical with its government, without which it still survives. Plato needs a better argument before he can help himself to all the implications of personal immortality.

The myth of Er (614b–621d)

Having argued for immortality, Socrates fleshes out his argument with detail about the events to come after death. Here too Plato is repeating ideas he has worked out before: both the *Phaedo* and the *Gorgias* conclude with myths of otherworldly judgment, while the *Phaedrus* (246b–256e) depicts the starting-point of the reincarnational cycle.

Er the Armenian, Socrates says on this occasion, died in battle. Rather than stay dead, he roused up on his own funeral pyre and told of the afterlife. According to Er's story, all freshly dead souls travel to an unearthly junction, where they are judged and sent either up to the heavens for a thousand years or down into earth for at least as long, depending on how incorrigible they are (614c–d). Meanwhile, other souls return from their millennial stays in the earth and in heaven and tell of the rewards and punishments they received (614d–616a). These souls travel to a second place, located so that they can see the stars and planets from a point outside the visible universe (616b–617b). Here they cast lots and choose which human or animal life they want for their next trip into existence (617d–618b). Some choose well and others badly, but all must live with their choices (619b–620d). Socrates enjoins Glaucon to heed the moral of this story, that a person ought to practice justice informed by practical wisdom (621c).

The myth of Er offers a supernatural incentive for justice, and also an explanation of people's present situations in life. As an incentive, the myth satisfies both brothers' complaints from Book 2. Glaucon gets his reassurance that, besides being its own reward, justice will generate further rewards for the just. All the deeds of our lives are rewarded and punished (615b–c), which means that even unreflectively decent people can enjoy a fair return on the moral effort they expended while alive.

Then the myth moves to a different point, because ordinary justice is not its only aim. A character much like Cephalus makes the worst possible choice about his next life, not because of any immorality in him, but because his previous life of habitual virtue, combined with a thousand years' reward for that life's good deeds, lulled him into complacency about virtue and the soul (619b–d). Indeed, most souls acquire no lasting instruction from their successive incarnations, but swing from justice to injustice and back again. Only philosophical justice, which alone leads to a wise choice of future lives, will offer permanent relief from Plato's karmic pendulum. As conceived in Book 9, philosophical justice reflects not merely harmony among the soul's three parts, but a positive attachment, by the highest, to philosophy. Only the just behavior that also entails theoretical understanding of justice will make one a good judge of lives (618b–e).

Socrates' warning about the complacency of the mindlessly just answers, at last, Adeimantus' complaint that traditional myths of reward and punishment insult what they pretend to praise, by describing disembodied lives in which none of the virtuous ever practices virtue (363a–e). Socrates has told a new kind of myth in which the greatest virtue needs constant exercise, as much in the next life as in this one.

The myth also reconciles people to their present lives. A noble lie to suit everyone in every city, it makes every circumstance of one's life the work of the gods – hence inescapable – but at the same time pins responsibility for those circumstances on the person living through them, so that one may not even resent the inescapable. This is one of the most conservative touches in Plato's work. It hints that even founding the good city would be wrong, since that act would divorce a huge number of people from the circumstances of their lives. There are moods in which Plato mistrusts any change at all, apart from the internal change from vice to philosophical virtue.

Finally, the myth of Er is another Aristophanic moment in the *Republic*. The *Frogs* ends as the *Republic* does, with a return from the underworld; in the *Frogs* that return is prefaced by a debate between two rival poets, Aeschylus and Euripides, whereas in the *Republic* it follows a debate between the tribe of poets, taken together, and the voice of philosophy that is to supplant all of them. The reference to Aristophanes, if the myth of Er is that, serves as a comment about what the otherworldly contest should really result in, and who deserves to be its victor.

Suggestions for further reading

Readers curious about Plato's conception of imitation are advised to begin with Nehamas, "Plato on imitation and poetry in *Republic* 10," in J. Moravcsik and P. Temko, eds., *Plato on Beauty, Wisdom, and the Arts* (Totowa, Rowman & Littlefield, 1982), pp. 79–124. *Mimēsis* is also the subject of Griswold, "The Ideas and the criticism of poetry in Plato's *Republic*, Book 10," *Journal of the History of Philosophy* 19 (1981): 135–50, Tate, " 'Imitation' in Plato's *Republic*," *Classical Quarterly* 22 (1928): 16–23, and "Plato and imitation," *Classical Quarterly* 26 (1932): 161–9, and Verdenius, *Mimesis* (Leiden, E. J. Brill, 1949). For an unorthodox treatment of Book 10, see Deleuze, "Plato and the simulacrum," *October* 27 (1983): 45–56. On other issues in Plato's critique of the arts, see Annas, "Plato on the triviality of literature," in Moravcsik and Temko, *Plato on Beauty*, pp. 1–27,

Lodge, *Plato's Theory of Art* (London, Routledge & Kegan Paul, 1953), Partee, "Plato's banishment of poetry," *Journal of Aesthetics and Art Criticism* 29 (1970): 209–22, and Woodruff, "What could go wrong with inspiration?" in Moravcsik and Temko, *Plato on Beauty*, pp. 137–50.

Plato's myths have inspired a range of interpretations. Stewart, *The Myths of Plato* (Sussex, Centaur Press, 1905), though older, is still a good general treatment. On the myth of Er, see Annas, "Plato's myths of judgment," *Phronesis* 27 (1982): 119–43, and Smith, "Plato's use of myth in the education of philosophic man," *Phoenix* 40 (1986).

Part three

General
issues

Chapter 10

Plato's ethics and politics

When Plato speaks of justice, is he defining a state of political stability or a state of psychological balance?

As Book 2 opens, Socrates, Glaucon, and Adeimantus have come to expect a defense of justice to discover the special characteristics of the just soul. Then the analogy between the city and the soul lets Socrates devote most of the time spent on justice in the *Republic* to justice as a trait of the city. Which is Plato really talking about, the human soul or the city of humans?

The difficult question is not which entity, city or soul, is logically prior to the other. Plato's political system gains much of its value by being based on his psychological theory, rather than the other way around. The city has three parts because the soul does. Assuming that every person possesses three general kinds of motivation, and that one of the three must be uppermost, we have a non-arbitrary way of classifying everyone into one of three large groups.

But to say this is to raise a further question about whether Plato is describing a coherent political system, or is rather ignoring issues essential to political justice. Can the *Republic* really be a work of political philosophy, or do its political pronouncements amount only to illustrations of the psychological theory?

Plato has at least two solid reasons for wanting his dialogue to be more than mere analogy. In the first place, the close relationship between soul and city provides an argument for the legitimacy of political institutions. If the good city contains three distinct classes corresponding to the parts of every soul, then its structure reflects natural laws of psychology. If even one city reflects the laws of psychology, political organizations are not intrinsically unnatural.

In the second place, Plato believes politics to be essential to the good life. At points the *Republic* tries to deny the importance of political institutions: in Book 9 Socrates assures Glaucon that the regime they have invented will produce a life worth living even when no such city exists, as long as a person's soul contains the same harmonious pattern (591d–e; cf. 434d, 472c). But this consolation falls flat, because Plato believes that communities are necessary, and that their governance can make life better or worse. The first belief surfaces with ⑤, according to which human beings are, taken separately, incapable of providing for their own needs (369b). The second becomes evident over the course of Book 8, in which each type of city, not only worse than its predecessor, is also less worth living in. At the end Socrates and Glaucon call tyranny the most wretched of all regimes (576e) and the most enslaved (577c). Since life is better and worse depending on the city's merits, the best life must require the best government. Political philosophy is no metaphor, but must work as genuine politics. Hence the political details of Book 5, which make no sense as images of the soul, but apply only to the city.

Trouble begins when we try to visualize the citizens of Plato's city. If the productive class resembles an individual's appetites, are the members of that class as thoughtless as lust can be? Are the rulers pure intellect, with no bodily appetites of their own? For the analogy to apply completely, we need to stop thinking of Plato's city as a society of human beings, and recognize it as a fiction in which the classes, not their members, are the real entities. But then we lose sight of the city as a genuine political possibility.

If we *keep* the idea of this city as a collection of individuals, it can retain its power as a political inspiration, but the analogy to the soul becomes tenuous. Socrates has said that the city owes its virtues to its citizens' virtues (435e–436a); the city's courage, for instance, amounts to the human courage of the auxiliaries. If that courage in turn is to meet Plato's criterion for virtue, it must be a state of the soul in which spirit, as one of three parts, behaves in a certain way. So every auxiliary has a tripartite soul, complete with reason and desire. If the city is an image of the soul, something in the soul must correspond to the individual soldier's reason and desires. It follows that every part of the individual's soul contains all three parts in miniature; the psychological theory cannot hope to accommodate such complexity.

The underlying problem is that the analogy demands that a city consist of classes, not individuals. But in evaluating a political theory, it is important to ask whether the city treats its citizens justly, hence to look at the citizens as human beings. For the *Republic*'s central analogy to work, therefore, the political system it describes, however harmonious, is apt to fall short on the count of keeping its citizens happy. Indeed, when we turn to the specifics of the political philosophy, that is where we find it most inadequate. This is not a consequence of Plato's intentions, but of the theoretical structure within which he is working. Certainly Plato would like the citizens to be happy if they can manage it (421c, 540c). He only never arranges the city so that they may enjoy a reasonable expectation of that happiness. What is worse, his large-scale vision of the city leads him to treat individuals as interchangeable parts of the much more important social classes, therefore to overlook systematically what they might prefer for their lives. As a result, the members of every class in the Platonic city may justifiably complain of having been denied essential benefits.

The productive class remains untouched by so many of the *Republic*'s political reforms that at times Plato seems to have forgotten about it altogether. He does not include the laborers and artisans in the guardians' communism or breeding rituals. Aside from nebulous restrictions on how much money they may accumulate (421d–422a) or what they can do with their property (552a), the producers will live as people always have, owning goods and belonging to families. Their freedom from government intrusion may make them loyal to the rulers, but their life will never feel like a life of their own making, for they share in none of the city's distinguishing institutions and cannot participate in its governance. The price of their privacy is total loss of autonomy. This is an odd development, because Plato clearly values the capacity for self-rule: as he originally defines reason, its outstanding feature is just that power of self-mastery and self-legislation. Most people, since they possess at least a rudimentary rational faculty (441a–b), are capable of running their lives. Why does Plato deny that capacity to the majority of his citizens? Because he does not regard them as people, but as members of the desiring class. His *analogy* makes it seem fair to deny self-rule to those who cannot manage it, although his *psychology* should tell him that such a large fraction of humanity cannot all lack the reason it takes to run a human life. To put it another way, his willingness to prescribe a political system that his own psychological theory tells him runs counter to most people's highest aspirations and capacities shows that for Plato the community is an assemblage not of people but of classes.

The guardians exercise their rational faculties, since they rule not only themselves but the city too. On the other hand, they have no privacy: no money, no room of their own, no say over whom they "marry." They may not even choose to engage in the philosophical deliberation that gives them private pleasure; the lion's share of their life and energy belongs to the state. After being raised to enjoy a finer pleasure than anyone else can know, they are denied the right to pursue it.

The philosophers' lives must be unhappy if the city is to operate well, not only because Socrates denies their right to happiness (420b–421c, 465e–466c, 519d), but because their suitability for rule presupposes their reluctance. Philosophizing is essential to ruling because it is the only activity one would prefer over ruling (519b–521b; cf. 347d). That means the guardians are not even allowed to get over their distaste for administrative work: their happiness would only signal their corruption. Thus the existence of the good city presupposes the loss, by its finest citizens, of any right to private joys and desires. No doubt Plato considers this an acceptable price to pay, even for his beloved philosopher-rulers. In his eyes they have not come alive as individuals with spirited and appetitive faculties, because they continue to function as personifications of reason, rather than as people for whom reason, however well developed, is one faculty among many.

The injustices Plato tolerates toward the members of his ideal society symptomatize a class-analytic approach to politics that does not let him make sense of, much less answer, as simple a question as whether his city treats its citizens unjustly. Since Plato conceives the subject of political philosophy to be a definition of the justice of a city, we cannot help suspecting that his inability to address the justice of the city's behavior toward its citizens discloses a shortcoming in his theory.

Is Plato a theorist of totalitarian government?

Obvious affinities

Since the rise of modern totalitarianism, many of its enemies have pointed out its resemblance to the Platonic state; their argument has only been made more persuasive by Nazi and Stalinist books happily claiming Plato for a predecessor. Between the big family of the city and the powers available to its rulers, we feel ourselves on all too familiar ground.

The popular image of communism comes first to mind when we hear of the guardians' lives together, propertyless in dormitories. Other specifics of the ideal city will remind a reader of modern fascism, and in particular the fascist fetishism of unity. Under fascism, the state has an identity above and beyond the collection of individuals who make it up. Citizens owe their lone allegiance to the state, which functions as everyone's family; family loyalty becomes a constant reinforcement of filial devotion to the state. And, in most appearances of fascism, the state gives itself over to military organization. When not at war or planning for war, the state expresses its militaristic nature in the rigid hierarchy of civil society. Normal life becomes boot camp.

On all counts, Plato bears a nasty *prima facie* resemblance to a fascist. Most offensive is his organic theory of the state, a sense that the state counts as an individual. The very possibility of an analogy between person and city presupposes a reality to the city's existence that will not let it remain a mere collection of human beings. Add to this Plato's dream of eradicating the family, so that the emotional attachments once pulling people toward private goals may produce a social oneness constantly keyed up to the level of beer-hall fraternity, and every feature of state worship is in place.

The Platonic state further reproduces totalitarian regimes in its authoritarianism. The philosophers' knowledge of the Form of the Good licenses their complete domination over the other citizens' lives: free political debate makes no more sense to Plato than asking children to vote on the multiplication table. As every government does, the guardians will make laws about contracts, libel, and insult, will levy taxes and regulate trade (425c–d). But we also see them lying to the people about their births (414d–415a) and to the guardians about their breeding partners (460a); planning the reproduction of the guardians in accord with eugenic theories (459a–e); restricting the speech and poetry permitted in the city; indoctrinating the young guardians.

An unsympathetic reader will think at once of the possibilities for abuse and blunder, assuming rulers with either character flaws or imperfect knowledge. Here lies the puzzle; for Plato acknowledges both the potential for character flaw in his rulers, and the imperfection of their knowledge about guardian-breeding. Socrates describes batteries of tests to separate the upright guardians from their unworthy siblings (413d–414a, 535a, 537a), institutes penalties for those who have not learned their moral lessons (468a–469b), and warns of the young candidates' corruption if they should learn dialectic too early (537c–539d). As for error, the excellent city begins its slide into injustice because of these same rulers' mistakes about breeding (546a–547a). To grant them the power they have on the grounds of either their goodness or their intelligence betrays a willingness on Plato's part to invest rulers with power even when they go wrong; that willingness marks a crucial difference between authoritarian expertise and what looks like veneration of the state.

Dissimilarities

Anyone out to compare Plato's city to modern totalitarian states must take care to keep certain differences in mind as well. The organic unity of the Platonic state lacks the furious nostalgia found in modern fascism, and for all his elucidations of the rulers' power, Plato still makes that power something much less than it became under totalitarianism.

First, the national unity invoked by fascist leaders is not a genuine phenomenon, but a sociological fiction of old communal forms lost in the modern world. The histrionic rhetoric of fascism betrays its attempt to impose that dream of community by force. By comparison, the Platonic community's idea of itself as an extended family was already in place in Athens. Plato does not deserve special scrutiny for repeating the platitudes of his day, nor the label "fascist"; what makes the patriotism of modern fascism so dangerous is its artificial imposition of a tradition on a context unfamiliar with it. It is also relevant here that the *Republic* contains no hint of racialism; as for Plato's typically Greek assumption that his people stand apart from barbarians, that is a nationalistic *prejudice* to which he brings no nationalistic *theory*.

Moreover, Plato does not personalize the state to the point of demanding irrational loyalty from its citizens. In Book 7 Socrates requires the good city's philosophers to rule, but exonerates the philosophers in existing cities from any debt; for they

> grow up spontaneously against the will of the regime in each [city]; and a nature that grows by itself and doesn't owe its rearing to anyone has justice on its side when it is not eager to pay off the price of rearing to anyone. (520b)

By this reasoning, political obligation depends on the city's merits. And in Book 9, Socrates claims that one owes loyalty only to the well-run city, or to the model of that city in one's soul (591d–e). Anyone with intelligence will care only for this regime, and "won't be willing to mind the political things" in the city that happens to exist (592a; cf. 592b). A theory that finds civic sentiment appropriate only in a perfectly governed city cannot resemble a point of view from which one venerates one's country "right or wrong."

Plato would be likely to find the furor over unanimity perplexing. For him it represents a necessary condition of politics. The city came into existence in the first place to compensate for its members' inadequacies (⑤). When Plato emphasizes unity, therefore, he understands himself not to be choosing one value among many, but to be holding to the one that makes human community possible. Given how often the citizens of a democracy call for widespread agreement about important matters, the agreement by itself is not totalitarian. And we must bear in mind that it is not to be coerced. Plato takes pains to keep the army from terrorizing citizens, on the grounds that a good state will base its legitimacy on persuasion rather than force (see 548b, 552e).

As for the manifestations of state power in Plato's city – and they are significant – we should remember that the overwhelming number of them concern only its ruling class. Every totalitarian state has had a ruling elite; none has imposed its intrusive laws only on that elite and let the majority live as they always had. None has divorced economic power from political power – indeed, Marxist theory considers that divorce impossible. None has begun with such elaborate provisions for keeping governance from settling into the hands of a dynasty.

Certain other differences between Plato and modern totalitarians have seemed too trivial or irrelevant to mention, but to my mind suffice to make him, at worst, a precursor to authoritarian theory, but not himself a totalitarian. First, there is the obvious fact that totalitarianism has only been possible in the modern age, because only our age gave it the tools it needed. Telephone networks, television, and guns help a state spy on its subjects, bombard them with misinformation, and keep them, whatever their numbers, at such a disadvantage in every confrontation as to guarantee their docility. We need not even speak of faster or fancier tools of the ruthless modern state. It may be true that Plato would have put these technologies to work if he could have imagined them; still, the absence of modern tools from his arsenal leads him to sketch a political entity that differs in kind, not merely in degree, from the worst of this century's states. In another world he may have proposed a more terrifying state apparatus. In the world he lived in he could no more describe a totalitarian state than he could write an English sonnet.

Secondly, the *Republic* is virtually free of one significant ingredient of the totalitarian imagination, namely its pathological attention to detail. Consider Ezra Pound's scheme of cards and stamps to discourage people from accumulating money in bank accounts; Stalin's arbitrary restrictions on the mathematics that Soviet economic planners could use; the Nazis' baroque determination of who counted as a Jew (to say nothing of their capacity for grislier details). These obsessions with the political structure itself, with exercising power in the minutiae of a plan, are absent from the *Republic*. Plato errs on the side of visionary haziness, not on that of finely wrought detail, and by doing so reveals his lack of fascination with the exercise of state control.

Finally, there are those who have called Plato a totalitarian because he believed that moral propositions can be known as surely as those of mathematics. He clearly did believe this; just as clearly, that belief cannot make him a totalitarian without condemning the great majority of religious belief, and the majority of moral theorizing. Plato's confidence may be false, even dangerously false; to call it totalitarian is not only unfair (and itself dangerous), but also false to the lives of all the believers in objective moral standards who never fell into totalitarian beliefs or practices.

A lingering worry about Platonic politics

One last worry is worth raising about Plato's style of political thought. He belongs with political philosophers of the Enlightenment in believing that tradition does no useful work in thinking about politics, and that "politics as usual," the quotidian process of horse-trading, is an evil to be avoided. Here the same visionary haziness that relieved us a moment ago convicts Plato.

When Socrates calls for everyone over ten to be expelled from a city, and philosophers to indoctrinate the remaining children (540e–541a), he removes all doubt as to the value of traditional culture in the Platonic state. Book 2's dismissal of whatever poetry contains false allegations about the gods has already made this attitude evident. The *Republic* retains a role for Delphi (427b–c, 461e, 540b), but otherwise finds no place for the traditions that Plato's contemporaries took pride in. Totalitarian government wants no brakes on its progress toward a new society; tradition, whether for good effect or bad, must be admitted to exercise a retarding effect on social change. Plato ushered into political philosophy a disregard for the customary that it has never abandoned, and that shows itself today in those fruits of political philosophy we call totalitarian governments.

Plato likewise gives no thought to politics as usual. He is a non-political thinker, in that he does not assume the existence of, or worry about managing, political opposition. This unconcern for the political is perhaps the *Republic*'s most dangerous legacy. It unleashed into the sphere of politics the habit of aiming for a result without caring about what process leads to it. It is this spirit that keeps political philosophy as divorced as it is from real politics, or finds a union for the two only in totalitarian states: as long as theory sets itself the task of describing a world without politics, it is likely to find itself put into practice only by totalitarians, for they will have no theoretical basis for respecting the daily grind of the political process.

Chapter 11

Plato's metaphysics and epistemology

How do the *Republic*'s mentions of Forms compare with one another?

The reader who wants to study Forms more closely should supplement the *Republic* with passages in the *Symposium* (210e–212a) and *Phaedo* (74a–75d, 100b–106e). Their more direct presentations help one return to the *Republic* with a better sense of what Plato is up to. After the *Republic*, every reader ought to read the first pages of the later dialogue *Parmenides* (128e–135d), in which Plato criticizes his own theory.

But before traveling so far afield, we need to make the best sense we can of the *Republic*'s three arguments about the Forms (Books 5, 7, 10) and one mention of them (Book 6), all of which have some detail to add to the picture.

As Table 1 shows, there are certain clear similarities among the discussions, such as the Forms' uniqueness; we may surmise that whatever else he was unsure of, Plato had made up his mind that for every

TABLE 1. Arguments for the Forms

	Book 5 475e–480a	Book 6 507a–b	Book 7 523a–524d	Book 10 599a–597d
1. Terms attached to Forms	1. Fair, ugly, just, unjust, good, bad; also 2. double, half, large, small, light, heavy (479a–b)	Fair, good (507b)	Big, little, thick, thin, soft, hard (523e)	Couch, table (596b)
2. Features of particular objects	1. Many (476a); 2. never X without also holding the contrary property non-X (479a–c); 3. objects of opinion (479d); 4. likenesses of the corresponding Form (476c)	1. Many things that share a single name (507b); 2. seen but not intellected (507b)	1. [in the case of specific properties X.] both X and non-X (524a–c); 2. visible and not intelligible (524c)	1. Many things that share a single name (596a); 2. "like" the corresponding Form (597a)
3. Features of Forms	1. Unique (476a); 2. really X for every property (476b–d); 2a. always the same in all respects (479a); 3. things that "are" (476e); 4. objects of knowledge (476d)	1. Unique (507b); 2. intellected but not seen (507b)	Intelligible and not visible (524c)	1. Unique (596b, 597c); 2. made by a god (597b)

property there could only be a single Form (see 597c). Note also the symmetry between rows 2 and 3: the characteristics of Forms named in a passage are, as a rule, antitheses to the characteristics of particular objects named in the same passage. Do the many things of experience hold their properties equivocally? Then the Forms will hold them univocally. Are particulars seen but not intellected? The Forms are intellected but not seen. Plato defines his Forms (as other philosophers have tended to define their ideals) in opposition to the things of this world. This opposition always makes for the Forms' non-identity with particulars, and usually also captures their self-predication, their characteristic of perfectly exemplifying their properties. So Table 1 bears out our earlier observation that uniqueness, self-predication, and non-identity comprise Plato's most general descriptions of Forms (see pp. 126–8).

Some of the columns go together better than others. The mention of Forms in Book 6 is intended as a digest of the argument in Book 5, so it is no wonder that the characteristics of Forms and non-Forms outlined there reiterate points from the earlier argument. As for the discussion in Book 7, it is not really about the Forms at all, but about a pedagogical value in the properties that can hold of individual things. What Book 7 has to say about particular objects is compatible with the argument in Book 5.

The misfit is Book 10, which in some respects repeats what the earlier passages say, in others violates their consensus. The things of experience are still called "many," as in Books 5 and 6; they are "like" their corresponding Form, as Book 5 asserts. But in Book 10 Socrates says that the Forms are made by a god, the only time that Plato ever mixes religion into his metaphysics. Nothing turns on this remark, but it warns us that Book 10 will differ from the other passages.

Book 10 also says that there are Forms of Couch and Table, whereas other mentions of Forms in the *Republic* name only evaluative and relative terms. But I will briefly put off the question of which things have Forms, and confront here the third difference between Book 10 and the other passages, namely the justification Socrates offers for the existence of Forms. "We are . . . accustomed to set down some one particular form for each of the particular 'manys' to which we apply the same name" (596a).

The idea behind this "one-over-many" argument (hereafter OM) is simple: consider any group of things – horses, just laws, large objects – called by a single name. The predicate applied to all the members of this group does not itself belong in the group: "that which all horses have in common" is not in turn a horse, but what you may call the essence of horses. As the single core set of properties common to horses, yet not one itself, this essence satisfies the three conditions of uniqueness, self-predication, and non-identity. So it is a Form.

The OM is well ensconced in Plato's metaphysics. Row 2 of Table 1 suggests that it is at work in Book 6, where Socrates says that "there is a fair itself, a good itself, and so on for all the things that we then set down as many" (507b). This *need* not imply a one-over-many argument; "the things that we then set down as many" may mean specifically the X things of Book 5, in which case Socrates is saying that there is a Form for each set of many things *of a certain sort*, not that belonging to a set of commonly named things suffices to generate a Form. But the *Parmenides* (132a) also announces the OM as an argument for Forms, and Aristotle's testimony confirms that Plato used it, along with other arguments, to generate Forms (*Metaphysics* 990b9–17, 1078b17–1079a4).

Plato therefore has more than one argument for the existence of Forms, and uses different ones in different contexts. Book 5's argument against knowledge of particulars (AKP; see pp.128–35) produces a Form for every property borne in a qualified or context-dependent way by particular objects. Whatever reason we give for the failure of things to bear their properties – that they decay, or that they rely on comparisons with other objects – the AKP only establishes the contrasting Forms for properties that in some way invite doubt or disputation. The OM requires only the property's application to a host of objects, and therefore yields a Form for every general predicate.

It would be strange to condemn a philosopher just for having more than one argument for an important doctrine. We might want to see Plato as deploying his arguments for the Forms strategically. In Book 5 he wants to demonstrate the superior clarity of philosophical knowledge, so he appeals to the argument that makes the Forms unambiguous bearers of their properties in all contexts. In Book 10 he wants paradigms of knowledge against which to pose a wide range of artistic images, and uses the argument that generates the greatest range of Forms. In both places the ultimate purpose of the theory remains to find support for our ambiguous and disputable moral vocabulary, to find essential moral truths that will not vacillate along with our loose ordinary talk of good and bad. If we know anything about the Forms, it is that Plato used them to continue Socrates' project of defining ethical terms, so that the general statements Socrates looked for about virtues might be true of some ideal objects (see Aristotle, *Metaphysics* 987b1–14); as long as that remains his goal, he may use more than one argument to reach it.

But what if the arguments prove incompatible with one another? Do the AKP and the OM do the same work when they show the existence of Forms?

The AKP works as an argument in favor of the Forms by criticizing the many X things of this world. Just and large things cannot teach us unambiguously about justice or largeness, so either Forms must exist – about which we know when we understand those properties – or we have no knowledge about the most important matters. If this critique of X things is right, it poses Forms as the only escape from a variety of skepticism. The OM, despite its merit of producing a wealth of Forms, fails to make a similar case for them, because it develops no critique of non-Forms. Horses are not all called horses because they fall short of being what they are – on the contrary, they seem to get the name of horse by virtue of *being* horses. (Recall that the passage in Book 7, which in crucial respects echoes the AKP, asserts the full standing of a finger – and, by implication, a horse – in its species.)

This difference between the two arguments' efficacy points to the deeper discrepancy between them. While the Form of X produced by the OM does stand "over" the many X things by virtue of not being a particular object – it is their metaphysical better – it does not so clearly hold the property of being X in a superior way. It is consistent with every particular X thing's being perfectly X, since it yields a Form of X as long as more than one thing is X. On this account Forms are *universal terms*, and not obviously the *perfect versions* of properties.

We can hardly see how Plato could have taken the OM and the AKP both to be arguments about the same entities. His attraction to the OM makes sense, given its power in generating such quantities of Forms so rapidly; but without any critique of non-Forms that would demonstrate the need for Forms, this power represents the advantages of theft over honest toil. And there are other problems. The OM leads to what has been called the "Third Man Argument" (*Parmenides* 131e–132b), whose reduction of the theory to absurdity Plato himself seems to have taken as a fatal blow. Even without the Third Man Argument, there is the problem that the OM commits us, as Aristotle argued, to Forms of negative properties. For since the predicate "not human" applies to a number of things, there must be a Form of Not-Human, a property so vague that it could hardly have an ideal version. We have seen how hard it can be to interpret the AKP, and it is far from a complete justification of Forms, but at least it avoids these defects.

What sorts of things have Forms associated with them?

This issue needs to be stated and treated carefully. The passages in the *Republic* and other dialogues that mention Forms tend to give different sorts of examples of which properties have Forms associated with them. Although the examples are not arguments, and so do not *commit* Plato to decisively different metaphysical theories, the range of examples does *suggest* that he did not hold to a single scope for his Forms. The examples given are also relevant because within the confines of a specific passage Plato largely restricts his examples of Forms to those implied by the argument that passage either sets forward or hints at. If the examples fit the argument, they can help us see which forms of which argument Plato is attached to.

For example, the only Form named in the *Symposium* (211a–b) is beauty, not, say, the largeness that pops up so frequently elsewhere (*Phaedo* 100e, *Republic* 479b, *Parmenides* 131c, perhaps *Statesman* 283d–e). In the *Symposium* Socrates claims that the failure of individual beautiful things inheres, *inter alia*, in beholders' disagreements about whether or not the things are beautiful. The argument from relativity to observers really only works for evaluative terms; hence its appearance here, when the only Form named represents an evaluative term.

Table 1 shows that no two *Republic* passages name exactly the same properties to which Forms correspond. Book 10 stands out, its couch and table rather dingy specimens next to the abstract thinness or lightness of Book 7; Book 6 does not mention those latter concepts, but only evaluative terms. The evidence from other dialogues compounds this complexity. Some mention of the Forms, explicit or implicit, has been claimed for the *Cratylus, Euthydemus, Hippias Major, Laws, Meno, Parmenides, Phaedo, Phaedrus, Philebus, Protagoras, Sophist, Statesman, Symposium, Theaetetus,* and *Timaeus*; the examples listed in those dialogues cover a broad range of properties, which we may summarize by collecting these examples into four groups: (a) evaluative terms; (b) relative terms and more specifically mathematical ones; (c) naturally occurring things; (d) human artifacts. (Apart from Book 10, artifacts only come up at *Cratylus* 389b–d, regarding the ideal shuttle.)

Some of this divergence may be the result of offhand remarks, but not all of it. The dialogues that examine the Forms in the greatest detail pull in opposite directions. The *Phaedo*, apart from the *Republic* the closest thing to a sustained defense of the Forms, counts only evaluative terms, and such very general relative concepts as equality and inequality, as terms to which Forms correspond (74a–b, 100b–e). The *Parmenides*, Plato's sustained *attack* on the Forms, expands the catalogue to include nearly everything, probably such terms as "man," "fire," and "water" (130c), and maybe even such ignoble ones as "hair" and "mud" and "dirt" (130c–e). When two reliable sources yield such different answers to our question, we know that the problem does not lie with the *Republic* alone, or with Plato's penchant for informal and untechnical language.

It is noteworthy that the four kinds of things that are said to have Forms are not equals. Rather, each category tends to presuppose the existence of Forms for the preceding category. When Plato has Forms of plants and animals, he also has Forms of mathematical objects; when he names relative terms as Forms, the group includes terms of praise or blame. So the question of what things have Forms will always be a question of more Forms or fewer; and every list will contain Forms for ethical and aesthetic terms. It is worth stressing again that Plato wants those last Forms, that nearly every argument with which he defends his theory produces Forms to shore up the language of ethics.

But here we need to exercise the greatest care regarding what we call Plato's arguments. Given Book 10's use of the OM, we may take an easy way out and associate that argument with the large set of Forms, and the AKP with a much smaller set, perhaps restricted to evaluative and relative terms. This is *too* easy. Though the *Republic*'s two sets of examples roughly go together with the two different arguments Plato uses for generating Forms in that dialogue, the connection need not be as close as it first appears. In the first place, the range of lists of Forms we have just looked at cannot be reduced to Plato's choice of the AKP and the OM. The dialogues that contain widely divergent extensions for the theory of Forms do not all use different arguments for the Forms. In the second place, the AKP by itself can produce varying sets of Forms. Even if we leave the OM aside for the purposes of defending one strand of Plato's theory, we find that which Forms the AKP produces is not determined by its critique of particular things' ambiguity, but also depends on how Plato *interprets* that ambiguity. We have seen how hard it is to decide just how Plato takes the world to fail; appealing to the AKP, then, does not settle the question of which Forms exist. If an X thing fails at being X by virtue of the same decay that infects the whole physical world, the AKP may imply a Form of X for every property X; then the AKP and the OM yield the same list of Forms. If it fails at being X because of disputes that people have over its X-ness, the AKP licenses us only to admit Forms of evaluative terms.

In short, even if we leave aside the more abstract complexity that results from Plato's use of more than one argument for Forms, we still have the concrete complexity before us concerning how he uses the AKP. The scope of the Forms, as well as their intrinsic nature, depends on what Plato takes to be most decisively wrong with the world of appearances.

Chapter 12

Plato's abuses
and uses
of poetry

How does the early censorship of poetry in Books 2 and 3 compare with the final rejection of all artistic imitation?

Table 2 covers most of the points at which we need to compare the *Republic*'s two discussions of poetry. It would be ridiculous to deny the differences between the two passages' argumentative strategies and assumptions; at the same time, the remarkable degree of agreement between the table's columns shows that the differences, considerable though they are, will work toward a single common purpose. Both these sections of the *Republic* reject the great majority of Greek literature, both ban it from the good city, and both justify their censorship (at least in part) by spelling out that literature's effect on its audience. The differences

209

TABLE 2 Arguments against poetry

	Books 2–3 377a–398b	Book 10 595a–608b
1. Authors at fault	Homer (377d, 379d–e, 381d, 383a, 386c–387b, 388a–c, 389a, 390a–391b, 393a); Hesiod (377d, e); Pindar (381d, 408b); Aeschylus (380a, 383a); Sophocles (381d); tragedians (394c–d, 408b)	Homer (595b, 598d, 599c–600e, 605c, 606e–607a); Hesiod (600d); tragedians (595b, 598d, 605c)
2. Audience susceptible to poetry	Children (377a–c), but also the adults of the city (378a, 380b–c, 383c, 386a, 391b)	Children (598c), but mainly adults (604e, 605b), "even the best of us" (605c)
3. Problem with poetry	1. Its falsehoods about the gods (377d–e, 379a); worse, 2. its bad effect on the guardians (378a, 386c, 387b–c, 388d, 391e)	1. Poetic imitation is an inherently ignorant process (598c–601b, 602a–c); worse, 2. it corrupts the soul (604d–606d)
4. Bad effects of poetry	Disrespect for ancestors (378b, 386a); disunity among citizens (378c, 386a); laughter (388e); lamentation (387d–e, 388d); cowardice (381e, 386b, 387c); indulgence of appetites (389d–e)	Laughter (606c); lamentation (605c, 606a); indulgence of appetites (606d)
5. Process of imitation	1. The poet's impersonation of a character's way of speaking (393a–b, 395a); 2. the actor's enactment of a character (396b)	1. The painter's imitation of the appearance of an object (598b–c); 2. the poet's impersonation of the appearance of a person's behavior to the untrained audience (604d–e)
6. Subjects of imitation	Human beings (392b, 393b–c, 395c–396d)	Human beings (604e, 605a–c)
7. Bad effects of imitation in particular	Bad habit (395c–e)	Arousal of the low parts of the soul (605a, 606a–d)
8. Permissible poetry	Imitations of the best men (396c–398b)	Hymns to the gods; imitation and celebration of the best men (604e, 607a)

between the two arguments may mean that certain poems will fail by the standards of one and not by the standards of the other. But such puzzle cases are inconsequential by comparison with the sameness of intent in both passages, namely to show that the great prize and pride of Athenian culture, far from conveying wisdom, delivered its teachings so confusingly as to accomplish more mischief and mystification than enlightenment.

Thus, two of the *prima facie* differences fail to translate into any practical inconsistency. Books 2–3 appear interested in excluding bits of specific poems, or at most certain genres, from the city, while Book 10 plunges into its argument without concern for such niceties; but in practice this difference will be negligible. Both passages censor nearly every line of Homer, and nearly every word spoken on the stage. What does not offend Socrates in the earlier discussion by its dubious morality is banned for its imitative form. Apart from Book 10's concession to religious hymns, the two purges will leave the city with the same few scraps of poetry.

Truth and falsehood seem to matter more in Book 2, while Book 10 addresses the psychological effects of poetry. But as Socrates warms to his discussion of the young guardians' education, he makes clear that apparent untruth in a poet's tales of the gods and heroes matters only insofar as it corrupts the poem's hearers. Nor is the charge of untruth absent from Book 10, for the analogy between painting and poetry establishes the deep inevitability of poetic ignorance.

The two treatments do conceive differently of poetry's audience. Books 2–3 are meant to map out a new curriculum, and therefore dwell on how children hear poems. Even though the censorship that Socrates advocates for young guardians spreads to include all the city's residents (see p. 68), one might still accuse him of thereby thinking of the adults *as* children, hence as incapable of grasping what poetry is doing to them. But in Book 10 he is wrestling with the more complex phenomenon of an educated, virtuous adult's response to sophisticated poetry. No simple warning about bad role models will do justice to that phenomenon, so Plato uses all the intellectual theories he has developed in the *Republic* to account for his harsh judgment of poetry.

This mention of the *Republic*'s technical theories brings us to the lines of Table 2 describing imitation, the principal feature of poetry in both discussions. The two accounts belong to different worlds, and the predictions of the *effects* of imitation also differ markedly. Whereas in one case imitation acts neutrally on its audience, in the other it is inherently inclined to produce bad effects. To put it another way, Books 2–3 identify a number of faults in existing poetry, but rather than blame poetry itself Socrates points the finger at the poets who have thus far written, the bad apples who spoil poetry for everyone else. Even imitation comes in for blame largely because it has thus far presented poor models to the young. Book 10 expects all imitation to go bad, as though by its nature it sought out those poor examples, as though imitation of good people were the oddity (see esp. 605a). In short, Book 10 argues for two positions that Book 3 never thinks of suggesting:

1. Imitation may be described not simply in terms of its literary form, but more deeply in terms of its epistemic status; it is the imitation of appearance.
2. Imitation is naturally inclined to imitate bad people and appeal to bad parts of the soul; hence, poetry is not a neutral form that might hold any content, but tends to hold the worst sort.

These differences take us to the most difficult parts of Plato's aesthetics. For one thing, it is notoriously difficult to nail down what he means by *mimēsis*. "Emulation," which seems to have been the original primary sense of the Greek word, does not come close to covering the uses Plato puts it to. Nor do "imitation" or "mimicry"; "representation" is itself so vague as to translate the problem into English without settling it. In Book 3 alone, Plato stretches *mimēsis* to cover the distinct processes of a poet's creation of a believable character, and an actor's enactment of the character, as if the process had no clear meaning. In Book 10 the first imitator identified is the painter; when the subject changes to poetry, the imitator is no longer tied to drama. Plato's example becomes Homer, with the tragedians his incidental epigones. In a broader sense, Book 10 refuses to approach imitation as Book 3 had; for while Book 3 is trying to define a term in order that the reader might recognize imitation, Book 10 assumes that the reader recognizes it, and sets out to explain what everyone has already seen.

The two developments in Book 10, the epistemological diagnosis of imitation and the claim of its inherent depravity, depend on propositions about the Forms and the soul that Socrates has argued for in the books between the two discussions. In Book 2 poets looked accidentally error-prone when they talked about the gods; in Book 10 we find the error built into their enterprise, thanks to what we have learned in the meantime about the physical world's susceptibility to equivocation. In Book 3 the dramatic process of imitation threatened to mislead the young when it showed them (as it inexplicably found itself doing) inappropriate role models; in Book 10 we can see the fascination with wicked characters as a natural aspect of poetic imitation, because Plato's psychological theory has prepared us to call any unphilosophical activity the work of a soul's nether regions.

Although a skim of Book 10 makes clear that Plato's warning about poetry requires his division of the soul into parts, that much psychological theory will not suffice. For in the course of his critique of art, Socrates assumes "the calculating part in a soul" to do the work of weighing and measuring (602d–e). This assumption deviates from the original definition of reason, which had assigned to it only the work of calculating the *relative worth of different desires* (439c–d). Reason could take on the task of weighing and measuring only after it grew – implicitly in Book 5 and explicitly in 9 – from a simple overseer of the soul into a philosopher. Thus ⑪, which grants reason its own desires, lets Plato surreptitiously attribute all interest in the sensuous world to the soul's irrational parts. Since artistic imitation obviously directs itself to the world of the senses, the conclusion in Book 10 that it appeals to unreason (605a, 606a–d) is a *fait accompli* before it is ever stated.

Still more patently than the tendency toward corruption in poetry, its tendency toward error follows from views that Socrates did not have at his disposal when he first defined imitation. Whether we focus on the distinction between intelligible and visible objects (507b–c), or on the intellect's need to investigate further where the report of the senses proves self-contradictory (523a–524c), we find an opposition in place between better and worse understanding, with the former connected to the Forms and the latter to objects of unphilosophical experience. Any such opposition will license a condemnation of the arts, as long as Plato can claim that the fundamental artistic process always yields objects of the lower class. Here is where Book 10 relies on the picture of reality developed in the Divided Line (509d–511e). The Line ranks every object on the basis of whether it is an original or the image of an original. Copies of copies of Forms belong at the bottom of the Line. Because a host of similarities link the "imitation" (*mimēsis*) of Book 10 to the "image" (*eikōn*) of Book 7, the fate of art has been sealed as soon as Plato identifies imitation as its essential property. We might even say that by introducing the language of original and image into his explication of the Divided Line, Plato has left himself little work to do in Book 10: purposely produced copies could stand little chance in a system whose most opprobrious word is "image."

How can the rejection of poetry be squared with Plato's own use of literary devices, myths, and images?

This question may seem too vague to take up, but some version of it comes to most readers of the *Republic*. Even as Plato banishes poetry, his plans for telling tales to the citizens find him smuggling poems back into town. Given the low place of images on the Divided Line, and Book 10's hostility toward the arts, it ought to follow that the noble lie, the parable of the ship of state, the Allegory of the Cave, and the myth of Er remain excluded from philosophy. Plato's reliance on image, metaphor, and myth either dooms his philosophical enterprise, or demands an explanation of why those tropes should not count as the kin of poetry.

Defending Plato requires that we find a distinction between his literature and the poetry he is so eager to expel from his city. What stops the dialogues, or the myths and allegories in them, from being imitations of appearance? To say that Plato's imitations imitate reality rather than appearance is attractive but misguided, for the point of Book 10 is that every artistic imitation, by its nature, imitates appearance alone. To say that a Platonic dialogue imitates only a good person (Socrates), with as little drama as possible, may be – however bland – true, as far as it goes; but it does not go far enough, for the person of Thrasymachus alone shows that Plato could include hugely imperfect characters in his dialogues.

Suppose we return to a question that arose in our reading of Book 10 (pp. 181–3): how do appearances differ from imitations of appearance? We noted that poetry was said to possess "charm" (601b, 607c). The *Republic* contains no hint of where that charm came from, but its effect is clear enough: the defining characteristic of artistic imitations resides in their power to stop their audience from asking rational questions about them.

By comparison, the lowly images that are not works of art may or may not lead their viewers into inquiry. A mason or physicist will treat the triangular tile pattern on the floor as a visible and physical thing whose significant properties include mass, hardness, brittleness, and so on. A geometer will treat the same object as a visual aid for thinking about and demonstrating the properties of triangles. I may use my reflection in the mirror to see if my coat is on right (in which case I treat the reflection as a means to finding out about the thing reflected), or focus on the blemishes in the mirror's surface (in which case I ignore my coat). Mirrors and floor tiles do not determine a single response; paintings and poetry do. Geometers who measured the dimensions of an object represented in a painting could be accused of misunderstanding the nature of painting, in a way that they could not be said to misunderstand floor tiles for treating them in the same way. Floor tiles, unlike artistic images, leave themselves receptive to rational inquiry. They allow themselves to be transcended, while artistic images make that transcendence impossible or unappealing.

For Platonic literature to stand apart from poetry, it must likewise leave itself receptive to inquiry. Plato tries to stop artistic imitation from working its effect, and thereby to reclaim control over the imitation. Artistic images produce a world of their own, an aesthetic domain in which the realities of life no longer hold, where only the internal principles of the painting, the melody, or the plot determine its details. Plato produces literary images that draw attention to their own inadequacy.

In a treatment so brief this can only be a hypothesis. I will content myself with pointing to two passages in the *Republic* designed to induce sober inquiry unseduced by the charms of imitation. As it happens, both passages are connected with astronomy – a nice coincidence, because the *Republic* depicts astronomy as a study that can treat visible images either productively or unproductively, either as aids to solid geometry or enticements for the eyes (529d–e).

In the myth of Er Socrates explains the structure of outer space (616b–617b). But rather than mention stars or planets, he describes eight concentric bowls mounted on a spindle; we understand these bowls to be the spheres in which first the stars, then the planets, then the sun and the moon all revolve. To understand this description one must already know how to think about celestial bodies and their orbits in terms of their geometric properties. The more that my interest in the afterlife draws me into the myth, the more I am inspired to decipher this account of the heavens: my attraction to the myth and its images leads me to find the mathematical pattern behind it. So the myth of Er accomplishes what Socrates has said all studies of astronomy should. It describes the orbits of heavenly bodies in terms of solid geometry, rather than acknowledge their material natures. To dig into that myth is to improve one's powers of intellection.

A passage from Book 7 serves a similar purpose. Glaucon praises astronomy for directing the soul "upward" (529a), and Socrates rebukes him. Glaucon has confused the upward drift of the soul in philosophical education with what is above in a physical sense (529a–c). Mindful of the misleading potential of metaphor, Socrates undercuts the image he has relied on, according to which greater abstraction corresponds to higher physical standing. In reminding Glaucon that this is only a metaphor, Socrates thereby undercuts the Divided Line and Allegory of the Cave. I take this exchange to remind the reader that metaphors are very well in their place, as shorthand for more elaborate accounts or as first descriptions of what a student will later grasp more fully; but when they begin to deceive the student the images do more harm than good, and a teacher needs to discard them. The dialogues differ from unenlightened literature in reminding their audience that there is a higher tribunal than the literary imagination, that even the most vivid and most pregnant images need to yield to the progress of reason, that in the world Plato dreams of inhabiting every likeness of reality will meet the same fate, and human life will keep every other goal subservient to its achievement of the Good.

Appendix

Fundamental premises in the *Republic*'s argument

① The unjust try to get the better of all others, the just only to get the better of the unjust (349b–c) – p. 45.

② Injustice is a force, with the power of promoting disunion, that can exist within an individual or a society (351d, e) – p. 47.

③ Everything has a work (*ergon*) that it alone can do, or that it does better than anything else can (352d–353a) – p. 47.

④ Justice is the virtue of the soul (353e) – p. 48.

⑤ Humans taken individually are not self-sufficient (369b) – p. 61.

⑥ People are naturally disposed to perform different tasks (370a–b) – p. 61.

⑦ The P-just soul = the soul of one who is most likely to perform O-just deeds – p. 95.

⑧ The P-just soul is the happiest possible soul – p. 94.

⑨ Virtuous and expert rule is possible if and only if the rulers are philosophers – p. 111.

⑩ The love of every kind of learning produces knowledge of ethical matters – p. 111.

⑪ The rational part of the soul has desires of its own (485d) – p. 114.

⑫ Every level of understanding requires a corresponding level of reality in the object of understanding – p. 129.

⑬ Poetry imitates appearance (595b–602c) – p. 174.

⑭ Poetry appeals to the worst parts of the soul (602c–606d) – p. 174.

Bibliography

This is a selection of books and articles for the reader who is getting to know Plato and the *Republic*, as well as an acknowledgment of the sources to which I have become most indebted in writing this book. **Boldface type** indicates the works especially suitable to beginning students, while SMALL CAPITALS indicate those with thorough references to other works on the *Republic*.

Plato and Socrates; Plato as author

Bambrough, R., ed., *New Essays on Plato and Aristotle*, London, Routledge & Kegan Paul, 1965.

BENSON, H. H., ed., *Essays on the Philosophy of Socrates*, Oxford, Oxford University Press, 1992.

Gadamer, H. G., *Plato's Dialectical Ethics: Phenomenological Interpretations relating to the Philebus*, trans. R. M. Wallace, New Haven, Yale University Press, 1991.

Goldschmidt, V., *Les dialogues de Platon: structure et méthode dialectique*, Paris, Presses universitaires de France, 1947.

Griswold, C., "Style and philosophy: the case of Plato's dialogues," *The Monist* 63 (1980): 530–46.

Grote, G., *Plato and the Other Companions of Socrates*, 3 vols., London, John Murray, 1975, originally pub. London, 1888.

Gulley, N., *The Philosophy of Socrates*, New York, St Martin's Press, 1968.

GUTHRIE, W. K. C., *A History of Greek Philosophy*, vol. IV: *Plato: The Man and His Dialogues: Earlier Period*, Cambridge, Cambridge University Press, 1975.

Hyland, D., "Why Plato wrote dialogues," *Philosophy and Rhetoric* 1 (1968): 38–50.

Kahn, C., "Did Plato write Socrates' dialogues?", *Classical Quarterly* 31 (1981): 305–20.

KRAUT, R., *Socrates and the State*, Princeton, Princeton University Press, 1984.

Kuhn, H., "The true tragedy: on the relationship between Greek tragedy and Plato," *Harvard Studies in Classical Philology* 52 (1941): 1–40, and 53 (1942): 37–88.

McPherran, M. L., "Socrates and the duty to philosophize," *Southern Journal of Philosophy* 24 (1986): 541–60.

Moors, K., "Plato's use of dialogue," *Classical World* 72 (1978): 77–93.

NUSSBAUM, M., *The Fragility of Goodness*, Cambridge, Cambridge University Press, 1986.

Patterson, R., "The Platonic art of comedy and tragedy," *Philosophy and Literature* 6 (1982): 76–93.

Santas, G. X., *Socrates: Philosophy in Plato's Early Dialogues*, London, Routledge & Kegan Paul, 1979.

Saxenhouse, A. W., "Comedy in Callipolis: animal imagery in the *Republic*," *The American Political Science Review* 72 (1972): 888–901.

Shorey, P., *What Plato Said*, Chicago, University of Chicago Press, 1933.

Tarrant, D., "Plato as dramatist," *Journal of Hellenic Studies* 75 (1955): 82–9.

Taylor, A. E., *Plato: The Man and his Work*, London, Methuen, 1926.

VLASTOS, G., ed., *Plato*, 2 vols., Garden City, Doubleday, 1971.

VLASTOS, G., ed., *The Philosophy of Socrates*, South Bend, University of Notre Dame Press, 1971.

VLASTOS, G., *Socrates, Ironist and Moral Philosopher*, Ithaca, Cornell University Press, 1991.

Adam, J., *The Republic of Plato*, 2nd ed., 2 vols., Cambridge, Cambridge

General works on the *Republic*

University Press, 1963.

ANNAS, J., *An Introduction to Plato's Republic*, Oxford, Oxford University Press, 1981.

Brann, E. T. H., "The music of the *Republic*," *St. John's Review* 39 (1989–90): 1–103.

Crombie, I. M., *An Examination of Plato's Doctrines*, 2 vols., London, Routledge & Kegan Paul, 1962.

Cross, R. C. and Woozley, A. D., *Plato's Republic: A Philosophical Commentary*, New York, St Martin's Press, 1964.

Murphy, N. R., *The Interpretation of Plato's Republic*, Oxford, Oxford University Press, 1951.

Nettleship, R. L., *Lectures on the Republic of Plato*, 2nd ed., London, Macmillan, 1901.

OPHIR, A., *Plato's Invisible Cities: Discourse and Power in the Republic*, Savage, Md., Barnes & Noble, 1991.

Reeve, C. D. C., *Philosopher-Kings*, Princeton, Princeton University Press, 1988.

Sesonske, A., ed., *Plato's Republic: Interpretation and Criticism*, Belmont, Calif., Wadsworth, 1966.

White, N., *A Companion to Plato's Republic*, Oxford, Blackwell, 1979.

Republic, Book 1

Adkins, A. W. H., "The Greek concept of justice from Homer to Plato," *Classical Philology* 75 (1980): 256–68.

Boter, G. J., "Thrasymachus and *pleonexia*," *Mnemosyne* 39 (1986): 261–81.

Garnsey, P., "Religious toleration in classical antiquity," in W. Shiels, ed., *Persecuting Toleration*, Studies in Church History 21, Oxford, Oxford University Press, pp. 1–27.

Gotoff, H. C., "Thrasymachus of Calchedon and Ciceronian style," *Classical Philology* 75 (1980): 297–311.

Hadgopoulos, D. J., "Thrasymachus and legalism," *Phronesis* 18 (1973): 204–8.

Joseph, H. W. B., "Plato's *Republic*: the argument with Polemarchus," in A. Sesonske, ed., *Plato's Republic*, Belmont, Calif., Wadsworth, 1966, pp. 6–16.

Kraut, R., "Comments on Gregory Vlastos, 'The Socratic elenchus,'" *Oxford Studies in Ancient Philosophy* 1 (1983): 27–58.

Lycos, K., *Plato on Justice and Power*, Albany, SUNY Press, 1987.

Reeve, C. D. C., "Socrates meets Thrasymachus," *Archiv für Geschichte der Philosophie* 67 (1985): 246–65.

Roochnik, D. L. "Socrates' use of the techne-analogy," *Journal of the History of Philosophy* 24 (1986): 295–310.

Sesonske, A., "Plato's apology: *Republic* I," *Phronesis* 6 (1961): 29–36, reprinted in A. Sesonske, ed., *Plato's Republic*, Belmont, Calif., Wadsworth, 1966, pp. 40–7.

Sparshott, F. E., "Socrates and Thrasymachus," *Monist* 50 (1966): 421–59.

Thayer, H. S. "Plato: the theory and language of function." in A. Sesonske, ed., *Plato's Republic*, Belmont, Calif., Wadsworth, 1966, pp. 21–39.

Tiles, J. E., "Techne and moral expertise," *Philosophy* 59 (1984): 49–66.

Vlastos, G., "The Socratic elenchus," *Oxford Studies in Ancient Philosophy* 1 (1983): 27–58.

Vlastos, G., "Elenchus and mathematics: a turning-point in Plato's philosophical development," *American Journal of Philology* 109 (1988): 362–96, reprinted in H. H. Benson, ed., *Essays on the Philosophy of Socrates*, Oxford, Oxford University Press, 1992, pp. 137–61.

Politics, ethics, and psychology

Bambrough, R., "Plato's political analogies," in P. Laslett, ed., *Philosophy, Politics, and Society*, Oxford, Blackwell, 1956, pp. 98–115.

Bambrough, R., ed., *Plato, Popper, and Politics*, Cambridge, Heffer, 1967.

Barker, E., "Communism in Plato's *Republic*," in A. Sesonske, ed., *Plato's Republic*, Belmont, Calif., Wadsworth, 1966, pp. 82–97.

Bluestone, N. H., *Women and the Ideal Society: Plato's Republic and Modern Myths of Gender*, Amherst, University of Massachusetts Press, 1987.

Calvert, B., "Plato and the equality of women," *Phoenix* 29 (1975): 231–43.

Cooper, J., "The psychology of justice in Plato," *American Philosophical Quarterly* 14 (1977): 151–7.

Cooper, J., "Plato's theory of human motivation," *History of Philosophy Quarterly* 1 (1984): 3–21.

Crossman, R. H. S., *Plato Today*, 2nd ed., London, George Allen & Unwin, 1959.

Demos, R., "A fallacy in Plato's *Republic*?", *Philosophical Review* 73 (1964): 395–8, reprinted in G. Vlastos, ed., *Plato*, Garden City Doubleday, 1971, vol. II, pp. 52–6.

Dover, K. J., *Greek Homosexuality*, London, Duckworth, 1978.

Halperin, D., *One Hundred Years of Homosexuality and Other Essays on Greek Love*, New York, Routledge & Kegan Paul, 1990.

Irigaray, L., "Plato's *hystera*," in *Speculum of the Other Woman*, trans. Gillian C. Gill, Ithaca, Cornell University Press, 1985, pp. 243–364.

Irwin, T., *Plato's Moral Theory*, Oxford, Clarendon Press, 1977.

Keuls, E., *The Reign of the Phallus: Sexual Politics in Ancient Athens*, New York, Harper & Row, 1985.

Klosko, G., "Implementing the ideal state," *The Journal of Politics* 43 (1981): 365–89.

Lesser, H., "Plato's feminism," *Philosophy* 54 (1979): 113–17.

Leys, W. A. R., "Was Plato non-political?" *Ethics* 75 (1965): 272–6, reprinted in G. Vlastos, ed., *Plato*, Garden City, Doubleday, 1971, vol. II, pp. 166–73.

Mabbott, J. O., "Is Plato's *Republic* utilitarian?" in G. Vlastos, ed., *Plato* Garden City, Doubleday, 1971, vol. II, pp. 57–65.

Morrow, G. R., "Plato and the rule of law," *Philosophical Review* 59 (1941): 105–26.

Neu, J., "Plato's analogy of state and individual: the *Republic* and the organic theory of the state," *Philosophy* 46 (1971): 238–54.

NUSSBAUM, M., "The *Republic*: true value and the standpoint of perfection," in *The Fragility of Goodness*, Cambridge, Cambridge University Press, 1986, pp. 136–64.

Ostwald, M., "The two states in Plato's *Republic*," in J. P. Anton and G. L. Kustas, eds., *Essays in Ancient Greek Philosophy*, vol. I, Albany, SUNY Press, 1972, pp. 316–27.

Pierce, C., "Equality: *Republic* V," *The Monist* 57 (1973): 10–11.

Popper, K., *The Open Society and Its Enemies*, London, Routledge & Kegan Paul, 1945.

Rankin, H. D., *Plato and the Individual*, London, Methuen, 1964.

Robinson, R., "Dr. Popper's defence of democracy," in *Essays in Greek Philosophy*, Oxford, Clarendon Press, 1969, pp. 74–99.

Ross, D. "The Sun and the Idea of Good" in *Plato's Theory of Ideas*, Oxford, Oxford University Press, 1953, pp. 39–44.

Sachs, D., "A fallacy in Plato's *Republic*," *Philosophical Review* 72 (1963): 141–58, reprinted in G. Vlastos, ed., *Plato*, Garden City, Doubleday, 1971, vol. II, pp. 35–51.

Santas, G. X., *Plato and Freud: Two Theories of Love*, Oxford, Basil Blackwell, 1988.

Santas, G. X., "Plato on goodness and rationality," *Revue Internationale de Philosophie* 156 (1986): 96–114.

Shorey, P., "Plato's ethics," in *The Unity of Plato's Thought*, Chicago, University of Chicago Press, 1903, reprinted in G. Vlastos, ed., *Plato*, Garden City, Doubleday, 1971, vol. II, pp. 7–34.

Sprague, R. K., *Plato's Philosopher-King*, Columbia, University of South Carolina Press, 1976.

Thayer, H. S., "Models of moral concepts and Plato's *Republic*," *Journal of the History of Philosophy* 7 (1969): 247–62.

Thorson, T., ed., *Plato: Totalitarian or Democrat?*, Englewood Cliffs, N. J., Prentice-Hall, 1963.

Versenyi, L. G., "Plato and his liberal opponents," *Philosophy* 46 (1971): 222–37.

Vlastos, G., "Justice and happiness in the *Republic*," in G. Vlastos, ed., *Plato*, Garden City, Doubleday, 1971, vol. II, pp. 66–75.

Vlastos, G., "Was Plato a feminist?", *Times Literary Supplement* March 17–23 (1989).

Metaphysics, epistemology, and dialectic

Allen, R. E., "The argument from opposites in *Republic* V," in J. P. Anton and G. L. Kustas, eds., *Essays in Ancient Greek Philosophy*, Albany, SUNY Press, 1972, vol. I, pp. 165–75.

Brentlinger, J. A., "Particulars in Plato's middle dialogues," *Archiv für Geschichte der Philosophie* 54 (1972): 116–52.

Burnyeat, M., "Platonism and mathematics: a prelude to discussion," in A Graeser, ed., *Metaphysik und Mathematik*, Berne, P. Haupt, 1987.

Cherniss, H., "The philosophical economy of the theory of ideas," *American Journal of Philology* 57 (1936): 445–56, reprinted in G. Vlastos, ed., *Plato*, Garden City, Doubleday, 1971, vol. I, pp. 16–27.

Elias, J. A., "'Socratic' vs. 'Platonic' dialectic," *Journal of the History of Philosophy* 6 (1968): 205–16.

FINE, G., "Knowledge and belief in *Republic* V," *Archiv für Geschichte der Philosophie* 60 (1978): 121–39.

Fine, G., "Separation," *Oxford Studies in Ancient Philosophy* 2 (1984): 31–87.

Gosling, J. C. B., "*Republic* Book V: *ta polla kala* etc.," *Phronesis* 5 (1960): 116–28.

Gulley, N., *Plato's Theory of Knowledge*, London, Methuen, 1962.

Hamlyn, D. W. "*Eikasia* in Plato's *Republic*," *Philosophical Quarterly* 8 (1958): 14–23.

Irwin, T. H., "Plato's Heracleiteanism," *Philosophical Quarterly* 27 (1977): 1–13.

Joseph, H. W. B., *Knowledge and the Good in Plato's Republic*, Oxford, Clarendon Press, 1948.

Kahn, C., "The Greek verb 'be' and the concept of being," *Foundations of Language* 2 (1966): 245–65.

Malcolm, J., "The Line and the Cave," *Phronesis* 7 (1962): 38–45.

Moravcsik, J., "Understanding and knowledge in Plato's philosophy," *Neue Hefte für Philosophie* 60 (1978): 1–26.

Morrison, J., "Two unresolved difficulties in the Line and the Cave," *Phronesis* 22 (1977): 212–31.

Nehamas, A., "Confusing universals and particulars in Plato's early dialogues," *Review of Metaphysics* 29 (1975): 287–306.

Nehamas, A., "Plato on the imperfection of the sensible world," *American Philosophical Quarterly* 12 (1975): 105–17.

Nehamas, A., "Self-predication and Plato's theory of Forms," *American Philosophical Quarterly* 16 (1979): 93–103.

Patterson, R., *Image and Reality in Plato's Metaphysics*, Indianapolis, Hackett Publishing Co., 1985.

Raven, J. E., "Sun, Divided Line, and Cave," *Classical Quarterly* 3 (1953): 22–32.

Robinson, R., *Plato's Earlier Dialectic,* 2nd ed., Oxford, Clarendon Press, 1953.

Robinson, R., "Analysis in Greek geometry," in *Essays in Greek Philosophy*, Oxford, Clarendon Press, 1969, pp. 1–15.

Ryle, G., "Dialectic in the academy," in R. Bambrough, ed., *New Essays on Plato and Aristotle*, London, Routledge & Kegan Paul, 1965, pp. 39–68.

Santas, G. X., "The Form of the Good in Plato's *Republic*," in J. P. Anton and A. Preus, eds., *Essays in Ancient Greek Philosophy*, vol. II, Albany, SUNY Press, 1983, pp. 232–63.

Vlastos, G., "Degrees of reality in Plato," in R.Bambrough, ed. *New Essays on Plato and Aristotle*, London, Routledge & Kegan Paul, 1965, pp. 1–19.

Wedberg, A., *Plato's Philosophy of Mathematics*, Stockholm, Almqvist & Wiksell, 1955.

Art

Annas, J., "Plato on the triviality of literature," in J. Moravcsik and P. Temko, eds., *Plato on Beauty, Wisdom and the Arts*, Totowa, Rowman & Littlefield, 1982, pp. 1–27.

Annas, J., "Plato's myths of judgment," *Phronesis* 27 (1982): 119–43.

BELFIORE, E., "'Lies unlike the truth': Plato on Hesiod, Theogony 27," *Transactions of the American Philological Association* 115 (1985): 47–57.

Deleuze, G., "Plato and the simulacrum," *October* 27 (1983): 45–56.

Frutiger, P., *Les mythes de Platon*, Paris, Alcan, 1930.

Gadamer, H.-G., *Dialogue and Dialectic*, trans. P. Christopher Smith, New Haven, Yale University Press, 1980.

Griswold, C., "The Ideas and the criticism of poetry in Plato's *Republic*, Book 10," *Journal of the History of Philosophy* 19 (1981): 135–50.

HALLIWELL, S., *Plato: Republic 10*, Warminster, Aris & Phillips, 1988.

Havelock, E. A., "Plato on poetry," in A. Sesonske, ed., *Plato's Republic*, Belmont, Calif., Wadsworth, 1966, pp. 116–35.

Lodge, R. C., *Plato's Theory of Art*, London, Routledge & Kegan Paul, 1953.

NEHAMAS, A., "Plato on imitation and poetry in *Republic* 10," in J. Moravcsik and P. Temko, eds., *Plato on Beauty, Wisdom and the Arts*, Totowa, Rowman & Littlefield, 1982, pp. 79–124.

Pappas, N., "The *Poetics'* argument against Plato," *The Southern Journal of Philosophy* 30 (1992): 83–100.

Partee, M. H., "Plato's banishment of poetry," *Journal of Aesthetics and Art Criticism* 29 (1970): 209–22.

Partee, M. H.,, "Plato on the rhetoric of poetry," *Journal of Aesthetics and Art Criticism* 33 (1974): 203–12.

Smith, J. E., "Plato's use of myth in the education of philosophic man," *Phoenix* 40 (1986).

Stewart, J. A., *The Myths of Plato*, Sussex, Centaur Press, 1905.

Tate, J., "'Imitation' in Plato's *Republic*," *Classical Quarterly* 22 (1928): 16–23.

Tate, J., "Plato and imitation," *Classical Quarterly* 26 (1932): 161–9.

Tate, J., "Plato, Socrates and the myths," *Classical Quarterly* 30 (1936): 142–5.

Urmson, J. O., "Plato and the poets," in J. Moravcsik and P. Temko, eds., *Plato on Beauty, Wisdom and the Arts*, Totowa, Rowman & Littlefield, 1982, pp. 125–36.

Verdenius, W. J., *Mimesis*, Leiden, E. J. Brill, 1949.

Woodruff, P., "What could go wrong with inspiration? Why Plato's poets fail," in J. Moravcsik and P. Temko, eds., *Plato on Beauty, Wisdom and the Arts*, Totowa, Rowman & Littlefield, 1982, pp. 137–50.

Index